STEWARDS OF THE GOSPEL

Stewards of the Gospel

Reforming Theological Education

Ronald E. Vallet

Foreword by

Bruce C. Birch

With Contributions by

Daniel Aleshire
David L. Bartlett
Bruce C. Birch
Terry Parsons
Eugene F. Roop
L. E. "Ted" Siverns

WILLIAM B. EERDMANS PUBLISHING COMPANY

GRAND RAPIDS, MICHIGAN / CAMBRIDGE, U.K.

© 2011 Ronald E. Vallet

All rights reserved

Published 2011 by
Wm. B. Eerdmans Publishing Co.
2140 Oak Industrial Drive N.E., Grand Rapids, Michigan 49505 /
P.O. Box 163, Cambridge CB3 9PU U.K.
www.eerdmans.com

Printed in the United States of America

16 15 14 13 12 11   7 6 5 4 3 2 1

Library of Congress Cataloging-in-Publication Data

Vallet, Ronald E., 1929-
Stewards of the Gospel: reforming theological education / Ronald E. Vallet;
foreword by Bruce C. Birch; with contributions by Daniel Aleshire . . . [et al.].
p.   cm.
Includes bibliographical references (p.   ) and index.
ISBN 978-0-8028-6616-5 (pbk.: alk. paper)
1. Christian stewardship — Study and teaching.
2. Theology — Study and teaching. I. Title.

BV772.V27 2011
254'.8 — dc22

2011014925

To Schools of Theological Education,

Denominations

and

Christian Congregations

in

North America

and

To Our Grandchildren

Matthew, Nikita, Nicholas, and Davahn

Taylor and Toby

Carly, Benjamin, Luke, and Hailey

Mbinintsoa M. Ramarolahy ("Ram")

Contents

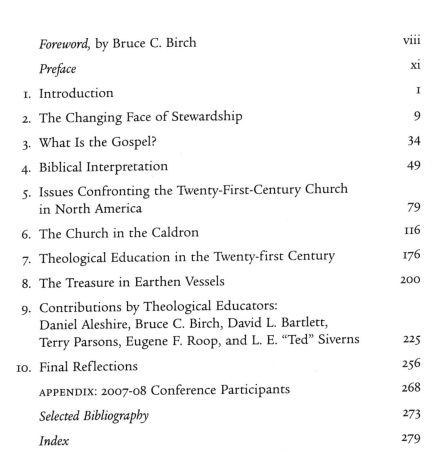

Foreword

The understanding of stewardship and its place in the life of local congregations and denominational bodies has undergone a dramatic change in the last thirty years. For me, and for many, the event that signaled the onset of this change was the publication of Douglas John Hall's seminal volume *The Steward: A Biblical Symbol Come of Age* in 1983.

As a young Old Testament scholar, I was blissfully unaware of the changing conversation that preceded the publication of Hall's volume, but in 1978, along with Larry Rasmussen as co-author, I had published a volume entitled *The Predicament of the Prosperous*. It dealt with the relationship of central themes in biblical theology to the ethical issues surrounding our responsible use of resources, both economic (poverty and wealth) and material (environment and human society). I was surprised and a bit puzzled when I received an invitation to speak, out of the context of that volume, at the Winter Meeting of the Commission on Stewardship of the National Council of Churches (NCCC) in 1983 in San Antonio. The other speaker was Douglas John Hall. My academic and ecclesiastical life has not been the same since.

The word and concept of stewardship had, in my experience, no place in the graduate education of an Old Testament scholar, even one wanting to understand his work as a biblical theologian. As a student coming of age in the sixties, I was keenly interested in the moral/ethical address of the biblical message, but like most growing up in the church in my generation, I regarded stewardship as mainly a matter of the annual financial campaign for a local congregation. But after hearing

Doug Hall and reading his book, after spending several days in interaction with the vibrant group of church leaders and teachers that made up the Commission on Stewardship for the NCCC, I was never again in doubt that many of my central biblical, theological, and ecclesiastical commitments were captured by the richness of the biblical concept of the steward. Stewardship studies, conferences, consultations, and courses have been a constant part of my vocational life since that time, and the influence of that ongoing conversation has infected many other parts of my scholarship and teaching.

Here is the significance of my personal testimony for this volume. Ron Vallet has been present along the entire way of this journey, not only for me, but also for many others like me. He was a stewardship executive for the American Baptist Churches in the USA and a member of the Commission on Stewardship for the NCCC when I came to speak at my first Winter Meeting. He succeeded Nordan Murphy as executive director of the Commission in 1987 and was the first executive director of the Ecumenical Center for Stewardship Studies (ECSS), when reorganization of the National Council of Churches made an independent venue for stewardship studies necessary. He has published a steady stream of the most helpful and insightful volumes on stewardship. He has been a creative and reliable resource for conferences and courses on stewardship even after retirement from directing the ECSS. He has been a constant encouragement to myself and others to think further and more boldly about the central role of stewardship in theological scholarship and in church life.

In this volume Ron Vallet takes us one further step on the journey to reclaim the role of steward as central to the life and scholarship of the church. He has long spoken to those of us in this conversation who are also theological educators about the implications of this revolution in understanding the role of the steward for the way in which leaders are prepared and equipped to serve the church. He has asked probing questions. Why are there so few courses directly devoted to the role of the steward in faithful discipleship? Why are connections not made to stewardship in the necessary courses on Bible, church history, theology, ethics, and ministerial practices? He has initiated conversations on stewardship and theological education in numerous times and places.

This volume is the fruit of those efforts by Ron Vallet to link stewardship to the very way in which all leaders for the church are educated and equipped. In the pages of this book the reader will find a chronicle of the effort to reclaim the role of steward for the church to which many have contributed. But here the reader will find, not unusually, Ron Vallet challenging us to take the next step and to revision theological education in a way that gives the role of steward its deserved central place. As usual he has enlisted allies in this challenge, but he has supplied the impetus and the vision, and in this volume brought together the mandate for a reconceived focus in theological education.

I hope the challenge of this volume will find a wide reading audience among those who care about the future of the church and the way in which we prepare leaders capable of meeting the challenge of a world and a church that badly need stewards. The invitation of this volume is not to a set of glibly offered prescriptions for the church's future, but to the joining of a conversation on what it means to be God's stewards that is as old as the creation itself and as pertinent to the present as the raging debate over use of resources that occupies both front pages and church agendas. No conversation could be more important for us as creatures of God and those called to be the faithful people of God.

BRUCE C. BIRCH
Wesley Theological Seminary
Washington, D.C.

Preface

Let a man regard us in this manner, as servants of Christ and
stewards of the mysteries of God.

1 Corinthians 4:1 (NASB)

As each one has received a special gift, employ it in serving one
another as good stewards of the manifold grace of God.

1 Peter 4:10 (NASB)

This book is written primarily for theological educators, denominational leaders, pastors, and lay leaders who are concerned for the institutions of which they are a part, but even more so for the overall well-
being of the Christian church as a vessel for the gospel of Jesus Christ.

In this book, as well as in previous books, I have used the word
"steward" as a metaphor. After introductory remarks in Chapter 1,
Chapter 2 gives a history of the word "steward" and the way in which I
use the word as I write of "stewards of the gospel." Chapter 3 offers my
best understanding of the meaning of the word "gospel." I use "steward" as a "metaphor," well aware that any metaphor has limitations,
and being equally aware of the reality that many persons view the word
"steward" as tired and limited in scope. Many persons in the church
have given up entirely on the word, except to talk about fundraising for
the budget of the church. I am not yet ready to forsake "steward" as a

metaphor that can enrich our understanding of our relationship to one another, to all of God's creation, and to God.

First Corinthians 4:1, quoted above, reminds us that we are stewards of the mysteries of God. For me, the mysteries of God are bound up in the phrase "gospel of Jesus Christ." In other parts of the Christian faith, some may understand "the mysteries of God" differently than I do as a "mainline Protestant." Those of other faiths may view "the mysteries of God" differently still: those of the Jewish faith may understand the phrase as referring to the Hebrew Scripture; followers of Islam may use the word Qur'an, the sacred Scripture of Islam. The list could go on for other faiths.

At several of the Conferences held in 2007-08 (see below), the question was asked if the word "disciple" might be a better metaphor for my purposes than the word "steward." The word "disciple," when used to mean a disciple of Jesus Christ, is a powerful image and usually is taken to mean a follower of the person and teachings of Jesus. However, in my view, the word "steward" carries a higher level of responsibility and accountability than does the word "disciple." Some argued that even the word "disciple" is much overused and "watered down."

My life journey has given me the privilege of serving as a pastor, a denominational executive at the regional and national levels, a national ecumenical executive, and an adjunct professor. I am grateful for each of these opportunities. Overall they have provided me with a wide perspective of the church in North America. As I worked on this manuscript and reflected on my experiences, I became increasingly aware of the disconnect among these differing worlds within the Christian faith. I believe that a connective and integrative link is needed. To move in that direction I am proposing a position that I have called "Ministry Integrator."

A brief history of events that led me to the writing of this book may be helpful:

In 1979, Bruce C. Birch and Douglas John Hall were co-speakers at a National Council of the Churches of Christ in the U.S.A.'s Commission on Stewardship event. Birch's account of his experience at that event is compelling:

> In 1979 I undoubtedly associated the word stewardship primarily with the annual budget pledge campaign in a local church. To hear Douglas John Hall (and to read his book as I quickly did) and to find

a multitude of convergences with my own interests as a biblical theologian was for me an intellectual and spiritual opening to an unexpected arena. I could never think of stewardship in such a narrow way again.[1]

Birch added in the same article: "I was struck by the comprehensiveness of the role of steward."

A year earlier, in 1978, Birch and Larry Rasmussen had co-authored a book, *The Predicament of the Prosperous,* that dealt with issues of hunger, poverty, and environmental responsibility. Later Birch wrote: "I have now come to understand this book as primarily concerned with stewardship."[2]

In 1988, Birch and M. Douglas Meeks engaged in informal dialogue at an annual ecumenical stewardship event of the Commission on Stewardship of the National Council of the Churches of Christ in the U.S.A.[3] At the beginning of the dialogue, Birch said: "We're long overdue for a discussion of stewardship concerns in relation to theological education, candidacy, entry into ministry, and what that means for the church."

Meeks continued:

In the long run seminaries tend to mirror the church, that is, they turn out to be what the church wants. So if you want things changed in the seminaries, it is important to open up discussion in the church.

You have to start where people live, in terms of their deepest faith, their deepest interests. I don't think anything will change until one asks that question, "What's true?" And if we say the gospel is true, then we have to question the assumptions of many other truth claims in our society. Any program of stewardship that fails to deal with the level of deepest human assumptions is not going to change much in the church.

The church is a place where we should be free to fight over the meaning of the gospel and the meaning of Jesus. And that fight is

1. Bruce C. Birch, "The Bible, Stewards, and Ministry," a paper prepared for the 2003 conference in Hamilton, Ontario. Excerpts of this paper appear in Chapter 9.

2. Bruce C. Birch, "The Bible, Stewards, and Ministry."

3. A condensation of the dialogue can be found in Bruce C. Birch and M. Douglas Meeks, "Stewardship and Theological Education: A Dialogue," *Journal of Stewardship* 44 (1992): 44-49.

not taking place often enough in the seminaries, in congregations, in church headquarters, or in stewardship staffs.[4]

For a hundred and fifty years or so, seminaries have been organized in terms of divisions or departments. There are the "Bible boys and girls" [professors of biblical studies], the "thought boys and girls" [professors of theology], and the "practice boys and girls" [professors of pastoral ministry]. These divisions are deeply ingrained in seminaries because similar divisions are deeply ingrained in our whole culture. When things are arranged that way, stewardship becomes one of the small questions of the "practice boys and girls," and it's basically a question of "how to." The "thought boys and girls" are glad not to have to think about things like that. We like to talk about higher things, things that are more spiritual and intellectual.

Most of us who are ordained have been socialized for three years of our lives in the seminary, and it's difficult to get rid of those thought patterns.

It is crucial that those who have a new vision of stewardship sit face to face with seminary faculty and say that stewardship is not just about programs to raise funds, but is rather a way of being in the world without which the church cannot be the church. If that is the case, stewardship belongs to the teaching of the Old and New testaments, to church history, to systematic theology, and to ethics.[5]

One of the worst things that can happen in seminaries is to shove something as important as stewardship is into a special studies program, as we have done sometimes with black studies and women's studies. What could have the effect of changing the whole curriculum then gets buried in a corner. And the rest of the faculty says, "Oh, thank God, I don't have to think about that anymore." That's the way we "thought boys and girls" often react. What could make a difference is for the church to say to seminaries, "Stewardship, when it is understood properly, is *the* question." I have tried to argue that stewardship encompasses the survival questions of the *oikoumene* and the whole creation. *Stewardship is a central way of shaping the research and teaching of all seminary fields.*

---

4. L. E. "Ted" Siverns wrote in response to this statement, "I've been surprised at how potentially good discussion and debate is avoided."

5. Siverns described this as a way to think and be holistic and not, as is the ordinary case, to be department voices seeking the welfare of our particular discipline.

In the dialogue, Birch pointed out the importance of the witness of those who are involved in ecumenical stewardship ministries:

> You who are involved in ecumenical stewardship ministries have a record of sponsoring serious scholarship in behalf of the church's interest. You have a witness to make to the denominations about the importance of scholars for the next generation and the renewal that comes out of that. Maybe it's time to testify to its importance in your area so that other areas of the church's life might think it would be important to them as well.

In 1992, Robert Wood Lynn spoke at a colloquy for theological educators about the history of theological education in North America. The last great reformation in theological education, he said, had begun near the beginning of the twentieth century with an effort to introduce the discipline of psychology into the curriculum. The effort was begun by a small group and took half a century to succeed. I would hope that a new reformation would not take half a century, but it may be so.

At the time of the colloquy, I was executive director of the Ecumenical Center for Stewardship Studies, sponsor of the event. At the end of his three presentations, Lynn spoke of the need for a new reformation of theological education. He issued a challenge to use the metaphor of steward as the organizing or core principle for the curriculum of theological education as a way to break down the compartmental divisions and to integrate theological education's curriculum. I remember clearly that he then looked directly at me and challenged me to take leadership in such a reformation. His words of challenge took hold of me. That experience and others since my "retirement" in 1994 led me to bend my efforts and energies to the reforming of theological education with the metaphor of steward as the organizing principle.

In 2001, I wrote a thirty-page proposal on reforming theological education. The proposal received strong endorsement from several noted theological educators, including Walter Brueggemann and Douglas John Hall. In a letter dated January 8, 2002, Walter Brueggemann wrote to me:

> Thank you so much for sending along the information about the project on "Reforming Theological Education." It is a thoughtful piece, and I think you are taking on an enormously important proj-

ect. It may well be that you will find the seminaries endlessly intransigent, but at least one must try.

While I am fully supportive of it, it is not possible for me to attend the Colloquy in 2003. . . . I do wish you well and will look forward to being kept informed about the matter, as I have no doubt that it is of enormous importance. With good wishes and gratitude for what you are doing.

Similarly, Douglas John Hall wrote to me in a letter dated February 3, 2002:

The project you have outlined is most impressive. I am much taken with it. You have given a great deal of time and thought to the plan, and it is presented in a most orderly and impressive way. You would know, too, that I am in general agreement both with the theological statements about stewardship and the necessity of reforming theological education to the end of incorporating that component.

I do, of course, deeply appreciate that you wished to have an opinion from me. It is entirely positive. I wish you the best with it — it will not likely be smooth sailing, but it is eminently worthwhile.

Planning for a conference to gather a number of theological educators in 2003 to reflect on the proposal was begun. Due to a number of factors, which are detailed in Chapter 1, the planned conference was not held at that time.

Despite this setback, the proposal and the project remained alive. Under the umbrella of Theological Education 21 (TE21), a small not-for-profit organization formed in 2001, I undertook the writing of this book. During the writing of the book, I sent it, in the whole or by chapters, to a number of persons inviting their feedback. The comments and resource suggestions received were invaluable to me, both in writing the first draft and in the revision. The "readers" who assisted me are: Leslee Alfano, Vincent Alfano, Bruce C. Birch, William H. Brackney, Walter Brueggemann, William A. Carlsen, Mark Caruana, Neal Fisher, Stephen D. Foulk, Grace Grimes, Victor Ling, Genevieve Ludemann, A. Roy Medley, Robert McFarland, David Movsovich, Donald R. Rasmussen, Heather Richards, Norman Richards, Paul Richards, Eugene F. Roop, Richard E. Rusbuldt, Jackie Shannon, L. E. "Ted" Siverns, Heather Vallet, Rose Marie Vallet, Wanda Vassallo, Robert Walczyk, Henry Walldorff, June Walldorff, and Bruce Wisenburn.

In 2007, after reading the first draft of this manuscript and as we prepared for the conferences to follow, A. Roy Medley, General Secretary of American Baptist Churches in the USA, wrote:

> In *Stewards of the Gospel: Reforming Theological Education*, Ron Vallet provocatively argues that stewardship is the crux for the formation of Christian leaders and disciples. In doing so, Ron challenges old stereotypes of stewardship. As he unpacks his thinking, Ron takes us along some refreshing streams of biblical exegesis and theology that offer local congregations a renewed sense of purpose and vigor as communities that steward the gospel through intimacy with Christ and engagement with the world. Theological educators, pastors, and lay leaders alike will find much here to help reshape their thinking about the formation of disciples and leaders for a church that lives its life from the margins of society as God's redemptive counterforce.

We set up six conferences in 2007-08 to bring together groups of theological educators and others to discuss and give additional feedback about the proposal and the book. A revision of this book in 2008-09 followed the six conferences.

Joining me on the Board of Directors of Theological Education 21 (TE21) at its founding in 2001 were Bruce C. Birch, William A. Carlsen, Stephen D. Foulk, and Rose Marie Vallet. I am deeply grateful to them for joining their names and energies to this fledging endeavor. We also thank those who provided contributions to TE21 in that first year. Special thanks go to First Baptist Church, Endicott, New York, for their initial gift that first year and for continuing support later as the work continued. Much gratitude goes to A. Roy Medley and Leo Thorne, general secretary and associate general secretary, respectively, of American Baptist Churches in the U.S.A. (ABC/USA). Under their leadership, ABC/USA agreed to be a cosponsor of all six conferences in 2007-08 and also made a special grant to TE21 towards the expenses of the conferences.

We appreciate the cooperation and assistance of the schools of theological education and others that hosted conferences:

- Association of Theological Schools in the United States and Canada, Pittsburgh, Pennsylvania (Daniel O. Aleshire, executive director)
- Columbia Theological Seminary, Decatur, Georgia (Laura S. Mendenhall, president; D. Cameron Murchison, dean of faculty and executive vice president)

- Emmanuel College of Victoria University, Toronto, Ontario (Peter Wyatt, principal; Betsy Anderson, continuing education coordinator)
- First Baptist Church, Manlius, New York (Leon Oaks-Lee, pastor)
- Palmer Theological Seminary of Eastern University, Wynnewood, Pennsylvania (Wallace Charles Smith, president; Elouise Renich Fraser, vice president and dean)
- Wesley Theological Seminary, Washington, D.C. (David F. McAllister-Wilson, president; Bruce C. Birch, academic dean)

I offer a special word of appreciation to Rose Marie, my wife of fifty-six years. Not only has she given me moral support, but she has also assisted greatly with logistical support, both in my writing and in arranging for the conferences. This manuscript is being completed as I am in my eighty-first year, having had two heart attacks (1995 and 2005) with emergency bypass surgery after the second, and having been diagnosed with prostate cancer in 2002, followed by surgery (2002), radiation therapy (2003-04), and hormone therapy (2007-11). I am grateful to the doctors and all those in the medical professions who have been part of this ongoing journey.

I am very grateful to the publisher, William B. Eerdmans Jr., and his staff who helped so much with the production of this book — Linda Bieze, Jennifer Hoffman, Victoria Fanning, and Willem Mineur.

Above all, I give thanks to God for bringing me to this point in my faith journey.

My hopes and dreams for reforming theological education and helping to forge or strengthen the links among schools of theological education, denominations, and congregations in this twenty-first century are high. It is my prayer that others will catch the vision and work with TE21 and the church of Jesus Christ to carry the dream and its implementation deep into the twenty-first century.

Do not go where the path may lead;
go instead where there is no path and leave a trail.
Ralph Waldo Emerson (1803-82)

Grace and peace,

RONALD E. VALLET
Manlius, New York

CHAPTER 1

Introduction

Stewardship

In 1983, William A. Carlsen, a colleague on the staff of American Baptist Churches of New York State (ABC/NYS), gave me a copy of *The Steward* by Douglas John Hall.[1] As I read the book, my interest and excitement grew as I moved through the pages of Hall's groundbreaking work. Though I had had twenty-six years of pastoral experience at that time and had provided pastoral leadership in annual financial stewardship "campaigns" for the congregations I served, I quickly realized that my theological and biblical insights in regard to stewardship barely scratched the surface of what it means to be a steward.

One passage in Hall's book particularly caught my attention, pointed me in new directions in my understanding of stewardship, and led to a new phase in my faith journey:

> The extent to which the steward metaphor has *suffered* from our stewardship practices is reflected in the fact . . . that for many churchgoers, including clergy, the term has a decidedly distasteful connotation. It at once conjures up the horrors of every-person visitations, building projects, financial campaigns, and the seemingly incessant harping of the churches for more money. Ministers cringe

1. Douglas John Hall, *The Steward: A Biblical Symbol Come of Age* (New York: Friendship Press for Commission on Stewardship, NCCC, 1982).

I

at the mention of Stewardship Sundays: must they really lower themselves to the status of fund-raiser once more? Must they again play the role of a Tetzel?[2]

Later in 1983, my faith journey took a different direction, as I became national director of stewardship services for American Baptist Churches in the USA. In that position, I soon realized that Hall's book had strongly influenced the stewardship leaders of the twenty-seven denominations in the United States and Canada who formed the Commission on Stewardship of the National Council of the Churches of Christ in the USA (NCCC). As a member of the Commission, it was my privilege to work alongside the forty or so members of the Commission as we learned and grew together.

When Nordan Murphy retired in 1987 as executive director of the Commission, I was privileged to be selected as his successor. When I attended and spoke to my first meeting of the Governing Board of the NCCC as a new staff member, I stated that there was no other position in the life of the church in which I would rather be.

Over the next several years, several theological educators, including Hall and others, wrote resources and led ecumenical stewardship events for the Commission and the Ecumenical Center for Stewardship Studies (ECSS).[3] Through those experiences, my understanding of and love for what it means to be a Christian steward grew and deepened.

Theological Education

One of the outreach ministries of the Commission, and later of the ECSS, was to hold annual Colloquies for Theological Educators. Two theological educators who had committed themselves to exploring and sharing deeper understandings of stewardship led the sessions. The responsibility that participants accepted was to teach a course on stew-

2. Hall, *The Steward,* p. 6.
3. In addition to Douglas John Hall, some of the other theological educators were Jouette Bassler, Bruce C. Birch, Walter Brueggemann, Juan Samuel Escobar, James Alexander Forbes Jr., Beverly Roberts Gaventa, Chris Levan, Rick Lowery, Robert Wood Lynn, Melanie A. May, M. Douglas Meeks, Lauree Hersch Meyer, David P. Polk, John Reumann, Gene F. Roop, Lyle Schaller, L. E. "Ted" Siverns, Max L. Stackhouse, Susan Brooks Thistlethwaite, John H. Westerhoff III, and Patricia Wilson-Kastner.

ardship or to incorporate stewardship principles and understandings into an already existing course that they would teach during the two succeeding academic years. During the years that I was actively involved with the Commission and the ECSS, we documented more than fifty courses that had been taught in some forty seminaries by those who had attended one or more of the colloquies.

This was a good result, but some of us began to realize that, as helpful as it might be for these courses to be taught, it did not achieve the desired result of changing the core curriculum of the theological schools involved. This became increasingly clear to me after I retired from ecumenical stewardship ministry in 1994. Returning to live in New York State, I rejoined the staff of ABC/NYS, this time as minister for stewardship and mission support. In 1995, I also became adjunct professor for Christian ministries at McMaster Divinity College in Hamilton, Ontario. These two positions gave me the opportunity to work directly within the context of a theological school, as well as to have regular ongoing contact with more than three hundred congregations.

In consultation with others, I became convinced that a reforming of theological education, with the concept of "steward" at the heart of the curriculum, would be a major contribution to theological education in North America. Over a period of time, I worked on a proposal to accomplish such a goal in the twenty-first century. A not-for-profit corporation, Theological Education 21, Inc., was formed. In 2001, I sent a thirty-page proposal to a dozen theological educators in the United States and Canada. The beginning part of the proposal read as follows:

On Reforming Theological Education

The work of the pastor is to help people understand the life-giving logic of the gospel of Jesus Christ in the totality of their lives.

A Proposed Thesis

The object of theological education is to develop Christian stewards who, in turn, can provide leadership for the development of Christian stewards in Christian congregations, denominations, and in the church at large.

To advance this proposed thesis we will:

1. Put forth an understanding that Christian stewardship is radically different from the prevailing view;
2. Look briefly at the roots and practices of theological education in North America; and
3. Explore how the concept of "steward" can bring a unifying purpose and focus to the several dimensions of theological education and the traditions of *paideia* and *Wissenschaft*.

An excellent description of the traditions of *paideia* and *Wissenschaft* is given by Daniel O. Aleshire in his book *Earthen Vessels: Hopeful Reflections of the Work and Future of Theological Schools*.[4] The Greek vision of education known as *paideia*, called "Athens" by David Kelsey, "seeks to cultivate excellence of the soul, 'which consists of knowledge of the Good itself.' This knowledge 'requires a conversion, a turning around of the soul from preoccupation with appearances to focus on reality, on the Good.'"[5]

A different and competing approach Kelsey called "Berlin." Aleshire noted, "The Berlin model has limited room for truth derived from revelation or for any kind of student formation other than critical intellectual formation. . . . These two traditions represent two very different goals, and they are currently present in current higher education practices." By way of illustration, Aleshire described his son's liberal arts education as *paideia* education. "By contrast," he wrote, "most faculty members in ATS schools completed their Ph.D.'s in research universities. For theological studies to have a place in these kinds of institutions, they needed to follow the model that was invented at the University of Berlin."[6] Siverns wrote that by the early twentieth century a Ph.D. with its research or "Berlin" approach was the necessary meal ticket to teaching.

My own educational experience followed a different sequence. My university education as a major in zoology definitely followed the *Wissenschaft* route. The first years of my theological education were based in *paideia* education. It took many years for me to understand the

---

4. Daniel O. Aleshire, *Earthen Vessels: Hopeful Reflections of the Work and Future of Theological Schools* (Grand Rapids: Eerdmans, 2008). See especially pp. 36-39.

5. Aleshire, *Earthen Vessels*, p. 36.

6. Aleshire, *Earthen Vessels*, p. 37.

difference and to appreciate the contribution that each makes. I am glad that I had the opportunity to participate in both.

Aleshire has noted: "theological schools . . . deeply identify with both educational models. Both are present in the ATS accrediting standards. He concluded this section by noting that "the two impulses that Kelsey identified as Athens and Berlin will continue to influence theological education."[7]

The response to the proposal "On Reforming Theological Education," mentioned above, was positive, and in 2002 plans were begun to hold a major conference at McMaster Divinity College in Hamilton, Ontario, in the spring of 2003. Two events intervened that led to the cancellation of the conference. One was the severe acute respiratory syndrome (SARS) epidemic that developed in 2003, leading to a lower-than-hoped-for number of advance registrations. The second factor was my diagnosis of prostate cancer in the spring of 2002 and subsequent surgery and radiation treatments.

Gospel

In retrospect, the postponement of the 2003 conference turned out to be a "blessing in disguise." At the time of the postponement, my understanding of what it means to be a Christian steward had progressed to the point where I often expressed the primary focus of Christian stewardship as being that we are called to be "stewards of the gospel." A happening in 2004 gave me both a broader and a deeper understanding of the meaning of the word "gospel."

That year, I read two issues of a publication from Fuller Theological Seminary.[8] The themes of the two issues were "What Is the Gospel?" and "The Challenge of Evangelism in the Twenty-first Century." Reading the articles confirmed in my mind what I had suspected before: by and large, the church in North America has an inadequate concept of the meaning of the gospel.

The lead article by Marianne Meye Thompson described how the entire faculty of Fuller Theological Seminary had read *StormFront: The*

---

7. Aleshire, *Earthen Vessels,* pp. 38-39.

8. *Theology, News and Notes,* published by Fuller Theological Seminary (Spring and Fall 2004 issues).

Good News of God[9] and then entered into discussions. Thompson described the motivating factor for the discussion in these words:

> We were impelled to take up the question in our discussion because of a common concern that the gospel as articulated in the Scripture is far too seldom heard in our churches today. Instead of the proclamation of the Gospel of God (Mark 1:1, Romans 1:1), we often hear a gospel of self-improvement and self-gratification. We have become consumers, seeking what satisfies and delights. Of course, preachers rarely put it that way, and few Christians deliberately advocate a gospel that focuses on them and their own satisfaction. But time and again, Christians bear witness to the modern American gospel: it is all about getting one's needs met, finding meaning and satisfaction, discovering a better and more comfortable way to live.[10]

The articles in the two issues were gripping and led me to read not only those articles but also the discussion book, *StormFront,* as well as a dozen or more other books and numerous periodical articles that related to the exploration of the question "What is the gospel?"

I came to a realization that the biblical gospel of God is not a gospel focused on me or you. Rather, the gospel concerns God's action. The good news of the gospel is the good news of the kingdom of God — that God reigns. Mark opened his Gospel with these words:

> The beginning of the good news of Jesus Christ, the Son of God. As it is written in the prophet Isaiah,
>
>> "See, I am sending my messenger ahead of you,
>>   who will prepare your way;
>> the voice of one crying out in the wilderness:
>>   'Prepare the way of the Lord,
>>   make his paths straight.'"

John the baptizer appeared in the wilderness, proclaiming a baptism of repentance for the forgiveness of sins. And people from the whole Judean countryside and all the people of Jerusalem were going out to him, and were baptized by him in the river Jordan, confessing their

9. James V. Brownson, Inagrace T. Dietterich, Barry A. Harvey, Charles C. West, *StormFront: The Good News of God* (Grand Rapids: Eerdmans, 2003).

10. Marianne Meye Thompson, "Reflecting on the Gospel," *Theology, News and Notes,* published by Fuller Theological Seminary (Spring 2004), p. 2.

sins. Now John was clothed with camel's hair, with a leather belt around his waist, and he ate locusts and wild honey. He proclaimed, "The one who is more powerful than I is coming after me; I am not worthy to stoop down and untie the thong of his sandals. I have baptized you with water; but he will baptize you with the Holy Spirit."

In those days Jesus came from Nazareth of Galilee and was baptized by John in the Jordan. And just as he was coming up out of the water, he saw the heavens torn apart and the Spirit descending like a dove on him. And a voice came from heaven, "You are my Son, the Beloved; with you I am well pleased." (Mark 1:1-11)

In this text, it is clear that the gospel is about what God has done, and will do. Our human tendency is to replace God's activity with human activity so that we end up with a "gospel of human doing." Siverns wrote, "The human sin is to think and act as if we are in charge (Berlin) vs. the proclamation that '[God] has the whole world in his hands' *(paideia)*. I'm a little reluctant to use the term 'Athens' because of the association of Athens and philosophy and the earlier argument about Greek thought versus Hebrew experience. I know the issue is 'control' versus wonder, awe, astonishment, etc."

A Look Ahead

In the next chapter, we will explore the evolution of the understandings and practices of stewardship by the church in North America over the past several centuries and re-explore the biblical and theological bases of Christian stewardship.

In Chapter 3, we will look in greater depth at the question "What is the gospel?" We will see that a competing false gospel of salvation is proclaimed in North America and around the world. We will address the question: Do we have two gospels — the gospel of the kingdom and the gospel of the cross — or one?

Chapter 4 will deal with what I think is one of the thorniest problems that face the church in the twenty-first century, that is, the question of biblical interpretation. How is it that so many Christians, and others, can study the Bible and come to such differing, and sometimes opposite, interpretations? What are valid criteria for biblical interpretation?

Chapter 5 will look at issues that plague and torment North America and the world, such as racism, poverty and hunger, war, health, science and faith, and the environment.

Chapter 6 will examine how these issues play out in the lives of Christian congregations and Christian leaders and how a better understanding of what it means to be stewards of the gospel might lead to real differences in the lives of congregations and their leaders. The image of the culture as the bubbling caldron in which the church is immersed is set forth, not as a place from which to escape, but as the place of ministry.

Chapter 7 will focus on theological education in the twenty-first century and what the implications would be if we better grasped the meaning of being stewards of the gospel. The church needs leaders who are willing to be salt in the boiling caldron. How does theological education equip men and women whom God calls to be leaders of the community that we call church?

Chapter 8 will view the gospel as the treasure in earthen vessels and the need for integration among all the vessels. We will address the question: "Can the concept of steward serve as an integrating center for theological education?"

With one exception, the responses and conversations in Chapter 9 were written in 2009 in response to reading the first eight chapters of this book. (The response by Bruce Birch is excerpted from an article that he wrote in 2003 in response to the proposal I wrote in 2001.)

In Chapter 10, the final chapter, I offer excerpts from the responses and conversations in Chapter 9 as well as my own final words. I am deeply appreciative of the conversations, responses, and insights given by Daniel Aleshire, Bruce C. Birch, David L. Bartlett, Terry Parsons, Eugene F. Roop, and L. E. "Ted" Siverns.

It is my prayer that when we discover that our lives are part of God's purposes in and for the world, we will also discover that which satisfies our deepest thirst and hunger. In my view, that is the great paradigm shift that is needed.

CHAPTER 2

The Changing Face of Stewardship

As a deer longs for flowing streams,
so my soul longs for you, O God.
My soul thirsts for God,
for the living God.

Psalm 42:1-2a

In an earlier work, I wrote: "Though many church leaders deny it and argue otherwise, stewardship is a critical component of congregational life. Denials of and arguments against this statement reflect a radical misunderstanding of the nature of stewardship."[1] One reason for negative opinions of stewardship is that over the centuries, stewardship in the life of the church has most often been linked to raising money for the church and its institutions. During those same centuries, the understanding of stewardship has changed significantly, as we shall see below. The question many stewardship leaders have struggled with is whether the word "stewardship" can be rescued from the misinterpretations and misunderstandings cast upon it and once again take on the intent and meaning of its usage — both explicit and implicit — in the Bible. At the end of this chapter, we will see that the word "stewardship" can regain its biblical usage when it is linked to a thirst for God

---

1. Ronald E. Vallet, *Congregations at the Crossroads: Remembering to Be Households of God* (Grand Rapids: Eerdmans, 1998), p. 17.

rather than fundraising for the church. Perhaps the secular world's increasing use of "stewardship" can also help the church to have a wider view of stewardship.

Evolution of Stewardship

The understandings and practices of stewardship in the Christian church are not static. A brief historical review of the past few centuries in England and North America reveals that they have evolved over time. In an earlier work, I gave an overview of how the church's understandings and practices changed from the seventeenth century to the end of the twentieth century.[2]

Tithing in Seventeenth-Century England Was Compulsory in Nature

Luther P. Powell, in an intriguing chapter, "Stewardship in the History of the Christian Church,"[3] provided fascinating details of the tithing system in England in the seventeenth century. Powell described a book titled *The Parsons Counsellor,* by Simon Degge, which was a guide to ministers in the Church of England regarding all matters with which they might be confronted. The last half of the book deals with the laws of tithes and tithing. Farmers, for example, were confronted with multiple rules and conditions concerning their tithes. Those who received wages and salaries were also covered by the system. According to Powell, "This intricate system of tithing was built on civil laws, ecclesiastical canons, and custom."[4] Once the premises and presuppositions on which the tithing system was built were challenged and called into question, the system began to collapse. L. E. "Ted" Siverns noted that this appears to be not very differ-

2. Vallet, *Congregations at the Crossroads,* pp. 62-84. The historical information was drawn from William H. Brackney, *Christian Voluntarism: Theology and Praxis* (Grand Rapids: Eerdmans, 1998).

3. Luther P. Powell, "Stewardship in the History of the Christian Church," in *Stewardship in Contemporary Theology,* ed. T. K. Thompson (New York: Association Press, 1960), pp. 76-131.

4. Powell, "Stewardship in the History of the Christian Church," p. 104.

ent from the first century with tithing/taxing by the Roman government and the ecclesiastical government.[5]

Since the tithing system in seventeenth-century England was compulsory in nature, the farmers had little alternative than to pay into a system that they derided and jeered. Pastors took the brunt of their protests, since they were perceived to be the main beneficiaries of the system. Hostilities against the tithing system grew, and farmers jeered the parsons and stoned auctioneers and bailiffs who were sent to collect the tithe. Rebellious farmers added this protest to an old harvest song:

We've cheated the Parson;
We'll cheat him again.
For why should a blockhead
Have one in ten
For prating so long like a book learned sot,
Till pudding and dumpling burn to pot?

Another song, sung to the tune of "The Old Hundredth," also voiced the bitter protest:

God save us from these raiding priests
Who seize our crops and steal our beasts,
Who pray, "Give us our daily bread,"
And take it from our mouths instead.[6]

Some clergy, who were displeased with the system, gave up their livings rather than collect the tithe by legal means. Those who opposed the system were fined and imprisoned. Some others were even martyred for holding that doctrines of compulsory tithing were contrary to the law of God. Avoiding paying tax was to be "scot-free."

The pattern of acceptance (or non-acceptance) of the compulsory tithing system in England was to affect how the concept of tithing was received and practiced by churches in North America.

---

5. See for example the background of the parables in William R. Herzog II, *Parables as Subversive Speech: Jesus as Pedagogue of the Oppressed* (Louisville: Westminster/John Knox Press, 2006).

6. "Revolt of British Farmers Against the Tithe," *The Literary Digest*, 23 September 1933, pp. 116-17, as cited by Powell.

Puritans' Mixed Motives: A Mission Cause and a Promise of Reward

Early on in North America, there was a shift from compulsory tithes as the basis of support for the institutional church to an appeal to mission and to personal reward. With the discovery of native peoples in the Puritan areas of New England, Puritan divines immediately accepted the responsibility of the conversion of the "Indians" as a God-given task. This discovery of a new "mission field" provided a new motive and opportunity to appeal for money to "promote the gospel." Brackney described the shift:

> With the Puritan Revolution, however, much changed abut the conduct of Christian mission and who should be involved. First the Puritan government was convinced it had a responsibility to conduct Christian mission. An important geographical prospect was New England, and the specific target was the aboriginal population. Leading Puritans like John Eliot, Edward Winslow (1595-1655), and Henry Ashurst all believed it was incumbent upon the Christian Commonwealth to use all practical means to civilize and convert the Indians. Their concern was threefold: to obey the gospel, to rescue the "savages" from the yoke of Spanish Catholicism, and to assert Protestant Christian responsibility in the New World.[7] The first two worthy goals contrasted with the imperialism of the third objective in a Parliamentary bill passed in July 1649, entitled "An Act for the Promoting and Propagating the Gospel of Jesus Christ in New England." This legislation established a corporation that could conduct legal business to achieve the evangelization of the American Indian. The New England Company thus became the oldest English Protestant missionary society.[8]

In 1651, Parliament was persuaded to incorporate what became the New England Company, which gave a legal foundation to Indian charity.

But the words of John Eliot (1604-90) spoke of another motive for giving:

7. From the perspective of the twenty-first century church as a steward of the gospel, the wording of the second and third of these goals seems inappropriate. Slandering native peoples as "savages" and writing of the "yoke of Roman Catholicism" is counterproductive to the goal of obeying the gospel.

8. William H. Brackney, *Christian Voluntarism: Theology and Praxis* (Grand Rapids: Eerdmans; Manlius, NY: REV/Rose Pub., 1997), pp. 52-53.

Come forth, ye masters of Money, part with your Gold to promote the Gospel; let the gift of God in temporal things make way for the Indians' receipt of spirituals . . . if you give anything into banke, Christ will keep account thereof and reward it. . . . And as far as the Gospel is mediately advanced by your money, be sure you will be remembered.[9]

Here was the promise that Christ would keep an account and reward those who gave to the cause. Among the Puritans, giving was motivated not by legal compulsion but by a mission cause and the promise of what they would receive for "giving to the cause."

Church Giving in Colonial America and in the Nineteenth Century: Two Opposing Philosophies

English beliefs, customs, and practices had other effects on church giving in North America. In the American colonies and on the frontier, two opposing philosophies of support for the church were used: voluntary and compulsory.

Separatists, who had come from England to America by way of the Netherlands, introduced the philosophy of voluntary support. The Puritans came with similar convictions. In later years, however, many New England churches turned to public taxation as their method of support. Congregational churches and then early Presbyterian churches followed the pattern of tax support. In the area that was to become New York, planters agreed to be taxed to support the Dutch church in return for the privilege of farming in the area. In the Virginias and Carolinas, taxes were collected for the Anglican Church.

Not surprisingly, the system of compulsory support destroyed much of the willingness to give voluntarily. "[E]ven where voluntary support was practiced, the giving generally was reluctant. In those denominations that held to voluntary giving, such as the Baptist and Methodist, the people frequently expressed by word and action that the ministers were expected to do the suffering for the cause of Christ."[10]

During the early American period, a number of methods of com-

---

9. J.D., a Minister of the Gospel, *The Glorious Progress of the Gospel Amongst the Indians in New England* (London: Edward Winslow, 1649), p. 27, as cited by Brackney.

10. Powell, "Stewardship in the History of the Christian Church," p. 112.

pulsory support for the church were tried, including church glebes,[11] pew sales or rentals, subscription lists, and lotteries.[12] "[E]ach method seemed to have within itself at least one factor which led either to its partial or complete defeat. . . . If there was an exception to the statement that all methods failed to supply the financial needs or had within themselves the defeating factor, it was the method of voluntary or freewill offerings."[13] By the latter half of the nineteenth century, the church was faced with a financial crisis because of the failure of compulsory forms of giving as well as changing social/economic realities. Compulsory taxation had been removed in all states soon after the turn of the nineteenth century. Pew rents did not meet the growing financial needs. By the end of the U.S. Civil War, compulsory support for the church had been interrupted so completely that it lost its effectiveness. A cash economy was replacing the older barter exchange system. The church responded in a number of ways, including tithing not as compulsory but as voluntary.

Many of the methodologies used were voluntary in nature:

- Agents of mission societies traveled a circuit persuading people to contribute financial support for the mission society they represented.
- Protestant women gathered money into what they called Widow's Mite Societies and, later, women's mission groups.
- The most common practice in fundraising was a subscription list. A subscription list was a piece of paper on which a person wrote his or her name, and then included the amount of money that they were ready to contribute to the cause. Benjamin Franklin, an expert in the use of subscription lists, encouraged people to sign up in such a way that the first person who signed at the top was invariably the largest giver.
- Collections for special causes multiplied.

11. In a letter to the author, Siverns wrote that the Presbyterian Church in Canada (PCC) still uses "glebe" in the call to a new minister; the call states that the congregation will "provide manse and glebe," then provides a confused explanation of "manse and glebe" as "rented house, apartment, or other dollars annually for housing allowance." It is confusing when both a manse and a glebe are promised.

12. The source (Powell) is not clear if the lottery was a pew lottery or a money (or other type of) lottery.

13. Powell, "Stewardship in the History of the Christian Church," pp. 113-14.

- Toward the end of the nineteenth century, a simple new device called an envelope began to be used. Instead of external pressure — as in a subscription list — the envelope led to an inner dialogue with the Bible and one's conscience. Giving became a *private* affair between the giver and the treasurer or the financial secretary.
- A second simple device — the every member canvass — was adopted around the turn of the twentieth century and took the place of the subscription list. A congregation would send out members to call on other members and present them with the challenge of making an annual pledge to be paid weekly.

Prior to 1850, the few attempts to institute tithing in the American church were generally met with hostility. But, beginning as early as 1885, tithing began to play an important role in the stewardship movement. Four factors led to a growing interest in tithing: (1) the missionary awakening; (2) a reaction against liberal theology and higher criticism;[14] (3) a growing dissatisfaction with many of the methods of church support then being practiced; and (4) the layman's movement inspired and led by Thomas Kane, a Presbyterian elder. As early as 1876, Kane began to circulate pamphlets on the subject at his own expense. Millions of copies were distributed.[15] Generally, the predominant motive was the material reward that was promised; testimonials abounded that tithing brought material blessings. "Cast your bread upon the water . . ." was a text often used and is still heard.

The Language of Giving in North America

The evolution of church giving also occasioned changes in nomenclature. Despite the aphorism "Sticks and stones may break my bones, but words will never hurt me," the names we give to persons, things, and actions and the language we use do matter. In an important work, Robert Wuthnow noted the importance of the language and vocabulary used by persons in such actions as compassion, evangelism, motiva-

14. Powell ("Stewardship in the History of the Christian Church," p. 120) wrote that the reaction against liberal theology and higher criticism "led to a strict literalism. Progressive revelation was rejected, and the authority of the Old Testament was made equal with the New."

15. Powell, "Stewardship in the History of the Christian Church," pp. 120-21.

tion, and therapy. For example, he used these words to talk about acts of compassion:

> When I talk about "acts of compassion," then, I do not mean a particular set of values, taken simply at face value, such as a visit to the hospital or an afternoon of volunteering at a center for abused women. I mean the cultural framework as well: the languages we use to make sense of such behaviors, the cultural understandings that transform them from physical motions into human action. The discourse in which such behavior is inscribed is no less a part of the act than is the behavior itself. The possibility of compassion depends as much on having an appropriate discourse to interpret it as it does on having a free afternoon to do it. To ask whether compassion is possible, therefore, is to ask about the languages on which its very conceivability depends.[16]

Language and vocabulary in relationship to acts of giving and sharing are no exception. It is important to be able to name the act of giving as indicative of motive and purpose.

Robert Wood Lynn made important contributions to a discussion of the evolution of the language of giving, as noted in the following sections.[17]

"Charity"

Language that had included the use of the word "alms" for much of the church's history began to change centuries ago. For a time, the word "charity" was used. In the mid-nineteenth century, the church was casting about for another name for the act of giving by Protestants to their churches. The word "charity" was considered stale and worn out by then. (It is interesting to note an exception, however, when United States President Abraham Lincoln used "charity" in his second inaugu-

---

16. Robert Wuthnow, *Acts of Compassion: Caring for Others and Helping Ourselves* (Princeton: Princeton University Press, 1991), p. 45.

17. The material from Robert Wood Lynn is taken from three sources: presentations at the 1991 Winter Event of the Ecumenical Center for Stewardship Studies; a presentation, titled "Christian Ideas of Money," at the 1994 North American Conference on Christian Philanthropy; and material found in *Why Give? Stewardship*, a series of articles published on diskette in 1996. In what follows, these sources will be cited by year.

ral address on March 4, 1865: "With malice toward none; with charity for all." The word "charitable" still retains a positive value, however.)

"Benevolence" and "Beneficence"

Two words used prominently in the nineteenth century as successors to the word "charity" were "benevolence" and its companion "beneficence." The word "benevolence" had been developed in the seventeenth and eighteenth centuries in writings of moral philosophers in Great Britain and elsewhere. (Merriam-Webster dates the word to the fourteenth century.)

One of the interpreters of benevolence in North America was Jonathan Edwards, often considered America's greatest philosopher and a prominent Calvinist Congregational minister of the eighteenth century. He defined benevolence in a way that is quite different from how we use the word today. For him, benevolence signified the sense of *joy and exaltation* that people feel when a neighbor is to enjoy a "good." These two words — "benevolence" and "beneficence" — were increasingly used by Protestant churches in the nineteenth century. In fact, the names of some of the church agencies that had responsibility for gathering funds often bore the name of systematic benevolence or systematic beneficence. Even today, The United Methodist Church uses the term "General Benevolences."

Some persons did not consider these words to be appropriate, however, and felt that a new biblical phrase or word was needed — one that would provide a moral constraint against the sin of covetousness. A deep anxiety about money and a spirit of covetousness, with all its attendant perils, developed. For example, in "The Revised Catechism," written in 1871, Mark Twain described the grip of greed. It was a bitter twist on the Westminster Catechism:

> What is the chief aim of man? — to get rich.
> In what way? — dishonestly if we can; honestly if we must.
> Who is God, the one and only true?
> Money is God. Gold and Greenbacks and Stock —
> Father, son, and ghosts of same, three persons in one;
> These are the true and only God, mighty and supreme.[18]

18. Mark Twain, "The Revised Catechism," *New York Tribune*, 27 Sept. 1871, quoted

"Stewardship"

Toward the end of the nineteenth century, churches in both Canada and the United States rediscovered a word. The word was "stewardship." This word had two advantages: (1) it was a biblical term that was familiar to a Bible-reading public, and (2) at the same time the word was fresh and relatively unused.

While the words "stewardship" and "steward" were used occasionally during the nineteenth century in relationship to possessions, Lynn reported that his research indicated that nobody focused on the word "stewardship" as the way of naming the Protestant act of giving during that period of time. Yet, almost overnight, it became popular and was used widely by the 1910s.

Why did such an abrupt change take place? The word "steward" is sometimes translated as "trustee." The word "stewardship" appealed to a rising middle class who thought of themselves as decision makers. The steward, it was said, is expected to exercise discretion on behalf of a master without receiving minute direction.

Yet, biblically, the *oikonomos* (steward) was usually also *doulos,* which is translated either "servant" or almost always in the NRSV as "slave." In fact the *oikonomos* was usually in the awkward position of trying to faithfully serve the master and those who worked for the master.

Nevertheless, the net effect was that stewardship was in the air. It was an idea whose time had come. The word fit very well for Protestant fundraisers whose job it was to raise money and articulate the relation between faith and money.

Josiah Strong, at the turn of the twentieth century, wrote a book titled *Our Country: Its Possible Future and Its Present Crisis,* and was the first to present a whole and complete understanding of stewardship. Though largely unknown now, *Our Country* sold more copies in the United States than any book since *Uncle Tom's Cabin.* He was the first advocate of stewardship. He wrote, "Christian stewardship is the perfect protection against the perils of wealth."[19]

The message of stewardship was also very attractive to a new generation of church bureaucrats in what came to be known as early-twentieth-century systematic benevolence. Today we tend to take

---

in Justin Kaplan, *Mr. Clemens and Mark Twain: A Biography* (New York: Simon and Schuster, 1966), pp. 124-25.

19. See "Vision and Money" in Lynn, *Why Give?* (1996), p. 272, and Lynn, 1991.

church bureaucrats for granted. In the early twentieth century, church bureaucrats were just coming into being.

Most denominations in United States and Canada had an office that was often named the Committee for Systematic Benevolence. In the 1910s, a new generation took over these agencies and provided extraordinary leadership. Some of the best of these leaders were returned missionaries.

Harvey Calkins, a returned Methodist missionary, wrote a book in 1914 titled *A Man and His Money*. He argued that we have two choices: we can talk about the Christian as a trustee who administers a trust under legal sanctions and restraints and who is under specific instructions from which he may not depart, or we can talk about the Christian as a steward who knows nothing about legal requirements. The steward's ambition is to know his master's mind and then, unbidden, fulfill the master's program. Calkins chose the second of these two options.[20]

Very soon, leaders in every denomination in Canada and the United States were repeating what Calkins had said. Lynn, speaking in 1991 at the Winter Event of the Ecumenical Center for Stewardship Studies, described how as stewardship was introduced in the 1910s, the giving record of the denominations began to ascend rapidly. This was especially true of the American churches, which were untroubled by World War I until 1917. Canada was deeply involved in the war three years earlier and thus had a different experience.

The giving rate in the United States went up as new programs — such as the every member canvass, the pledge, and weekly contributions — were introduced. All of these bore the name of "stewardship." By 1918, leaders of the church stewardship offices in the United States were at the top of the status ladder. The spirit was, "We can do anything." In that spirit of invincibility, stewardship leaders launched what was to be a humbling lesson: an American debacle called the Inter-church World Movement.

Lynn reported that an interchurch committee was formed to raise money for all of the denominations simultaneously. The campaign was to be supported by an interchurch staff who would raise $1.3 billion

20. Siverns noted that The Presbyterian Church in Canada likes defining a congregation's trustees as a pen directed by the hand of the congregation. "I guess Calkins illustrated how one word, in this case *oikonomos*, leads to two related but almost incompatible definitions."

over a period of five years. When they gathered in January 1920, after a year of preparation, the work involved 140 different boards representing 34 Protestant denominations. The coalition covered between 80 and 90 percent of all American Protestant mission work. By early 1920, the staff had grown to 2,612 and had to be housed in a major building in midtown Manhattan. Plans to create a new skyscraper, to be known as the Interchurch Center, were begun. As it turned out, the campaign was a disaster. The denominations were stuck with the bill for millions of dollars that had been spent in building a staff. They left behind a heritage of debts and disillusions. In the 1910s the stewardship people had been at the top of the status ladder. By the 1920s they were the culprits and considered to be the people who had misled the church in this hapless venture. Calkins returned, disillusioned, as a missionary to India. He realized that stewardship education is a process that takes a long time and that it is a disastrous mistake to link stewardship to short-term financial goals.

Scarcity and Abundance

From the early days of the missionary movement in North America in the early nineteenth century through the televangelists of recent years, one stream of Protestants assumed *an abundant supply of money,* in contrast to others who worried about *the scarcity of money.* Lynn said:

> Whereas other Protestants worried about the scarcity of cash, these movement leaders characteristically assumed an abundant supply of money. In that vein, for example, one movement stalwart assured his audiences in the 1820s that "there is capital enough to evangelize the world in a short period of time, and without the retrenchment of a single comfort."
>
> No, the true scarcity lay in the dimension of *time,* not in the realm of money. These folk lived under the pressure of an intense awareness of an eschatological crisis — the crisis of great opportunity. *Now* was the time for giving. God's future was coming. Any invitation to give money to this cause was more than a "once in a lifetime" opportunity. These challenges were, in effect, "once in history" occasions for making a difference in the whole human race.[21]

21. Lynn, "Christian Ideas of Money" (1994).

John R. Mott stood out among this group. Born near the end of the U.S. Civil War, he lived into the 1950s. He was a missionary and ecumenical leader who popularized the watchword of the movement — "the evangelization of the world in this generation." Considered by many to be the most accomplished fund-raiser in the history of North American Protestantism, Mott demonstrated that, when the meaning of money was presented, money became a powerful force. He described money as "stored up power" and spent his life, in his words, "liberating the money power of the world."

Methodologies of Giving

A study done by the Commission on Stewardship of the National Council of the Churches of Christ in the U.S.A. in the mid 1980s listed eight categories of generic congregational commitment enlistment plans that were currently in use and that built on the older patterns mentioned above:

1. Every Member Visitation
2. Mail Appeal
3. Telephone Appeal
4. Personal Delivery, such as Pony Express
5. Loyalty Sunday
6. Congregational Dinner
7. Small Group Meetings in Homes
8. Faith-Promise Plan.[22]

For those readers interested in an overview of money and the Protestant church in America, an intriguing book by James Hudnut-Beumler provides many insights into how Protestant churches in America raised money from colonial times (1750) to the present (2007). The title and subtitle of the book indicate the scope of the book: *In Pursuit of the Almighty's Dollar: A History of Money and American Protestantism*. It is abundant with helpful illustrations, tables, and figures. E. Brooks Holifield is quoted on the back cover: "The book will both inform

22. Robert J. Hempfling, "An Enlistment Plan That Fits," *Journal of Stewardship* 39 (1987): 22-29.

church executives and pastors and exemplify the benefits of approaching religious studies through material culture."[23]

A Summary

A close look at the preceding historical accounts of the understandings and practices of stewardship in the Christian church reveals an underlying pattern of change in regard not only to the methodologies used and practiced, but also substantial changes in both the theological assumptions and the motivations of contributors and the receivers of giving to the church.

Law and custom, as we have seen, compelled the "givers" of tithes in seventeenth-century England. The contributors had no positive motive. From their point of view, the motive was negative: fear of imprisonment, or worse, if they did not comply. From the point of view of the receivers of the tithe, the motive had a positive cast, though it was of questionable worth to others: to insure the life (and growth) of the institutional church. Mixed with this institutional motive would have been the material welfare of church officials.

Among the Puritans in America, giving was voluntary, but involved mixed motives: to support both a God-given mission to convert the Native Americans and also to receive a promised material reward.

In the American colonies and on the frontier, two opposing philosophies of support for the church were used: voluntary and compulsory, but the voluntary philosophy won out. Giving to the church compelled by state law had disappeared after the beginning of the nineteenth century. Legal compulsion to give to the church became a thing of the past in the United States. The tension between compulsory and voluntary giving swung to giving being entirely voluntary.

The issues being debated and tested in practice had to do with motives and with methodologies of giving. Over time, the prevailing moti-

---

23. James Hudnut-Beumler, *In Pursuit of the Almighty's Dollar: A History of Money and American Protestantism* (Chapel Hill: University of North Carolina Press, 2007). I was especially intrigued to find on pp. 116-18 a description and reproduction of a recommended household budget used at a Sunday night fireside discussion in the 1920s at Delaware Street Baptist Church, Syracuse, New York. Coincidentally, this is the congregation (now relocated and renamed Fay Road Baptist Church, Syracuse, New York) of which my wife and I are members.

vation moved from being a response to external pressures, that is, to support the institutional church, to inner motivations, such as the "need of the giver to give" and/or an expression of gratitude to God. At least, this was the "lip service" given by church leaders. Sometimes, the motive of gratitude that was being expressed and taught masked the motive of institutional survival. When push came to shove, the latter (the external motivation) trumped the former (the inner motivation).

Throughout the latter half of the twentieth century, stewardship was often presented as a way to express thanksgiving to God. Some stewardship leaders wrote and said that the *only* reason to give is to express thanksgiving to God. At the same time, they often pointed out the importance of denominational and other mission causes. The motives appear to have been mixed. Certainly Scripture is clear that we are called on by God to praise God and to express thanksgiving for God's gifts and blessings. But a question lingers: Is gratitude the only motive to give to God (and church causes)? Is gratitude even the primary reason? In my view, there are other factors.

Attitudes about Money and More Recent Stewardship Practices

In the early years of the twenty-first century in North America, two opposing attitudes about money are expressed within the church. Both attitudes recognize that the Bible speaks extensively about money, and each side of the "prosperity debate" points to passages that support its point of view. Yet they come to opposite conclusions.

One side teaches that prosperity is God's gift and quotes passages such as those found in Deuteronomy 8:17-18, Ecclesiastes 5:18-19, Malachi 3:10, Luke 6:38, and John 10:10.

The other side, maintaining that prosperity is not automatically a sign of God's blessing, uses texts such as Psalm 49:16-20, Matthew 6:19-21, Mark 10:24-26, Luke 12:33, and James 5:1-3.

The Bible, with a variety of sometimes competing theologies, seems to provide leeway in the debate about the prosperity debate. How does one decide which side to come down on in terms of biblical interpretation? In Chapter 4, we will explore the subject of biblical interpretation and some of the criteria that can be helpful.

In three of the Gospels, Jesus called on his disciples to deny self and "take up his cross." "For what does it profit a man if he gains the whole world and loses his own soul?" This is a hard saying. Some Christians, like George Adams, restate Jesus' question, "Why not gain the whole world *plus* my soul?" The contrast is clear.

Some megachurch pastors, such as Rick Warren, have not supported prosperity theology. Warren wrote, "This idea that God wants everybody to be wealthy. There is a word for that: baloney. It's creating a false idol. You don't measure your self-worth by your net worth. I can show you millions of faithful followers of Christ who live in poverty. Why isn't everyone in the church a millionaire?"[24] Ron Sider, evangelical antipoverty crusader, wrote, "They [proponents of prosperity theology] have neglected the texts about the dangers of riches. Prosperity Gospel Lite is one of the most powerful forms of neglect of the poor."[25]

In March 2006, Ben Witherington of Asbury Seminary wrote, "we need to renounce the false gospel of wealth and health — it is a disease of our American culture; it is not a solution or answer to life's problems."[26]

Because the subject is money, many pastors are unwilling to enter into serious teaching or preaching on this "taboo" subject. Collin Hansen, an editor at *Christianity Today* noted that "Jesus' words about money don't make us very comfortable, and people don't want to hear about it." Princeton University sociologist Robert Wuthnow said the church "talks about giving but does not talk about the broader financial concerns people have, or the pressures at work. There has long been a taboo on talking candidly about money."[27]

A sharply contrasting attitude was expressed in the words of megachurch pastor and author Joel Osteen: "I think God wants us to be prosperous. I think he wants us to be happy. I think he wants us to enjoy our lives. I don't think I'd say God wants us to be rich."[28] I do not think that the distinction Osteen made between the words "prosper-

24. George Adams and Rick Warren, as cited by David Van Biema and Jeff Chu, "Does God Want You to Be Rich?" *Time,* 18 Sept. 2006, p. 50.

25. Ron Sider, as cited by Van Biema and Chu, "Does God Want You to Be Rich?" p. 54.

26. Ben Witherington, as cited by Van Buren and Chu, "Does God Want You to Be Rich?" p. 55.

27. The quotations from Hansen and Wuthnow are taken from Van Biema and Chu, "Does God Want You to Be Rich?" pp. 48-55.

28. Joel Osteen, as cited by Van Biema and Chu, "Does God Want You to Be Rich?" pp. 48-55.

ous" and "rich" is valid. Indeed, the distinction seems to be nothing more than a play on words.

Toward a Deeper Understanding of Stewardship

Happiness and Money

An article by Gregg Easterbrook in *Time* magazine gave insights about the role of and understandings about money in late-twentieth-century and twenty-first-century American culture.[29] The author made an observation that "If you made a graph of American life since the end of World War II, every line concerning money and the things that money can buy would soar upward, a statistical monument to materialism." Easterbook continued, "But if you made a chart of American happiness since the end of World War II, the lines would be as flat as a marble tabletop."

Yet, by contrast, a poll by *Time* referred to by Easterbrook in the same article found that happiness in the United States tended to increase as income rose to $50,000 a year. (The median annual U.S. household income at the time of the poll was around $43,000.) After that, income did not have a dramatic effect. The poll indicated a slightly more nuanced view than Easterbrook concluded: persons at a poverty or near poverty level were not as happy as those whose incomes were at a level of $50,000 or more.

Another study by Edward Diener, a psychologist at the University of Illinois, based on interviews of members of the *Forbes* 500, indicated that they were only a tiny bit happier than the public as a whole.[30] Why do those with wealth feel only a little happier than the public as a whole? Diener concluded that it is "Because those with wealth often continue to feel jealousy about the possessions or prestige of other wealthy people, even large sums of money may fail to confer well-being."[31] Sociologists call this phenomenon "reference anxiety" — or, as it is sometimes called, "keeping up with the Joneses."

---

29. Gregg Easterbrook, "The Real Truth about Money," *Time*, 17 Jan. 2005, pp. A32-A34.

30. Easterbrook, "The Real Truth about Money," p. A33.

31. Easterbrook, "The Real Truth about Money," p. A33.

Robert M. Martin offered these intriguing thoughts on happiness and desire:

Let's put the problem in more picturesque terms. I know the genie who lives in a lamp will grant three wishes — change three things to make them the way you want them to be. I know you'd like to meet this genie; unfortunately I've lost his address. But I can get you in touch with his cousin Fred who is also a genie who can make the world match your desires. Fred does this not by changing the world, but by changing your desires. If something isn't the way you want it to be, Fred will change what you want. Are you eager to avail yourself of Fred's services? Why not. . . ?

Maybe you think there's more to life than getting what you really want. What? Why?[32]

Robert Wuthnow gave his insight into this subject:

And yet studies over time show little change in the proportions [of those] who register various levels of happiness or unhappiness. Here the solution is obvious. Happiness is a relative concept. At any given time, those who are better off are generally happiest, but as overall economic development occurs, expectations shift, causing the less well off still to compare themselves unfavorably with the better off.[33]

Easterbrook concluded in his article:

Psychology and sociology aside, there is a final reason money can't buy happiness: the things that really matter in life are not found in stores. Love, friendship, family, respect, a place in the community, the belief that your life has purpose — those are the essentials of human fulfillment, and they cannot be purchased with cash. Everyone needs a certain amount of money, but chasing money rather than meaning is a formula for discontent. Too many Americans have made materialism and the cycle of work and spending their principal goals. Then they wonder why they don't feel happy.[34]

32. Robert M. Martin, *There Are Two Errors in the the Title of This Book: A Source Book of Philosophical Puzzles, Problems, and Paradoxes* (Peterborough, Ont.: Broadview Press, 1992), pp. 195-96.

33. Robert Wuthnow, *Christianity in the Twenty-first Century* (New York: Oxford University Press, 1993), p. 114.

34. Easterbrook, "The Real Truth about Money," p. A34.

Though these reports have a degree of ambiguity, they merit a conclusion that, except at or near the poverty level, the amount of money one has is not directly correlated with the degree of happiness one is experiencing. These observations about the relationship between money and happiness may well indicate a coming consensus that money does not lie at the root of happiness. It may remind us again of the depth of the meaning of the words in 1 Timothy 6:10: "The love of money is a root of all kinds of evil, and in their eagerness to be rich some have wandered away from the faith and have pierced themselves with many pains." A thirst for money does not bring the happiness that people seek.

Probing More Deeply

In these early years of the twenty-first century, the time seems right to probe more deeply and to consider other factors in relationship to stewardship. These questions merit consideration:

- Is the term "stewardship" any longer an appropriate term?
- Is, or should, the survival of the institutional church be the primary motive for giving to the church? How willing, or not willing, is the church to lay down its institutional life? Does Christian stewardship exist primarily as a way to fund the church?
- Should stewardship principles and understandings be based on rules or obligations? What is the dilemma of hierarchical assumptions?
- What does it mean to present stewardship as covenant: obedience and promise?

If one takes a long historical view, it is evident that the motivations for giving and the methodologies used have not been successful, whether measured from a personal satisfaction point of view or by a utilitarian, fundraising point of view.

Loren B. Mead pointed to a partial success of stewardship methodologies in these words:

Techniques of stewardship have helped us fund the church and its ministry for a century. These techniques have made possible miracles of mission. These techniques have undergirded strong and vibrant institutional forms of enlarging ministry. In the coming generations, as financial resources continue to diminish, more and more pressure will be put on stewardship to respond to financial crises.[35]

While there is much truth in Mead's words, in that techniques of stewardship did help fund the church and many of its ministries for a century, it is also true that the success was never as complete or as long-lasting as his words seem to imply. The more common story of stewardship has been of disappointments and frustrations experienced by denominational and other stewardship officials who were charged with "funding" the ministries of the church. When Mead wrote of "more and more pressure [being] put on stewardship to respond to financial crises," his assumption apparently was that the primary role of stewardship is to fund the ministries of the church. If stewardship leaders accept this assumption, overall results will continue to be as unsatisfactory as they have been for the past several centuries. I am not ready to accept this assumption.

On the other hand, Mead seemed to be on solid ground when he contended that "the issue is not really money or budgets, but the deep anxieties and fears we have about our relationship with God."[36] His concluding paragraph in the article includes this sentence: "The real work of stewardship is to help us grow spiritually."[37] I agree with these words, but the question lingers, "What does it mean to grow spiritually?" This leads to an even more basic question: Is there a deeper understanding of stewardship that is not based on some combination of external rules or obligations, that does not rest on funding the institutional church, that is not necessarily an expression of thanksgiving, and that underlies an understanding of covenant based on obedience and promise? My conclusion is that the answer to each part of this question is a resounding yes.

Mead's words in the same article also described a *critical spiritual anxiety.* He wrote that "'wealth' and 'money' are key words to the critical spiritual anxiety of almost everybody in every congregation in the country." He continued, "our tools of stewardship (all of them that I

35. Loren B. Mead, "Wealth and Stewardship: An Interactive Exploration of Law and Grace," *Journal of Stewardship* 49 (1997): 40.

36. Mead, "Wealth and Stewardship," p. 39.

37. Mead, "Wealth and Stewardship," p. 40.

know of) fail to take into account the deeply spiritual dilemmas we each hear in how we relate to what we have and whose we are."[38] In these words, I think that Mead is squarely "on target."

Mead's statements about critical spiritual anxiety resonate with the words of Walter Brueggemann. In an important address given at Trinity Presbyterian Church, Atlanta, Georgia, on October 29, 1996, Brueggemann described the experience of being pulled in two directions, or being haunted by two different versions of one's life.[39] His address described two stories that operate in his life:

1. One story that competes for our loyalty is *the money story*.
2. But we also know about and take seriously a different account of our lives, *the story of the gospel*.

The money story, he said, is "the story of self-sufficiency and merit and being safe on our own terms." The sign of this story is *more*. It insists that no matter now much one gathers together, it is not yet enough for happiness and safety. "The outcomes of this story are *anxiety and worry*" (emphasis added). At this point, both Mead and Brueggemann have similar analyses of the human condition: a symptom of the quest for money is a critical spiritual anxiety.

But Brueggemann then described in detail the second story, the story of the gospel: "It is an account of God's generosity that we are able to see in the mystery of God's creation, that we know crucially in God's love in Jesus of Nazareth, and that we trust because we have experienced it in intimate, concrete ways in our own lives."

He continued, indicating that the sign of this alternative story is baptism. "The outcome of the story is a life of communion with God shaped like gratitude, a capacity for deep generosity because all that we have is a gift, and a valuing of neighbor, whereby we live to transform our world into a viable neighborhood where *justice and mercy for all brothers and sisters* is assured" (emphasis added).

The first story of anxiety and greed — the money story — has great power and is the dominant story of our culture.

The question then is how do we move our lives toward the second

38. Mead, "Wealth and Stewardship," p. 40.

39. The address is published in Walter Brueggemann, "Follow Your Thirst," *Journal of Stewardship* 49 (1997): 41-48.

story? Brueggemann said: "The move from the story of anxiety to the story of generosity does not happen by accident or by osmosis. It happens by intentional resolve and by incremental discipline. It happens not only with our money but with every aspect of our lives."

How does it happen? Brueggemann proposed a way, one with which I resonate and that, in my view, has major implications for what it means to be a steward of the gospel and for the world of theological education. Brueggemann listed three dimensions of what it means to be imbedded in the gospel story.

1. The God with whom we want to live is a God of deep love, but also of great demand.

2. What God cares for is the world. God cares for every creature in creation, and intends that every creature must have the safety and dignity of a full life.

This is also a point that Douglas John Hall has made consistently, both in writing and in conversations of which I was a part, declaring that God's passion is for this world and that we are called to live in this world. In his 1982 publication, *The Steward,* Hall wrote:

> This world, for all its pain and anguish of spirit, in spite of its injustice and cruelty, the deadly competition of the species and their never-wholly-successful struggle to survive — this world is the world for which God offered up "his only begotten Son." It was precisely the belief in a God crucified that gave Bonhoeffer the courage to go to his own death affirming the life of the world.[40]

3. Communion with God and generosity for the neighbor are linked to our baptismal sense of self. "The community of the baptized believes that God, in the very mystery of creation, has created us to be giving, caring, sharing, generous creatures." That is who we really are! Stewardship, thus, is a practice of *our true selves.*

Brueggemann went on to make the main point of his address. Drawing from his observations of commercials during the time of the 1996 Olympic Games in Atlanta and also from his trip to Kruger National Park in South Africa, he talked first about beer commercials that had the theme "Follow Your Thirst." His point was not that it was a

---

40. Douglas John Hall, *The Steward: A Biblical Symbol Come of Age* (New York: Friendship Press for Commission on Stewardship, National Council of the Churches of Christ in the U.S.A., 1982), p. 68.

beer commercial, but rather that the underlying motif of the commercial was to urge more — "more thirst, more drink, more self-indulgence, more satisfaction."

His reflection then turned to Psalm 42, which begins with the metaphor of a deer thirsting for water. The psalmist links this deep thirsting with the believer yearning for communion with God the way that a deer yearns for water.

> As a deer longs for flowing streams,
> so my soul longs for you, O God.
> My soul thirsts for God,
> for the living God. (Psalm 42:1-2a)

The human need for God's presence is as real as the human need for water. The Psalm, Brueggemann said, is an invitation to "follow your thirst." If one lives in the story of "more," one will go to beer (or Coca Cola or iced tea).

The story of the gospel, of which baptism is the sign, is that our true thirst is for God. In Brueggemann's words, "That is who we truly are, and only that will quench."

But there is danger and risk in coming to the waterhole, as Brueggemann observed in a visit to Kruger National Park. When an animal leans down to drink, it is vulnerable, off-guard, and easy prey. But because the thirst is so great, the animal must come despite the danger.

For those who are baptized, there are also dangers and risks that must be taken. Because it is the waterhole of the gospel, when we drink there "God will draw us into new purposes that will be costly and demanding. Drinking there will change our lives."

Another danger is that "those schooled in the ways of the world will find us easy prey, innocent, easily exploited and taken advantage of. But we must drink there and only there, because it is the only offer of the water of true life."

In Isaiah 55:1-2, an Old Testament poet issued an invitation to persons of faith:

> Ho, everyone who thirsts, come to the waters; and you that have no money, come, buy and eat! Come, buy wine and milk without money and without price. Why do you spend your money for that which is not bread, and your labor for that which does not satisfy? Listen

carefully to me, and eat what is good, and delight yourselves in rich food.[41]

In Matthew 6, Jesus said:

Do not store up for yourselves treasures on earth, where moth and rust consume and where thieves break in and steal, but store up for yourselves treasures in heaven, where neither moth nor rust consumes and where thieves do not break in and steal. For where your treasure is, there your heart will be also. . . . Therefore I tell you, do not worry about your life, what you will eat or what you will drink, or about your body, what you will wear. Is not life more than food, and the body more than clothing? (Matthew 6:19-21, 25)

A Proposed Definition of Stewardship

In his 1996 address, Brueggemann defined stewardship as "a resolve to move beyond the tale of anxiety." His definition is more a verb than it is a noun! He noted that stewardship is not about cunning budgets. It is about our true selves. Where does this leave us? Here are my conclusions:

1. Though stewardship relates strongly to one's attitudes about money and possessions, it is not about funding institutions or ministries, even those of the church. The words of Douglas John Hall are instructive in this regard:

   What if the mission itself requires something like the biblical metaphor of the steward if it is to be grasped imaginatively and engaged in faithfully? What if at least part of what is intended by the overall theme of these issues — "North America as Mission Field" — demands of us that we take up this metaphor and incorporate it into our theology of mission as such? What if stewardship, instead of just being the *means* of our mission, were a vital dimension of its *end* — that is an indispensable aspect of what Christian mission actually *is*.[42]

41. Instead of "living water," commercial interests are directing us to bottled water.

42. Douglas John Hall, "Stewardship as a Missional Discipline," *Journal for Preachers*, Advent 1998, pp. 19-20.

2. Stewardship relates to a theological imperative; it is not based on legal or mandatory obligations. It originates inside a person and compels him or her to act.

3. Though stewardship can relate to a feeling of gratitude to God, it is not based on pressures, such as guilt or pressures of feeling obligated to express thanksgiving.

4. Stewardship is not based on motivations such as responding to promises of prosperity or favoritism.

5. Stewardship is based on the human being's need for God, which can be described as an all-consuming thirst. It is a move from thirst based on anxiety and the felt need for "more," to a thirst for the gospel of God. In the words of the prayer of St. Augustine, "You have made us for yourself and our heart is restless until it rests in you."[43]

Stewardship then may be defined as drinking deeply from the waters of the living God by moving from the stagnating waterholes of "more" to the living water of the gospel of Jesus Christ, and inviting others to do the same.

Looking Ahead

But what then is the gospel of Jesus Christ? In Chapter 3, we will seek a better answer to that question. As we shall see, far too often the gospel has been substituted for by a false gospel, or diminished into something that Jesus would not have recognized.

---

43. Augustine, *Confessions* I.I.I.

CHAPTER 3

What Is the Gospel?

What the gospel offers . . . is the opportunity to be drawn into something larger than ourselves — into God's overflowing love that moves out in ever-widening circles, embracing the whole of creation. The gospel sees our humanity not in terms of needs to be met, but in terms of capacities and gifts to be offered in God's gracious service. We are created not to consume but to know God, not merely to meet our own needs but to participate in God's life and mission.

James V. Brownson et al., *StormFront*

What is the gospel of Jesus Christ of which we are called to be stewards? If stewardship is seen as drinking deeply from the waters of the living God by moving from the stagnant waterholes of "more" to the living water of the gospel of Jesus Christ and inviting others to do the same, as we argued in Chapter 2, what is the gospel toward which we are to move?

The importance of addressing this question was framed in words written by Miroslav Volf:

If we can neither state what the gospel is nor have a clear notion of what constitutes the good life, we will more or less simply float along, like jellyfish with the tide. True, a belief in our ability to shape the wider culture is woven into the fabric of our identity. So we complain and we act. But in the absence of determinate beliefs and practices, our criticism and activism will be little more than one more way of floating along.[1]

A False Gospel

To be a steward of the gospel is to do more than simply float along. However, before trying to answer the question, "What is the gospel?" it will be helpful to look at a competing, false gospel. An insightful article by Mark Lau Branson, "Escaping a False Gospel: On Changing Stories," depicts the gospel of consumer capitalism and globalization as a parody of the Christian gospel. This parody, he wrote, "is neither simple greed nor the 'health and wealth' gospel that is often appropriately criticized." He continued, "I am attempting to describe a narrative, a story, that competes with the narrative of the gospel of God."[2] This competing false gospel of salvation is proclaimed in North America and around the world.

What are the critical issues related to this false gospel? Branson identified the cultural contexts of Israel's exile and colonization as examples of the first issue. The second issue is addressed by the questions, "What is the relationship between the gospel and the churches? Is congregational life one option among many, or is the formation of congregations somehow critical to the essence of the gospel?" As more and more people seek ordination to non-congregational ministries, these questions become increasingly pertinent. We will discuss this second issue later in this chapter.

In regard to the first issue, Branson wrote, "The images of exile (the people of Israel living in Babylon) and colonization (Jews and Christians living under the coercive presence of the Roman Empire) have something in common: *some other power has gained dominance* (emphasis added). A 'big' story seeks to recast the story of God's people-forming narrative." He continued, "The narratives of Israel, the words and works of Jesus, and the Spirit-created churches of the New Testament provide us with a gospel that is sufficient to our salvation, powerful to transform us into something we cannot be on our own. If that gospel is not tangible in our churches, then we are amiss."

1. Miroslav Volf, "Floating Along?" *Christian Century,* 5 Apr. 2000, p. 398.
2. Mark Lau Branson, "Escaping a False Gospel: On Changing Stories," *Theology, News and Notes,* Spring 2004, pp. 16-19.

As the authors of *StormFront* stated clearly, we are not created to consume, nor merely to meet our own needs:

> What the gospel offers . . . is the opportunity to be drawn into something larger than ourselves — into God's overflowing love that moves out in ever-widening circles, embracing the whole of creation. The gospel sees our humanity not in terms of needs to be met, but in terms of capacities and gifts to be offered in God's gracious service. *We are created not to consume but to know God, not merely to meet our own needs but to participate in God's life and mission* (emphasis added).[3]

What Is the Gospel?

What then is the authentic gospel of God? One of my memories as a student at Fuller Theological Seminary was seeing founder Charles Fuller in the hallways and in the library of that institution. A few years later, Robert A. Guelich reported a conversation he had with Fuller following a forum. Fuller asked him, "Aren't you the student who chaired the forum on inspiration?" When Guelich acknowledged the fact, Fuller commented, "I long for the day when we can have a forum at Fuller Seminary on 'What is the gospel?'" Guelich described how the question haunted him then and continued to haunt him. He addressed this question from a deeply biblical and theological perspective in an article "What Is the Gospel?"[4] His article is a key source for much of the material that follows.

Guelich addressed the question of whether or not the Bible answers the question of "What is the gospel?" with two answers: the gospel of Christ crucified and the gospel of the Kingdom.

1. The Gospel of Christ Crucified

In regard to the gospel of Christ crucified, Guelich mentioned 1 Corinthians 15:1-5 where Paul offers one of the church's earliest expressions

---

3. James V. Brownson, Inagrace T. Dietterich, Barry A. Harvey, Charles C. West, *StormFront: The Good News of God* (Grand Rapids: Eerdmans, 2003), p. 34.

4. Robert A. Guelich, "What Is the Gospel?" *Theology, News and Notes,* Spring 2004, pp. 4-7.

of the gospel *(euangelion)*. First Corinthians 15:3b-5 reads: "Christ died for our sins according to the scriptures, was buried and arose on the third day according to the scriptures, and appeared to Cephas, then to the Twelve." Far too frequently this text has been reduced to become simply, *"Christ died for our sins."* *Christos,* of course, is the Greek word that is more accurately rendered as "Messiah," rather than being thought of as a name, "Christ," as it often is. Instead of "Christ died for our sins," we should read, "the Messiah died for our sins." A common denominator in Paul's writings is the death of Christ. Other texts with this theme include Hebrews 9:28 and 1 Peter 2:21-24. One ready answer to the question "What is the gospel?" seems to be: the death of Christ — the cross — is the heart of the gospel. For most of us, this answer seems to be no surprise. Isn't it obvious? We assume it is the biblical answer. "But," Guelich asked, "is the death of Christ and its resultant benefits really the heart of the gospel?"

2. The Gospel of the Kingdom

Other texts seem to point in a different direction. Do the four Gospels tell a different story than do the Pauline texts?

Mark's Gospel, written several years after Paul's letters, opens with a reference to "the gospel concerning Jesus Messiah, Son of God" (Mark 1:1). Mark's summary of Jesus' mission and message comes in 1:14-15: "Jesus came preaching the gospel from God, saying, 'The time has been fulfilled, the Kingdom of God is at hand, repent and believe the gospel!'" Guelich summarized in these words: "The Gospel according to Mark, therefore, is the gospel concerning Jesus Messiah, Son of God, who proclaimed the 'gospel from God.' And the 'gospel from God' is Jesus' announcement of the fulfillment of time, the coming of God's Kingdom. This is the Gospel (concerning Jesus Messiah, Son of God) according to Mark."

Matthew actually identifies the content of Jesus' teaching and preaching as the gospel of the Kingdom: "Jesus went about entire Galilee teaching in their synagogues and preaching the gospel of the Kingdom and healing every illness and disease among the people" (Matt. 4:23). Matthew showed that Jesus is the promised Messiah who both announced the "gospel of the Kingdom" and inaugurated the Kingdom as well.

Luke's Gospel does not use the actual noun "gospel." His account of Jesus' public ministry, however, begins with Jesus quoting Isaiah 61:1-2 in a synagogue in Nazareth. A new age of salvation for the poor, the prisoner, the blind, and the oppressed dawned with Jesus' announcement of the "year of the Lord's favor":

> Then Jesus, filled with the power of the Spirit, returned to Galilee, and a report about him spread through all the surrounding country. He began to teach in their synagogues and was praised by everyone. When he came to Nazareth, where he had been brought up, he went to the synagogue on the sabbath day, as was his custom. He stood up to read, and the scroll of the prophet Isaiah was given to him. He unrolled the scroll and found the place where it was written: "The Spirit of the Lord is upon me, because he has anointed me to bring good news to the poor. He has sent me to proclaim release to the captives and recovery of sight to the blind, to let the oppressed go free, to proclaim the year of the Lord's favor." (Luke 4:14-19)

In the fourth Gospel, John includes John the Baptist's public introduction of Jesus with these words: "Behold the Lamb of God who takes away the sin of the world!" One might then expect John to follow the themes familiar in Paul's writings. But consider how John concluded his Gospel with a clear statement of purpose: "Now Jesus did many other signs in the presence of his disciples, which are not written in this book, but these are written so that you may believe that Jesus is the Messiah, the Son of God, and that through believing you may have life in his name" (John 20:30-31).

What are we to make of the presentations of the gospel in the four Gospel accounts? Guelich summarized his response to this question in these words:

> We have four Gospels known respectively in the early church as "the Gospels according to Matthew, Mark, Luke and John." But not one presents the gospel as simply Christ crucified. Rather, each expresses the gospel in its own way as Jesus' announcement of the Kingdom either directly as in Mark's summary and Matthew's "gospel of the Kingdom," or indirectly as in Luke's announcement of the "acceptable year of the Lord," the dawn of the promised age of salvation, and John's statement of purpose to show that Jesus is indeed "the Messiah, the Son of God."

3. Two Gospels, or One?

Do we then have two gospels: one presented by Paul and some other New Testament texts, and a second expressed in the four Gospels? Several answers to this important question were offered by Guelich:

One solution has been to take the gospel of the Kingdom found in Jesus' words to be a *prelude* to the gospel of the cross — Christ crucified. In this view, the Gospels portray a Jesus who came to die. As Guelich described this solution, "The Gospels, then, portray a Jesus who came to die. In short, their content — the Gospel of the Kingdom — is interpreted in light of the gospel of the cross."

A second possible solution is to say that, yes, there are *two gospels*. The gospel of the Kingdom is *another* gospel, an earlier gospel that was preached by Jesus and his earlier disciples. The gospel of the cross is a reflected gospel of the early church that shifted the gospel of the kingdom to the gospel of *personal salvation*. Much of the American "evangelical" church has concluded that there are two gospels, and de facto opted for the church's gospel of the cross. The gospel then becomes basically, "Christ died for my sins," without resolving how the gospel of the cross relates to the gospel of the Kingdom.

The first "prelude" solution fails to find support in the biblical materials. The second "two gospels" solution results in two separate gospels and a disjunction between the teachings of Jesus and the preaching of the early church. How can the dilemma be resolved? To explore this question will involve looking again at the meaning of the word "gospel."

4. An Integrated Understanding of the Gospel

We come now to the heart of the question we are addressing in this chapter. The authors of *StormFront* suggested the following:

Gather a dozen Christians into a room and ask them the question, "What is the gospel?" The likelihood is that you will receive a dozen different answers. Some Christians will speak about forgiveness of sins, entering into a personal relationship with God by faith in Jesus Christ, and the gift of eternal life. They may add to this the incorporation of the believer into the body of Christ — the new humanity begun in Christ. Other Christians will speak of the liberation from oppression and injustice, of reconciliation, or of the restoration of creation. Still others will speak of the power of the Holy Spirit, healing miracles, freedom from demonic powers, and of a joy so intense that words simply cannot express it. Still other Christians will speak of strength in the midst of weakness, courage in the face of suffering, comfort, peace, and the capacity to face death unafraid.[5]

L. E. "Ted" Siverns observed that when we think we have arrived at a definition, the dynamic of the gospel escapes us; we find that gospel is a verb not a noun. It reminded him of a Jiha story:

> When a woman spoke proudly and profusely of her son who had just finished his studies at the Great Learning Centre, this little turbaned wise man urged her to be consoled. "Never mind, madam, he may have finished his studies but rest assured that God will surely send him more."

In my own experience, most Christians to whom I have addressed the question "What is the gospel?" respond with words that include the phrase "good news." But Guelich argued that the New Testament word "gospel" became a technical term and that simply describing it as "good news" robs the word of the little technical meaning that it might have. What might this technical meaning be? How far back does it go?

Guelich pointed to the opening words of the Gospel according to Mark: "The beginning of the gospel concerning Jesus Messiah, Son of God, as written by the prophet Isaiah . . ." (Mark 1:1-2a). These words link the "beginning of the gospel" back to the prophets' promise of a messenger (see Malachi 3:1 and Isaiah 40:3) and forward to the events summarized in Mark 1:4-15. These events include the coming of John the Baptist, the baptism and temptation of Jesus and summary of Jesus' teaching: "The time is fulfilled, the Kingdom of God is at hand; repent, and believe the Gospel."

"If, as Mark indicates," Guelich wrote, "we are to understand Jesus' 'preaching the gospel from God' (1:14-15) together with the coming of the Spirit upon him at his baptism (1:10) in light of what is written in Isaiah (Mark 1:1-2a), then Isaiah 61:1 comes immediately to mind":

---

5. Brownson et al., *StormFront*, p. 35.

The Spirit of the Lord God is upon me,
because the Lord has anointed me to bring good tidings to the
    afflicted. . . .

At the outset of his Gospel, Mark portrayed Jesus as Isaiah's promised one upon whom the Spirit of the Lord has come and whom God has anointed to preach the "gospel from God."

Matthew aligned the first four beatitudes of "the Sermon on the Mount" with Isaiah 61 to show that Jesus had come to proclaim the gospel promised in Isaiah 61.

In Luke, Jesus is presented as reading from Isaiah 61 in his hometown synagogue at the beginning of his public ministry and declaring that Isaiah's promise "has been fulfilled this day in your hearing" (Luke 4:16-21). Jesus knew the limits of his own people's understanding when they assumed that their lives were at the center of the world. When he tried to explain the reality of God's rule elsewhere, they wanted to domesticate it, make it something safe and harmless. "What gracious words," they said. They didn't get it.

Matthew, Mark, and Luke all presented Jesus and his ministry as expressing the "gospel" of Isaiah 61, which announces God's day of salvation for the afflicted, the captives, the blind, the oppressed, and those who mourn.

Elsewhere in the Gospels, we read that Jesus himself explained his ministry with references to passages from Isaiah. For example, in Matthew 11:2-6, when disciples of John the Baptist asked Jesus if he was the one expected, Jesus' response was drawn from Isaiah 35:5, 42:7, and 61:1: "the blind receive their sight and the lame walk, lepers are cleansed and the deaf hear, and the dead are raised up, and the poor have the gospel preached to them." Jesus was using texts from Isaiah to explain his ministry, even as the writers of the Gospels later drew on Isaiah to shed further light on Jesus' mission.

But, one may ask, where does Jesus' preaching of the Kingdom come into such a view of the gospel? Isaiah 61 does not specifically mention the Kingdom of God. Guelich answered this question: "Again, Mark supplies the clue (1:1-2) and, again, an indirect reference to Isaiah rounds out the picture. Jesus' preaching of the 'gospel from God' is found in the declaration that 'the kingdom of God is at hand.' And, again, this must be understood in the light of the prophet Isaiah." The combination of the announcement of the gospel and the message of the Kingdom can be found in Isaiah 52:7:

> How beautiful upon the mountains
> Are the feet of him
> Who brings good tidings [gospel],
> Who publishes peace,
> Who brings good tidings [gospel] of good,
> Who publishes salvation,
> Who says to Zion, "Your God reigns." (RSV)

In these words, the one who brings the "gospel" is the one who declares peace; the one who brings the "gospel" is the one who declares salvation. The content of "peace" and of "the good tidings" of "salvation" is made specific in the phrase "Your God reigns." Mark's rendering is Jesus' distinctive phrase, "the Kingdom of God." Thus we might fairly state, as Geulich did, "The gospel is the announcement of God's Kingdom, God's rule in history."

Jesus' gospel of the Kingdom was his expression of what God was doing in history and was doing through him to effect *shalom*. And, also, Jesus saw his way of effecting *shalom* as God's "anointed one" (messiah) to lead, as God's servant, to death and vindication: "For the Son of Man came not to be served but to serve and to give his life a ransom for the many" (Mark 10:45). Jesus saw his impending death and vindication as integral to God's promise of *shalom* — an integral part of the coming of God's rule or Kingdom into history. Jesus' death, then, was not merely the result of a misunderstanding of his message or a miscarriage of justice by the Jewish and Roman authorities.

Here then is the answer to the questions listed above about whether there is one gospel (and if so which one) or two gospels. In Guelich's words:

> The answer to how the gospel of the Kingdom and the gospel of the cross relate is that the gospel of the cross is integral to the gospel of the Kingdom in Jesus' ministry. But the gospel of the cross is only integral to the gospel of the Kingdom if we understand both to be an expression of the same "gospel," namely Isaiah's promised "gospel" of God. The "gospel," then, is the message that God acted in and through Jesus Messiah, God's anointed one, to effect God's promise of *shalom* — God's reign.

With this understanding of the gospel, "Christ died for our sins" is transformed into "the Messiah died for our sins according to the Scriptures" and in doing so combines the gospel of the Kingdom (the "Messiah") with the gospel of the cross ("died for our sins") as the biblical gospel ("according to the Scriptures"). It is not merely "good news" because of what it means to me.

Another important point needs to be made here. The New Testament contains various expressions of the gospel. Each expression reflects continuity with the theological substance of the gospel, while also using biblical and contemporary language and imagery to articulate that message. No one expression is more normative than the others.

So where does that leave the church in North America in the twenty-first century? Do we simply pass on traditional formulas, such as "justification by faith," "redemption," "salvation," "atonement," "Kingdom of God," "born again" that come from another era? Does not the presence of diverse New Testament expressions of the gospel that were drawn from and sensitive to that time and place challenge us to explore how we express the gospel in our day and place? I believe that the answer is yes. Could it be that even as the understandings and practices of stewardship have evolved, as we saw in the previous chapter, so our understanding of the gospel will evolve as we move more deeply into the twenty-first century?

The Gospel and the Churches

This brings us again to questions raised by the second issue mentioned near the beginning of this chapter: What is the relationship between the gospel and the churches? Is congregational life one option among many, or is the formation of congregations somehow critical to the essence of the gospel?

Branson expressed the core of his concern in these words: "Paul and Matthew, reflecting, I believe the teachings of Jesus, create a strong link between the gospel narrative and congregational life. The light is to be made visible to others. In a national norm akin to life in a food court (e.g. commuter lives, transient careers, temporary commitments, church hopping, etc.) we have adopted narratives antithetical to that gospel narrative."[6] He asked the question: "Have our minds, our theologies, our ecclesiologies been colonized?"

The link between the gospel and congregational life is vital. We must work to strengthen that link, not let it be "hijacked" by a "food court" mentality. As we saw in Chapter 2, our understanding of stewardship has changed and continues to change. Likewise, our understanding of gospel is being broadened and deepened. The issues that confront congregational life are also changing, as we shall see in Chapter 5. In Chapter 6, we will look at the church in the cultural caldron, while Chapters 7 and 8 will propose new possibilities for linking congregations and the world of theological education.

Darrell L. Guder wrote these words that help us understand that God's reign is multi-dimensioned and cannot be reduced to simple definition:

> God's reign is defined by the very character and action of God, which means that it cannot be reduced to simple definition nor made to serve human purposes. It is God's concrete self-disclosure in human history making a new relationship with God possible and thus a new life with a new future. So the good news of the kingdom of God is always, at any particular moment, partial; it always emphasizes this or that dimension of the wonder beyond telling, which is God's reign in our midst. Jesus teaches about the kingdom by telling parables that illustrate its various dimensions and the many ways in which we can encounter it. Always, however, the message focuses upon the loving, gracious, inviting reality of God in our human history; it creates the radically new option of submission to God's rule and thus entry into God's kingdom. This submission to God's rule is, paradoxically, the liberation of the believer from all that separates from God. To enter into the kingdom means to experience the forgiveness of sins, the liberation from all the demons which possess us, the gift of new life, and the invitation to a new kind of community.[7]

What does this mean for twenty-first-century congregations? The response of the congregation to whom Jesus spoke in Luke 4, as we noted above, can be instructive to congregations of today. Perhaps we

6. Branson, "Escaping a False Gospel."

7. Darrell L. Guder, *The Continuing Conversion of the Church* (Grand Rapids: Eerdmans, 2000), p. 37.

need to feel more of Jesus' impatience. But the trend of twenty-first-century congregations too often seems to be otherwise. The words of John Stendahl can provoke our thoughts:

> We inhabit a strange culture in which self-absorption and solipsism are mass-marketed, a culture in which our churches participate, compete and cater to please. Its assumptions may sit so deep and unspoken in us that it takes a voice of adolescent anger to put them into words. We shall perish if we cannot see a larger world and understand what we are doing to this globe and to strangers beyond the compass of our lives.[8]

A historical perspective on what "membership" in the church means, or does not mean, was put forth by Guder. The next paragraphs offer a summation of his research and thoughts.[9]

In the Western tradition of Christianity, Christian identity is usually defined as church "membership." This usage is probably rooted in Paul's terminology, especially in 1 Corinthians: "Now you are the body of Christ and individually members of it" (1 Cor. 12:27). This passage, of course, is describing the organic unity of Christ's body and the way in which Christians are linked to one another in Christ and depend upon one another. Gospel reductionism has led us far from that incarnational understanding of membership. As the church focused more on the benefits of salvation enjoyed by the individual Christian, membership came to mean "saved." The church redefined itself as the institution that administers salvation. To be a member was to enjoy the rights and privileges of salvation. Baptism was the event that put a person into the category of "saved." Nonmembership meant "unsaved": *extra ecclesiam nullus salus* — "outside the church there is no salvation" (Cyprian). Excommunication was threatening because it put one's salvation in jeopardy.

Guder argued that this reduced understanding of membership has persisted over the entire history of Western Christianity, through the Reformation into the modern period. One of the results of this understanding of membership has been "nominal" (or "inoculated") Christianity, that is, people who "name" themselves Christian, "who maintain a minimal level of faith commitment and practice, but for whom the vocation to serve Christ does not define their lives." Each period of

---

8. John Stendahl, "The Offense," *Christian Century*, 21 Jan. 1998, p. 53.
9. Guder, *The Continuing Conversion of the Church*, pp. 169-80.

church history has struggled with such a lowered understanding of what it means to be a "member" and the resultant shallowness of general church membership. We need to identify and learn from congregations in which "membership" is more than nominal.

Guder described the church's need for conversion in these words.

> This reductionism of the concept and practice of membership is a compelling example of the church's need for conversion. It reveals how far from the missional understanding of her vocation the church has moved in practice. We reveal what we think Christian witness is all about with the standards and practices we establish for becoming a Christian. If we accept a "lowest common denominator" definition of Christian commitment, then we should not be surprised that our congregations evidence so little commitment to gospel mission.
>
> This problem is clearly seen by many theologians. Karl Barth's comprehensive discussion of baptism, and especially of infant baptism, fleshed out many of the fundamental problems of nominal Christian membership as practiced in the churches of the Western tradition. William Abraham has suggested that evangelism must be understood as "initiation into the kingdom" and should require a process over time that is "corporate, cognitive, moral, experiential, operational, and disciplinary." This means that there must be a process of initiation which moves from pre-baptismal instruction, through baptism, to thorough grounding in the creeds and spiritual disciplines of the church. Rather than a low threshold, there will be a carefully conducted catechetical process which leads to an understanding and practice of membership that is shaped by the mission of the kingdom of God.[10]

We need congregations that are truly faith communities — gripped by the gospel. We do not need congregations of "nominal Christians." Just as Jesus took risks, so today we as disciples of Jesus are called to take risks. One of the risks we are called to take as stewards of the gospel is to break with the familiar to follow Jesus. One example of such risk taking may be the Ethiopian eunuch (Acts 8:27-39).

Matthew 9:10-13 relates Jesus' table fellowship with tax collectors and sinners. In fact the text says, "*Many* tax collectors and sinners came

---

10. Guder, *The Continuing Conversion of the Church*, p. 173.

and dined with Jesus." Not only was Jesus present; he was the host. The Pharisees asked the disciples, "Why does *your teacher* eat with tax collectors and sinners?"

Jesus took a major risk. He was regarded as being a friend of tax collectors and sinners (Matt. 11:19). The Pharisees were accustomed to separating the world into "good guys" and "bad guys" — clean and unclean. The boundary lines were distinct. Jesus' words and actions threatened such a world. That did not sit well with "religious" people. And it still doesn't.

We have seen above the importance of the prophet Isaiah in the words of Jesus as given in the Gospels. In his book *Using God's Resources Wisely*, Walter Brueggemann wrote that Isaiah 1:21-26 gives a synopsis of the whole history of the city of Jerusalem, "the model city of urban crisis and possibility." He continued, "The poet lays out the crisis and the possibility in three quick rhetorical moves."[11]

1. The city as it is intended by God is for faithfulness, justice, and peace.
2. But the city runs amok and forsakes justice and righteousness. "Then come murder and bribes, disregard of widows and orphans. This sorry state, says the poet, will lead to suffering, displacement, and exile."
3. "And then, in verse 26," wrote Brueggemann, "the poet abruptly and wondrously asserts a third season of the city yet to come . . . afterward!" A different future is still to come — a city of righteousness. It is a city mindful of widows and orphans in which God's resources are managed for the well-being of the weak and marginalized. The great poem (Isa. 65:17-25) that stands at the end of the book of Isaiah is an embodiment of the "afterward" that is anticipated in the first chapter of Isaiah. The "third season" is the future where humans manage God's resources as God intended. This is very close to what it means to be stewards of the gospel. This is a powerful clue to the life of what a Christian congregation can and should be.[12]

11. Walter Brueggemann, *Using God's Resources Wisely: Isaiah and Urban Possibilities* (Louisville: Westminster/John Knox Press, 1993), p. 77; see also pp. 77-81.

12. Gene M. Tucker noted that, although nineteenth-century scholarship demonstrated that the book of Isaiah was to be attributed to not one but three "Isaiahs," in the last two decades of the twentieth century the attention of scholarship turned to the in-

The authors of *StormFront* described the glowing sweep and scope of the message of the gospel:

> In the final analysis, the biblical understanding of salvation is not merely that our lives will be set right again at last. The biblical understanding of salvation is that our lives become swept up into something larger and greater than ourselves, into God's purposes for the world. In other words, the receiving of salvation and the call to mission are not to be conceived sequentially, as if one followed the other (first salvation, then grateful obedience in mission). Rather, to receive salvation *is* to be called into something larger and greater than we are, to be invited to participate in God's saving purpose and plan for the world. That is why the gospel is primarily about God, and only secondarily about us.[13]

To be a steward of the gospel is to so thirst for and respond to God's purposes that we become servants of Jesus Messiah in fulfillment of the gospel that integrates the gospel of the Kingdom with the gospel of the cross, according to the Scriptures. The good news is for all of God's creation, not just for "me."

In the next two chapters, we will address two questions: "What are valid principles of biblical interpretation in light of the evolving nature of our understanding of 'stewardship' and 'gospel'"? (Chapter 4) and "What are some of the major issues that confront us as stewards of the gospel in the twenty-first century?" (Chapter 5).

---

terpretation of the book as a whole. "The move to consider the book as a whole is long overdue." See Gene E. Tucker, "The Book of Isaiah 1-39: Introduction," in *The New Interpreter's Bible*, vol. 6 (Nashville: Abingdon Press, 1994), p. 28.

13. Brownson et al., *StormFront*, p. 34.

CHAPTER 4

Biblical Interpretation

The authority of the Bible is a perennial and urgent issue for those of us who stake our lives on its testimony. This issue, however, is bound to remain unsettled and therefore perpetually disputatious. It cannot be otherwise, since the biblical text is endlessly "strange and new." . . . Rather than proclaiming loud, dogmatic slogans about the Bible, we might do better to consider the odd and intimate ways in which we have been led to where we are in our relationship with the scriptures.

Walter Brueggemann,
"A Personal Reflection: Biblical Authority"

Introduction

Personal Experience

In my undergraduate work at the University of California, Los Angeles (UCLA), I received a B.A. degree with a major in zoology. Working on the thesis for my first seminary degree at California Baptist Theological Seminary (now American Baptist Seminary of the West), I chose as my thesis topic "The Validity of the Theory of Evolution and Its Relation to Theology." The thesis was my attempt to reconcile my understanding of the scientific method and, in particular, the theory of evolution, with

49

my understanding of theology and biblical interpretation. In the thesis, I argued that the theory of evolution was entirely consistent with Scripture. I took the point of view of theistic evolution, arguing that evolution was the method of creation that God had chosen and that this was consistent with the creation stories in the Bible and with my understanding of the nature of God. The thesis was accepted "as is."

A few months later, I met with the Ordination Council of the Los Angeles Baptist Association. One of the members of the Council was a young man who had been a fellow seminary student and who knew what had been my thesis subject. He asked me to explain my views on the Bible and evolution. I answered much as I had argued in the thesis. The floodgates were opened. I became intensely aware that there were differing interpretations of Scripture among the participants, though this was not a surprise to me. Many persons present thought and stated that their own interpretation of the Bible was correct, and that anyone who interpreted Scripture differently than they did was wrong and needed to be corrected.

The Council had three possible decisions to choose from: (1) approve the candidate for ordination and recommend that ordination take place; (2) recommend that ordination of the candidate not take place; or (3) recommend that ordination be deferred until the candidate would meet with a subsequent Ordination Council. The Council adopted the third option.

This was, of course, a time of distress and conflicting emotions in me. As it turned out, it was nearly one and a half years later before I met with another Ordination Council, with representatives from a different group of churches from the Los Angeles Baptist Association, and I was approved for ordination. I learned at an existential level that no one should advocate a principle of biblical interpretation that makes no leeway for differing interpretations of Scripture reached by persons of integrity under the guidance of the Holy Spirit. That principle of biblical interpretation can be described in these words: God has spoken to us unambiguously in the Bible. There is only one "right" interpretation of any given biblical passage. Of many different interpretations, there is only one that is valid. While a particular passage may have many *applications,* it must have only one *meaning* — the one the author (through inspiration of the Holy Spirit) intended.

It is my belief that such a limited view of biblical interpretation has caused much harm to the church and, even more, has led to conflicts and bloodshed over the centuries. The evidence is that the interpretation of many biblical texts has changed significantly over time, even centuries, and that views once popularly supported by Scripture are now neither generally accepted nor considered scriptural. Walter Brueggemann has reminded us that the basic premise of the Bible is relational: "We live not just because we happen to exist but because the One who has called the world into covenant is the same One who calls us to a relationship of responsibility. . . . [C]reation is a call to be in a continuing relation with the caller."[1]

Many factors related to biblical interpretation move far beyond the simplistic notion that there is only one "right" interpretation of any given biblical passage. Brueggemann noted several in his insightful article " A Personal Reflection: Biblical Authority":

> The authority of the Bible is a perennial and urgent issue for those of us who stake our lives on its testimony. This issue, however, is bound to remain unsettled and therefore perpetually disputatious. It cannot be otherwise, since the biblical text is endlessly "strange and new." It always and inescapably outdistances our categories of understanding and explanation, of interpretation and control. Because the Bible is "the live word of the living God," it will not compliantly submit to the accounts we prefer to give of it. There is something intrinsically unfamiliar about the book; and when we seek to override that unfamiliarity, we are on the hazardous ground of idolatry.[2]

In other words, it resists being object and persists in being subject.

In the article, Brueggemann listed "six facets of biblical interpretation" that he believed are likely to be operative among us all. These will be detailed later in this chapter.

Historical Examples

Next we turn our attention to four historical examples that the Bible is "the live word of the living God." These four are but a few examples

1. Walter Brueggemann, *The Bible Makes Sense,* rev. ed. (Cincinnati: St. Anthony Messenger Press, 2003), p. 19.

2. Walter Brueggemann, "A Personal Reflection: Biblical Authority," *Christian Century,* 3-10 Jan. 2001, p. 14.

among many over the centuries. The evidence of history in regard to the evolution of the interpretation of many biblical texts is powerful. The reader will also observe that the evolutionary process of interpretation is initiated and spurred on by crisis and controversy. We shall look in some detail at these four examples:

1. the theological controversy about the relationship between faith and works that erupted in the sixteenth century, still reverberating in the twenty-first century;
2. the conflict between the Bible and science about the solar system (and by implication the structure and movement of the entire physical universe) that peaked in the seventeenth century and was still being dealt with in the late twentieth century;
3. the struggle between proslavery and antislavery views and practices in the nineteenth century and the underlying conflicts about racism that continue into the twenty-first century; and
4. the genocide during the Holocaust conducted by the Nazis in the twentieth century and its still lingering effects in the twenty-first century.

Faith and Works

When one thinks of the relationship between faith and works, one thinks almost immediately of Martin Luther. From 1510 to 1520, Luther, then a Catholic priest, lectured on the Psalms and the books of Hebrews, Romans, and Galatians. As he studied these portions of the Bible, he began to understand terms such as "penance" and "righteousness" in new ways. He taught that salvation is a gift of God's grace through Christ received by faith alone. The first and chief article is this, Luther wrote, "Jesus Christ, our God and Lord, died for our sins and was raised again for our justification . . . it is clear and certain that this faith alone justifies us."

On October 31, 1517, Luther wrote to Albert, Archbishop of Mainz and Magdeburg, protesting the sale of indulgences in his episcopal territories and inviting him to a disputation on the matter. He enclosed the 95 Theses, a copy of which, according to tradition, he posted that day on the door of the Castle Church in Wittenberg.

Luther had already preached against indulgences, but he wrote the

95 Theses partly in reaction to the promotion of indulgences by Johann Tetzel, papal commissioner for indulgences in Germany, to raise funds for the renovation of St. Peter's Basilica in Rome. In thesis 28, Luther objected to a saying attributed to Tetzel: "As soon as the coin in the coffer rings, the soul from purgatory springs." The 95 Theses denounced such transactions as worldly and also denied the pope's right to grant pardons on God's behalf in the first place. The only thing that indulgences guaranteed, Luther said, was an increase in profit and greed. Luther did not deny the pope's right to grant pardons for penance imposed by the church, but he made it clear that preachers who claimed that indulgences absolved buyers from all punishments and granted them salvation were in error.

Others had attacked abuses in the church, but Luther's approach unleashed a doctrinal revolution in the reform movement. By rejecting papal and ecclesiastical practices that Luther deemed were in conflict with Scripture, he asserted the primacy of scriptural authority over the church, that is, Scripture over tradition.

The 95 Theses were quickly translated into German, printed, and widely copied, making the controversy one of the first in history to be fanned by the printing press. Within two weeks, the theses had spread throughout Germany, within two months throughout Europe.

Luther, taking the revival of the Augustinian notion of salvation by faith alone to new levels, borrowed from the humanists the sense of individualism, that each person can be his (or her) own priest and that the only true authority is the Bible.

The Reformation's principal arguments were based on "direct" biblical interpretation. When Luther and the other reformers adopted the standard of *sola scriptura,* making the Bible the sole measure of theology, they made the Reformation a reaction against the humanism of that time. Previously, the Scriptures had been seen as the pinnacle of a *hierarchy* of sacred texts.

The Protestants emphasized such concepts as salvation by "faith alone" (not faith and good works or infused righteousness), "Scripture alone" (the Bible as the sole rule of faith, rather than the Bible plus tradition), "the priesthood of all believers" (all people are individually responsible for their status before God such that talk of mediation through any but Christ alone is unbiblical). Because they saw these teachings as stemming from the Bible, they encouraged publication of the Bible in the common language and called for universal education (at least for males).

The Reformation did not happen in a vacuum, as there were movements for centuries calling for a return to biblical teachings, the most famous being from John Wycliffe and Jan Hus. It is no surprise that their teachings were later found in the Reformation. The spark that started the Reformation was a doctrinal issue brought up by the Bible. (There was also a secular or political side with the rise of the various states that sought to undermine the power of Rome or, what is the same thing, to increase their own power.)

Evidence of the evolutionary nature of biblical interpretation can be found in the agreement reached in 1999 between the Lutheran World Federation and the Roman Catholic Church, 482 years after Luther's 95 Theses. The Joint Declaration stated that salvation is achieved through God's grace, which then encourages Christians to undertake good works. As we have seen above, the doctrine of justification, or how human beings reach salvation, was one of the reasons for the breach between Luther and the papacy in the sixteenth century.

In 2006, the world's Methodist churches signed on to the agreement that had brought Catholics and Lutherans closer together on a key issue that rent them apart at the time of the Protestant Reformation. On July 23, 2006, Ishmael Noko, general secretary of the Lutheran World Federation, spoke in Seoul, South Korea, to the World Methodist Council, an umbrella organization for churches in 132 nations: "We have overcome a theological difference which has divided Western Christianity since the time of the Reformation."[3] Cardinal Walter Kasper, the Vatican's top official for promoting Christian unity, said in Seoul: "Today is one of the most significant dates in the history of our churches."[4]

A statement issued by the Methodist group representing nearly 70 million said: "It is our deep hope that in the near future we shall also be able to enter into closer relationships with Lutherans and the Roman Catholic Church."[5]

This history of the interpretation of the Bible, in regard to the relationship between faith and works, indicates once again that the Bible is "the live word of the living God," even when, as in this case, centuries pass as new understandings break forth.

---

3. "Lutherans, Catholics, Methodists in Accord," *Christian Century,* 22 August 2006, p. 11.

4. "Lutherans, Catholics, Methodists in Accord."

5. "Lutherans, Catholics, Methodists in Accord."

The Bible and Science: The Solar System

One of the most vexed areas related to biblical interpretation is the relationship between the Bible and science. As we noted above, some see the Bible as completely factual on all matters, including science. If there is a conflict, they say, then the Bible must be right and science wrong. Others say that if there is an apparent conflict, science must be reinterpreted or recast in such a way that the recasting of science matches their interpretation of particular biblical passages. Still others maintain that the Bible is not a book of science, but is a book related to God's relationship with God's creation, including human beings, and how human beings respond in faith to the living God.

One of the classic examples of "conflict" between the Bible and science was the dispute between Galileo and the church in the seventeenth century. Galileo Galilei (1564-1642) was an Italian physicist, astronomer, and philosopher who was closely associated with the scientific revolution.

Several passages in the Bible speak of the "firm" and "established" position of the earth:

The LORD is king, he is robed in majesty;
the LORD is robed, he is girded with strength.
He has established the world; it shall never be moved.

(Ps. 93:1)

Say among the nations, "The LORD is king!
The world is firmly established; it shall never be moved.
He will judge the peoples with equity."

(Ps. 96:10)

You set the earth on its foundations,
that it shall never be shaken.

(Ps. 104:5)

The world is firmly established;
it shall never be moved.

(1 Chron. 16:30b)

A generation goes and a generation comes,
but the earth remains forever.

The sun rises, and the sun goes down,
and hurries to the place where it rises.

(Eccles. 1:4-5)

For centuries, the church had interpreted literally[6] such passages as these, with the result that the church held a point of view that the universe is geocentric, that is, the earth is the fixed center of the universe and everything else revolves in circular orbits around the earth.

Over time, however, a contrary view began to emerge. The emerging view was that the sun is the center of the universe and everything else, including the earth, revolves in orbits around the sun. Galileo, among others, defended this view, known as heliocentrism, and claimed that it was not contrary to Scripture. He took Augustine's position on Scripture: not to take every passage literally, particularly when the Scripture in question is a book of poetry and songs, not a book of instructions or history. The writers of the Scripture wrote from the perspective of the terrestrial world, and from that vantage point the sun does rise and set. In fact, it is the earth's rotation that gives the impression of the sun in motion across the sky.

By 1616, when the attacks on Galileo peaked, he went to Rome to try to persuade the church authorities not to ban his ideas. In the end, Cardinal Bellarmine delivered to him an order not to "hold or defend" the idea that the earth moves and the sun stands still at the center. For the next several years, Galileo stayed away from the controversy.

In 1623, Galileo revived his project of writing a book on the subject, encouraged by the election of Cardinal Barberini as Pope Urban VIII. Barberini was a friend and admirer of Galileo and had opposed the

---

6. L. E. "Ted" Siverns wondered if the conclusion in this paragraph is correct. In a note to the author, he noted: "The conclusion hinges in part on what we meant and what we now mean by 'literal.' My understanding is that an earlier use of 'literal' was 'in a literary manner,' i.e., not so much what is said but what is meant. Considering the works of Origen, Augustine, and Chrysostom, of Albertus Magnus, Duns Scotus and Thomas Aquinas, of Luther, Calvin and the 'Scottish Realists' of the last century at Princeton Seminary, Jack Rogers, *Biblical Authority*, concluded that 'it is historically irresponsible to claim that for two thousand years, Christians have believed that the authority of the Bible entails a modern concept of inerrancy in scientific and historical details.' My sense is that the contemporary literal approach has been shaped by the scientific method — a method that suggests that the meaning, say of chemistry text, is what is plain and obvious on the pages. That is, science had led us to the contemporary form of literalism."

condemnation of Galileo in 1616. Galileo's book, *Dialogue Concerning the Two Chief World Systems,* was published in 1632, with formal authorization from the Inquisition and papal permission.

Pope Urban VIII had personally asked Galileo to give arguments for and against heliocentrism in the book, and to be careful not to advocate heliocentrism. He made another request, that his own views on the matter be included in Galileo's book. Only the latter of those requests was fulfilled by Galileo. Whether unknowingly or deliberately, Simplicius, the character defending the Aristotelian geocentric view in *Dialogue Concerning the Two Chief World Systems,* was portrayed as a fool who was often caught in his own errors. As a result, the book was perceived as an attack on Aristotelian geocentrism and a defense of the Copernican theory. To make matters worse, Galileo had put the words of Pope Urban VIII into the mouth of Simplicius. Most historians agree Galileo did not act out of malice and felt blindsided by the reaction to his book. However, the pope did not take the public ridicule lightly, nor the blatant bias. Galileo had alienated one of his biggest and most powerful supporters, the pope, and was called to Rome to explain himself.

With the loss of many of his defenders in Rome because of *Dialogue Concerning the Two Chief World Systems,* Galileo was ordered to stand trial on suspicion of heresy in 1633. The sentence of the Inquisition was in three essential parts:

1. Galileo was required to recant his heliocentric ideas; the idea that the sun is stationary was condemned as "formally heretical."
2. He was ordered imprisoned; the sentence was later commuted to house arrest.
3. His offending *Dialogue* was banned; and in an action not announced at the trial and not enforced, publication of any of his works was forbidden, including any he might write in the future.

After a period with the friendly Ascanio Piccolomini (the Archbishop of Siena), Galileo was allowed to return to his villa at Arcetri near Florence, where he spent the remainder of his life under house arrest, dying on January 8, 1642. While Galileo was under house arrest, he dedicated his time to one of his finest works, *Two New Sciences.* This book later received high praise from both Sir Isaac Newton and Albert Einstein. As a result of this work, Galileo is often called the "father of modern physics."

Galileo was formally "rehabilitated" in 1741, when Pope Benedict XIV authorized the publication of Galileo's complete scientific works (a censored edition had been published in 1718). In 1758, the general prohibition against heliocentrism was removed. On October 31, 1992, Pope John Paul II expressed regret for how the Galileo affair had been handled.

The controversy between the Bible and science continues to rage. Though the disagreement about the structure and movements of the solar system is resolved in the minds of most people, conflicts rage about the Bible's view related to other branches of science, especially in the life sciences. We will explore this more in Chapter 5.

Slavery

Over the centuries, indeed the millennia, much of the world has practiced slavery. America is no exception. One of the greatest evils in American history was slavery, when certain human beings were treated as though they had no human rights.

In the years before and during the American Civil War, Christian ministers and others in the North and in the South spoke with authority about the overriding purposes of God, but they came to strikingly different conclusions about slavery. A layperson named Abraham Lincoln framed the issue in these words: "Both sides read the same Bible and pray to the same God." But, he concluded, since they prayed for different outcomes, "the prayers of both could not be answered."

Aidsand Wright-Riggins III, in an article titled "Opposing Words of Horror," described a visit to America's Black Holocaust Museum in Milwaukee, Wisconsin. He wrote that what troubled him most deeply about his visit to the museum was reflecting on "how American Christians justified slavery and subordination of black people for hundreds of years based upon what they thought Scripture taught and sanctioned. *Christians owned slaves and justified it with Scripture.* With Bibles in hand, Christians lynched black men as their crosses blazed bright across southern nights."[7]

In 1852, Harriet Beecher Stowe's book *Uncle Tom's Cabin; or, Life*

---

7. Aidsand Wright-Riggins III, "Opposing Words of Horror," *Mission in America,* Sept./Oct. 2006, p. 4; emphasis added.

Among the Lowly was published. It was the best-selling novel of the nine-teenth century (and the second best-selling book of that century, fol-lowing the Bible) and is credited with helping to fuel the abolitionist cause in the 1850s. In the first year after it was published, 300,000 cop-ies of the book were sold in the United States alone. The book's impact was so great that when Abraham Lincoln met Stowe at the start of the Civil War, Lincoln is often quoted as having declared, "So this is the lit-tle lady who made this big war."

The book provided a powerful example of the abolitionist appeal to the general spirit of the Bible. The book had a tremendous influence in parts of the United States, though very little in the South. Stowe questioned widespread notions about the self-interpreting power of the Bible:

> For example, she had one of her slave-owning characters, Augustine St. Claire, suggest that scriptural interpretation was driven more by interest than intellect. "Suppose that something should bring down the price of cotton once and forever, and make the whole slave prop-erty a drug in the market, don't you think we should have another version of the Scripture doctrine? What a flood of light would pour into the church, all at once, and how immediately it would be dis-covered that everything in the Bible and reason went the other way!"[8]

One of the riveting passages in her book is set in Ohio, in the home of Senator and Mrs. Bird. Both of them appeal to the Bible to support their arguments. She appeals to the spirit of the Bible, while the sena-tor cites chapter and verse. Here is some of the discussion and action, presented in dramatic form:

> NARRATOR: After the slave Eliza escapes over the ice-clogged Ohio River with her young son, she comes, exhausted, to the home of Senator and Mrs. Bird just as they have finished discussing the senator's support for Ohio's version of the Fugitive Slave Law.[9]

---

8. Mark Noll, "The Impasse over Slavery: Battle for the Bible," *Christian Century*, 2 May 2006, p. 20.

9. A word of explanation: the "fugitive slave law" was a law stating that, even in a free state, a runaway slave was to be recaptured and returned to his or her owner. To pro-vide refuge for a runaway slave was illegal — a criminal offense.

When Mary Bird surprises her husband by attacking all such laws as "shameful, wicked, [and] abominable," John Bird replies with arguments paralleling the biblical defense:

SENATOR BIRD: "But Mary, just listen to me. Your feelings are all quite right, dear, and interesting, and I love you for them; but, then, dear, we mustn't suffer our feelings to run away with our judgment."

NARRATOR: In response to the arguments in favor of fugitive slave laws, which regularly included a proslavery use of the Bible, Mary Bird blows away the equivalent of chapter-and-verse argumentation with a larger [context] of scriptural sentiment:

MRS. BIRD: "Now, John, I don't know anything about politics, but I can read my Bible; and there I see that I must feed the hungry, clothe the naked, and comfort the desolate; and that Bible I mean to follow."

SENATOR BIRD: "But in cases where you're doing so would involve a great public evil — "

MRS. BIRD: "Obeying God never brings on public evils. I know it can't. It's always safest, all round, to do as He bids us."

SENATOR BIRD: "Now, listen to me, Mary, and I can state to you a very clear argument to show — "

MRS. BIRD: "O nonsense, John! You can talk all night, but you wouldn't do it, I put it to you, John — would you now turn away a poor, shivering, hungry creature from your door because he was a runaway? Would you now?"

NARRATOR: At that very point the fugitive slave Eliza arrives at their door, and the senator proves his mettle by setting aside his arguments and moving Eliza in the dead of night away from danger.

The senator's innate desire and passion for justice overcame his narrow and biased interpretation of Scripture.

The significance of Stowe's *Uncle Tom's Cabin* for the biblical debate over slavery lay in the novel's emotive power. Stowe exemplified — rather than just announced — the persuasive force of what she regarded as the Bible's overarching general message.

The Christian faith makes the stunning moral demand, here it is actually a command, that we love our enemies. In order to love our enemies, we must presuppose the best about them; we must attempt to see their lives lovingly, with charity, clenching our fist, gritting our teeth, and, in an act of daring love, show our determination to love them no matter what.

A remarkable book by Mark A. Noll portrayed the "dilemma" faced by proslavery and antislavery forces in mid-nineteenth-century America. Chapter 3 of that book, titled "The Crisis over the Bible," offers fascinating details of the "dilemma."[10]

In October 1845, two Presbyterian ministers took up the fight in a public debate in Cincinnati. The debate went on for eight hours a day through four long days. Jonathan Blanchard, who had been a student of Moses Stuart at Andover Seminary, defended the abolitionism that Stuart would later attack in his 1850 monograph. Nathaniel Rice, who had studied at Princeton Theological Seminary, defended Stuart's position that, although the Bible pointed toward the eventual, voluntary elimination of slavery, it nowhere called slavery evil as such. The two debaters agreed to base what they said on the Bible as their only authoritative source. Noll described the debate in these words:

> As Rice methodically tied Blanchard in knots over how to interpret the proslavery implications of specific texts, Blanchard returned repeatedly to "the broad principle of common equity and common sense" that he found in Scripture, to "the general principles of the Bible" and "the whole scope of the Bible," where to him it was obvious that "the principles of the Bible are justice and righteousness." Early on in the debate, Blanchard's exasperation with Rice's attention to particular passages led him to utter a particularly revealing statement of his own reasoning: "Abolitionists take their stand upon the New Testament doctrine of the natural equity of man. The one-bloodism of human kind [from Acts 17:26]: — and upon those great principles of human rights, drawn from the New Testament, and announced in the American Declaration of Independence, declaring that all men have natural and *inalienable* rights to person, property and the pursuit of happiness."[11]

Noll drew the following conclusions as to why the prevailing interpretative practices favored democratic, republican, antitraditional, and commonsensical exegesis. The biblical pro-slavery argument

10. Mark A. Noll, *The Civil War as a Theological Crisis* (Chapel Hill: University of North Carolina Press, 2006), pp. 31-50.

11. Noll, *The Civil War as a Theological Crisis,* p. 41.

seemed strong, the biblical anti-slavery argument seemed "religiously dangerous," and the more nuanced biblical argument against the American form of slavery did not fit well with "democratic practice and republican theory." Yet, many people in the North, who opposed any use of Scripture to attack slavery because of their commonsense interpretation of the Bible, "were nonetheless uneasy with the system." These were joined by a few from the South. "Though conservative in their attachment to traditional views of the Bible, they continued to struggle against the all-out proslavery biblicism of the South's great champions."

> On the eve of the Civil War, interpretations of the Bible that made the most sense to the broadest public were those that incorporated the defining experiences of America into the hermeneutics used for interpreting what the infallible text actually meant. In this effort, those who, like James Henley Thornwell, defended the legitimacy of slavery in the Bible had the easiest task. The procedure, which by 1860 had been repeated countless times, was uncomplicated. First, open the scriptures and read — at, say, Leviticus 25:45, or, even better, at 1 Corinthians 7:20-21. Second, decide for yourself what these passages mean. Don't wait for a bishop or a king or a president or a meddling Yankee to tell you what the passage means, but decide for yourself. Third, if anyone tries to convince you that you are not interpreting such passages in the commonsensical, ordinary meaning of the words, look hard at what such a one believes with respect to other biblical doctrines. If you find in what he or she says about such doctrines the least hint of unorthodoxy, as inevitably you will, then you may rest assured that you are being asked to give up not only the plain meaning of scripture, but also the entire trust in the Bible that made the country into such a great Christian civilization.[12]

This was the situation with regard to biblical interpretation just before the Civil War. "With debate over the Bible and slavery at such a pass, and especially with the success of the proslavery biblical argument manifestly (if also uncomfortably) convincing to most southerners and many in the North, difficulties abounded." This created a terrible problem for the whole country, "because its most trusted religious authority, the Bible, was sounding an uncertain note." The problem for

---

12. Noll, *The Civil War as a Theological Crisis,* pp. 49-50.

the evangelical Protestant churches was that "the mere fact of trusting implicitly in the Bible was not solving disagreements about what the Bible taught concerning slavery." The trouble was not limited to the churches, of course, but became a problem for the whole country, "because the remedy that finally solved the question of how to interpret the Bible was recourse to arms. The supreme crisis over the Bible was that there existed no apparent biblical resolution to the crisis. It was left to those consummate theologians, the reverend doctors Ulysses S. Grant and William Tecumseh Sherman, to decide what in fact the Bible actually meant."[13]

Wright-Riggins's description of his visit to America's Black Holocaust Museum ended with these words:

> I wondered, "How is it that generations of intelligent, converted and committed Christians could not see back then what we now commonly recognize as mitigating factors in the biblical record? How did we come to change our minds about what the texts actually said? What caused our churches to change course?"
>
> Somehow, I think it has something to do with affirming the primacy of Jesus Christ as God's Word over and against affirming any word or selection of words as "the Word." "Holocaust" is a word of horror and hopefully never the last word. It describes the deplorable depersonalization and destruction of people somehow deemed inferior or blighted or cursed. In each generation, it threatens to raise its ugly, beastly head to ravage another group of people whom God claims as God's own. Who is attacking now? How are biblical texts used to extend this terror? Who are those of our generation that Martin Niemoller would describe as truly concerned?[14]

Slavery ended in the United States in the nineteenth century, though it still exists in some other parts of the world. Racism — the underlying festering disease that led to slavery — lingers. We have treated symptoms, but the cause of the disease is still rooted deep underneath veneers of polite words and token actions. In the next chapter, we will look at the issue of racism, as well as other issues that face the church in the twenty-first century.

---

13. Noll, *The Civil War as a Theological Crisis,* p. 50.
14. Wright-Riggins III, "Opposing Words of Horror," p. 4.

Genocide and the Holocaust

The Holocaust in Nazi Germany (1938-45) began with a boycott of Jewish shops and ended in the gas chambers at Auschwitz and other concentration camps as Adolf Hitler and his Nazi followers attempted to exterminate the entire Jewish population of Europe. The total number of Jews murdered is generally set at 6,000,000 men, women, and children. Ironically, and tragically, even in the twenty-first century there are persons who deny the historical reality of the Holocaust. In 2006, the government of Iran sponsored a conference whose main objective was to deny that the Holocaust really happened.

The roots of the Nazi Holocaust began in January 1933, when, after a ten-year political struggle, Adolf Hitler came to power in Germany. During his rise to power, Hitler repeatedly blamed the Jews for Germany's defeat in World War I and subsequent economic hardships. He advocated racial theories that Germans with fair skin, blond hair, and blue eyes were the master race. The Jews, according to Hitler, were the racial opposite.

Almost as difficult to comprehend as the Holocaust itself were the acceptance of and acquiescence to Hitler's theories of racial purity by German theologians. A 1985 book by Robert P. Ericksen, titled *Theologians Under Hitler,* and later a film with the same title, detailed the strong theological support that most of the church's major theologians gave to Hitler. The book and the film detail the views of three of these theologians: Gerhard Kittel, Emanuel Hirsch, and Paulo Althaus.

Filmmaker Steven D. Martin made it clear that Kittel, Hirsch, and Althaus "were more representative of the church than the confessors and martyrs who opposed Hitler and are often invoked these days in sermons."[15] He continued:

> A particular telling remark comes from an interview with Hartmut Lehmann of Göttingen about the bishop of Hanover. After the *Kristallnacht* in 1938, the large synagogue in Hanover was still burning as the bishop arrived for work; the fire was within sight of his cathedral. The bishop's secretary expected him to express outrage, mar-

15. Jason Byassee, "Documenting the Church's Failure: Theologians and Nazis," *Christian Century,* 30 May 2006, p. 11.

shal resources to help — do something. Instead he sat down and began his administrative work for the day. What an image of the church during the Nazi horrors — doing nothing, oblivious to the flames. Often the church's behavior was even worse: it provided a rationale for those committing the horrors.

Lehmann, the liveliest individual interviewed in the film, makes another point that has application in our time. The church in Germany was eager to reacquire cultural prestige, and it was worried that it was perceived as overly effeminate. The Nazis offered an opportunity to be more tough and manly. The German Christians were thrilled when World War I navy hero Ludwig Muller was named *Reichsbischof,* the first head over a newly unified Protestant church in Germany. And they were delighted by the legions of Brownshirts who filled the churches to consecrate their marriages before altars draped with swastikas.[16]

Kittel's multi-volume *Textual Notes on the New Testament* is still the standard reference work on the etymologies of biblical Greek. Ironically he prepared for that work by befriending Jews and learning their literature, as his Hebrew-scholar father had before him. But then his viewpoint changed: "He later clarified (or changed his mind): his love was for *biblical* Judaism, from which secular contemporary Jews had long since fallen away."[17] Kittel came to think that Jews were a problem in Germany. Jason Byassee delineated Kittel's thoughts expressed in Kittel's lecture titled "The Jewish Problem" and the subsequent response by the Nazis:

> Why were Jews dominant in such crucial German institutions as the universities, the government and the press? Had this predominance weakened Germany, perhaps fatally? For Kittel the answer was yes, and something had to be done. He ruled out moving the Jews to the Middle East — the Arabs would never allow it. He ruled out annihilating them as "impractical." He also ruled out their assimilation into Germany society — such intermingling was precisely the problem. Therefore the only solution to the Jewish question was to remove them from their employment and separate them from the rest of society. Kittel warned that the world would call Germany's actions

16. Byassee, "Documenting the Church's Failure," p. 10.
17. Byassee, "Documenting the Church's Failure," p. 10.

"brutal" but insisted that this was "no one else's concern" — and that God did not call Germans to be weak.

Little wonder that the Nazis avidly reprinted the lecture. Kittel was later employed in the Nazis' Research Section on the Jewish Question — which decided that one of his proposed alternatives was not so impractical.[18]

The linchpin of Hirsch's theology was the German *Volk*, or "people," which included

the whole of Germany's great history in literature, the arts, and statecraft. Ericksen describes the concept of *Volk* as almost untranslatable: a "mystical, transcendent" link that bound Germans to one another and their tradition in a manner "almost beyond description." The *Volk* was more important to Hirsch than democracy, especially in the wake of the ruining of Germany in World War I and in light of the need to rebuild the country's greatness, which, he insisted, depended on the piety of the *Volk*.

Indeed, the *Volk* was for him as essential to God's work as Israel was to any Jew or Christian. "There is absolutely no contradiction to make it difficult as a German to be a Christian or as a Christian to be a German," Hirsch insisted. Little wonder that he greeted Hitler's rise to Germany's chancellorship in 1933 as "a sunrise of divine goodness." While other ecclesial supporters of the Nazis expressed some remorse later in life, Hirsch never did.[19]

Byassee concluded his article with these words:

[Filmmaker] Martin makes clear that a crucial precursor to removing Jews from Germany was the effort by theologians championing the Enlightenment to remove particular cultural baggage from the gospel, including the reality of Jesus' Jewishness. Ideas have consequences — something academics, of all people, sometimes forget.[20]

Here we observe that German theologians in an effort to promote Enlightenment ideas "sanitized" the biblical accounts of Jesus to remove the cultural baggage of Jesus as a Jew.

18. Byassee, "Documenting the Church's Failure," p. 10.
19. Byassee, "Documenting the Church's Failure," pp. 10-11.
20. Byassee, "Documenting the Church's Failure," p. 11.

By contrast, a minority of Christians of that time, such as Dietrich Bonhoeffer, Maximilian Kolbe, Corrie ten Boom, and the residents of the mountain village of Le Chambon in France who hid several thousand Jews, heroically opposed the Nazis.

Of these, probably the most familiar to Americans is Bonhoeffer, whose early and ongoing resistance to the Nazis is well known. He was involved in the Confessing Church and directed an underground seminary at Finkenwalde. After the forced closing of Finkenwalde, he continued to train students to serve in the Confessing Church through underground pastorates. On September 4, 1940, the Nazi government banned Bonhoeffer from public speaking, including teaching and preaching. This forced silence gave Bonhoeffer the opportunity to work on his magnus opus, *Ethics*. While staying committed to the Confessing Church, Bonhoeffer also became an agent for military intelligence and became involved in a plot to overthrow Hitler's regime. As Craig L. Nessan wrote about Bonhoeffer's "double life" during this time, "Under what conditions, if any, does one choose to become an interruption in order that other interruptions may cease? One can only imagine how this double life appeared to those who saw the decision only from the outside." Even Karl Barth, his colleague and confidant, wondered about Bonhoeffer's trustworthiness.

> As this volume [*Ethics*] amply documents through both Bonhoeffer's own writings and other original source material, he became deeply enmeshed in treasonous activities aimed at overthrowing the government of his beloved Germany. For a Protestant theologian, such engagement was unprecedented. Among these activities was his involvement in Operation 7, which smuggled 14 "non-Aryans" into Switzerland under the guise of an operation of military intelligence. While initially it was the charge of avoiding conscription that led to his arrest, Bonhoeffer's connection to Operation 7 offered further evidence of sedition, which deepened his legal predicament.
>
> Under the pretext of gathering intelligence, Bonhoeffer also made trips to Switzerland and Sweden, where he used his ecumenical contacts to negotiate on behalf of a post-Hitler German government.[21]

An assassination attempt on Hitler's life on July 20, 1944, failed. Bonhoeffer had been imprisoned in 1943. The failed attempt sealed

---

21. Craig L. Nessan, "A Life Interrupted," *Christian Century*, 17 Oct. 2006, p. 55.

Bonhoeffer's fate. He was executed on April 9, 1945, at the Flossenburg concentration camp, shortly before the end of the war.

The question before us is, "What led Bonhoeffer to live and to die as he did?" Robin Lovin noted that in the introduction to the English edition of *Ethics,* volume 6 in the Dietrich Bonhoeffer Works series, edited by Clifford Green, the editor helps to locate *Ethics* in relation to the rest of Bonhoeffer's works. The editor's notes give an account of how certain sources influenced *Ethics.* Lovin wrote:

> Foremost among these sources for Bonhoeffer's generation was the work of Karl Barth, whose return to the "strange world of the Bible" inspired his younger German counterpart's early lectures. Barth's theology marked a complete break with the adjustments to modern culture and Prussian political order that Bonhoeffer had learned from his mentors in Berlin, and it provided the starting point for the Confessing Church.[22]

Sixty-one years after the end of the Nazi holocaust, in April 2006, some twenty religious leaders came together to watch and comment on the film *Theologians Under Hitler.* The only Jewish participants were Arthur Waskow and Phyllis O. Berman. Following the viewing of the film and the discussion that followed, they wrote an article that gave their response as Jews to the colloquium.[23]

The colloquium was intended to face the questions: Could theologians and other religious leaders of our own generation make such a profound moral mistake as those in Germany in the 1930s? What could prevent such a betrayal? One of their observations afterward was this:

> The gathering was unanimously horrified by the film's demonstration that almost all the most respected theologians and other religious leaders and institutions of Germany had either acquiesced in or triumphantly celebrated the ideas and actions of Nazism. The gathering was also unanimous in wanting to prevent any analogous acquiescence or celebration of American theologians and religious communities *vis-à-vis* any practice or power that might be analogous to Nazism.

22. Robin Lovin, "What Would Bonhoeffer Do? Ethics for This World," *Christian Century,* 19 Apr. 2005, p. 26.

23. Arthur Waskow and Phyllis O. Berman, "Courtesy or Clarity? A Jewish Response to *Theologians Under Hitler,*" *The Progressive Christian,* Jan./Feb. 2007, pp. 11-12, 48.

Yet the whole spectrum of religious folk present — conservatives, liberals, progressives — held their tongues about their own specific concerns: Who or what might bear the potential of "Hitler" or "Hitlerism" in America today? Against what sort of acquiescence might we need to gird our moral and spiritual strength? No comment. Courtesy triumphed over clarity.[24]

Waskow and Berman concluded that though they joined in the cautious courtesy that may have been necessary for the gathering to be comfortable enough to have any useful discussion at all, they believe that "there must come a point when clarity is more important than caution or comfort, when clarity must be expressed with all possible courtesy . . . even if it makes all participants uncomfortable."[25]

If participants in such discussions could agree to seek clarity, with courtesy, many of the "cultural wars" related to issues of biblical interpretation could be mitigated and/or agreement more often reached. Perhaps the parties involved could "agree to disagree" more often then they do under the far too prevalent "I'm right and you're wrong" mindset. Can we seek both clarity and courtesy?

Dimensions of Biblical Interpretation

We consider further the "strange world of the Bible" as we return to Brueggemann's six facets of biblical interpretation, which he believed are likely to be operative among us all.[26] In the summaries of the six facets that follow, direct quotations from Brueggemann appear in quotation marks.

- *Inherency.* The Bible is inherently the living word of God; it reveals the character and will of God, and it empowers us for an alternative life in the world. Under this point he listed four sub-points, in the fourth of which he wrote, "the Bible is so endlessly a surprise beyond us that Karl Barth famously and rightly termed it 'strange and new.' The Bible is not a fixed, frozen, readily exhausted read; it

24. Waskow and Berman, "Courtesy or Clarity?" p. 11.
25. Waskow and Berman, "Courtesy or Clarity?" p. 48.
26. Brueggemann, "A Personal Reflection: Biblical Authority," pp. 15-20.

is, rather, a 'script,' always reread, through which the Spirit makes all things new."

- *Interpretation.* "[T]he Bible is not self-evident and self-interpreting," Brueggemann wrote. "The process of interpretation which precludes final settlement is evident in the Bible itself." As an example, he cited the Mosaic teaching in Deuteronomy 23:1-8 that bans from the community all those with distorted sexuality and all those who are foreigners. Moreover, in Deuteronomy 24:1-4, Moses taught that marriages broken in infidelity cannot be restored, even if both parties want to get back together. However, he pointed out, in Jeremiah 3, in "a shocking reversal given in a pathos-filled poem," God indicates a willingness to violate this teaching for the sake of restored marriage to Israel. "The old teaching is seen to be problematic even for God." The Jeremiah text shows God prepared to move beyond the old prohibition of Torah. Brueggemann's conclusion is that the interpretative project that gave rise to the final form of the text is itself "profoundly polyvalent, yielding no single exegetical outcome, but allowing layers and layers of fresh reading in which God's own life and character are deeply engaged and put at risk."
- *Imagination.* "Responsible interpretation requires imagination." Interpretation is more than simple reiteration of the text; rather, it is "the movement of the text beyond itself in fresh, often formerly unuttered ways." Jesus' parables are a good example. In ancient Israel and the early church there was an observant wonder. Just as eyewitnesses formed texts out of miracles that they observed and remembered, these "texted miracles" then became "materials for imagination that pushed well beyond what was given or intended even in the text." We, too, must follow the same process if we want to insist that the Bible is a contemporary word to us. "We transport ourselves out of the twenty-first century back to the ancient world of the text or, conversely we transpose ancient voices into contemporary voices of authority. . . . [W]e have figured out that a cold reiterative objectivity has no missional energy or moral force."
- *Ideology.* Whether we admit it or not, our interpretation is always affected and distorted by our own self-interests. "There is no interpretation of scripture (nor of anything else) that is unaffected by the passions, convictions and perceptions of the interpreter." Toward the end of this chapter, I will deal with this factor in more detail.
- *Inspiration.* "[T]he force of God's purpose, will and capacity for liber-

ation, reconciliation and new life is everywhere in the biblical text." We affirm this even though we do not fully understand how this is true. All we can do is to acknowledge that, in each text, "God's wind blows through and past all our critical and confessional categories of reading and understanding." That "powerful and enlivening force" does not simply ordain the text as Scripture but also affects "its transmission and *interpretation* among us" (emphasis added).

- *Importance.* Biblical interpretation that is done imaginatively, with a willingness to risk ideological distortion, and open to God's inspiring Spirit, is of great importance. The church dares to affirm that "the lively word of scripture is the primal antidote to technique, the primal news that fends off trivialization. Thinning to control and trivializing to evade ambiguity are the major goals of our culture. The church in its disputatious anxiety is tempted to join the move to technique, to thin the Bible and make it one-dimensional." The church is also tempted to trivialize the Bible by acting as though it is important only because it may solve "some disruptive social inconvenience." Thinning and trivializing the Bible reduce "what is rich and dangerous in the book to knowable technique and what is urgent and immense to exhaustible trivia." Brueggemann insisted: "The Bible is too important to be reduced in this way because the dangers of the world are too great and the expectations of God are too large. What if liberals and conservatives in the church, for all their disagreement, would together put their energies to upholding the main truth against the main threat? The issues before God's creation (of which we are *stewards*) are immense; those issues shame us when our energy is deployed only to settle our anxieties. The biblical script insists that the world is not without God, not without the holy gift of life rooted in love. And yet we twitter! The Bible is a lamp and light to fend off the darkness. The darkness is real, and the light is for walking boldly, faithfully in a darkness we do not and cannot control. In this crisis, the church must consider what is entrusted peculiarly to us in this book" (emphasis added).

A Summary of Principles of Biblical Interpretation

Reviewing Brueggemann's six dimensions and the dimensions drawn from the four historical examples of biblical interpretation has led me to the nine principles listed below, which I believe will be helpful to those engaging in biblical interpretation.

These nine principles, while listed separately, are flexible and, in many ways, interrelated and interconnected. Because of this, some of them could be combined in different ways or differentiated more finely. Nevertheless, I offer them as useful tools for the purpose of biblical interpretation.

They will evolve over time as our understanding of the "live word of God" grows and as the cultural environment in which we find ourselves changes from year to year and from place to place.

They are not listed in a specific order of priority, though my sense is that the pitfall of self-interest (number 4 below) is a dominant factor. For that reason, I have added more detail to that principle.

1. Inherency

The Bible is the live word of God. As such, it is always strange and new, not fixed and frozen.

Conflicts have raged, and continue to rage, about the Bible and science. In earlier centuries conflict was often about the physical sciences. In this century, it is far more often about the life sciences.

In *Uncle Tom's Cabin*, Mary Bird appeals to the spirit of the Bible, while her husband, the senator, cites chapter and verse. She blows away the equivalent of chapter-and-verse argumentation with a larger context of scriptural sentiment.

Wright-Riggins pointed to the primacy of Jesus Christ as God's Word over and against affirming any word or selection of words as "the Word."

Foremost among the sources for Bonhoeffer and his generation was the work of Karl Barth and his return to the "strange world of the Bible."

2. Interpretation

The Bible is not self-evident and self-interpreting.

The Protestants encouraged publication of the Bible in the common language.

Augustine's position on Scripture was not to take every passage too literally, particularly when the Scripture in question is a book of poetry and songs, not a book of instructions or history.

Stowe questioned the widespread notions about the self-interpreting power of the Bible. In her novel, Senator Bird's innate desire and passion for justice overcame his narrow and biased interpretation of Scripture.

Abolitionist Blanchard returned repeatedly to "the broad principles of common equity and common sense" that he found in scripture, to "the general principles of the Bible" and "the whole scope of the Bible," where to him it was obvious that "the principles of the Bible are justice and righteousness."

3. Imagination

Responsible interpretation requires imagination.

"A cold reiterative objectivity has no missional energy or moral force," as Brueggemann said. Imagination enables us to transport ourselves out of the twenty-first century back to the ancient world of the text or, conversely, transpose ancient voices into contemporary voices of authority. We experience what it is like to be in the other person's seat.

4. Ideology

Our interpretative work is shot through with self-interest, of which we are seldom aware.

The sale of indulgences by the church in sixteenth-century Germany is a strong example of self-interest as a determining factor.

In the antebellum southern United States, Christians owned slaves and justified it, based upon what they thought Scripture taught and sanctioned. Scriptural interpretation was driven more by interest than intellect. The remedy that finally solved the question of how to interpret the Bible was recourse to arms in the Civil War.

The two Jewish participants in the symposium on the film *Theologians Under Hitler* reminded us that there must come a point when clarity is more important than caution or comfort, when clarity must be

73

expressed with all possible courtesy, even if it makes all participants uncomfortable.

In the law, there is a basic rule known as the "hearsay rule," which states that testimony or documents that quote persons not in court are not admissible. Because the person who supposedly knew the facts is not in court to state his/her exact words, the jury cannot judge the demeanor and credibility of the alleged first-hand witness, and the other party's lawyer cannot ask questions of him or her. However, as significant as the hearsay rule itself are the exceptions to the rule, which do allow hearsay testimony. One of these exceptions is a statement by the opposing party in the lawsuit that is inconsistent with what he or she has said in court, called "declarations against interest." The principle is "that a statement asserting a fact distinctly against one's interest is unlikely to be deliberately false or heedlessly incorrect."[27] Stephen Foulk wrote:

> Statements qualifying for the exception are those which are contradictory or inconsistent with the author's or speaker's penal, pecuniary, or proprietary interests. (Most hearsay exceptions are made because there is some assurance of the statement's trustworthiness even though the speaker or author is not in court. Prior inconsistent statements are not within a hearsay exception and, in fact, are not considered hearsay because they are used to impeach the speaker or author who is then testifying in court.)[28]

The principle behind the hearsay rule and this exception to the hearsay rule suggest strongly that a person's credibility is much higher if statements being made by that person are against that individual's own self-interest. I suggest that this same principle can be applied to biblical interpretation. If a person's interpretation of a biblical text works against his or her own self-interest, the credibility of that interpretation is greatly enhanced.

This principle of "against self-interest" is especially operative when a particular interpretation of the Bible is held by a group of persons in

---

27. John Wigmore, *Evidence in Trials at Common Law*, vol. 5, section 1457, p. 329 (3rd edition, 1974), as cited by Attorney Stephen Foulk in a private communication to the author dated 24 Jan. 2007.

28. Attorney Stephen Foulk in a private communication to the author dated 24 Jan. 2007.

a majority position or in a position to enforce their interpretation by coercive means.

"Against self-interest" is also entirely consistent with Brueggemann's dimension of "ideology." His statements that "We are seldom aware about the ways in which our work is shot through with distorting vested interests" and that "It is so, whether we know it or not" stand as major warning signals as we do our work of biblical interpretation. The historical examples detailed above tell me that guarding against self-interest would have changed the conduct of the church and "Christians" if that principle had been taken more seriously. Consider the church in the sixteenth century as it continued to sell indulgences despite Luther's protests. Recall the lonely stand of Galileo and a few others against the position of the church that "the earth does not move." Think of American slaveholders who gained great economic benefit from the enforced labor of human beings of a different race. Remember churches and pastors in Nazi Germany who basked in the glory and prestige of being part of a glorious regime and ignored the brutality, imprisonment, and death that it brought fellow Germans (and others) who were Jewish.

Our human dilemma is that no interpretation of Scripture is unaffected by the passions, convictions, and perceptions of the interpreter. But perhaps we can guard against falling into the trap of biblical interpretation based on our own interests. For example, if my interpretation of the Bible seems to favor me and/or my group over against the interests of another person or another group, I should consult with those other parties. This is especially critical if my social or economic status, my racial or ethnic category or nationality, or any other factor has placed me (or could place me) in a position of power over or conflict with another person or group. Perhaps taking such precautions could reduce the effects of the "blindfolds" that we are too likely to wear when we open the Bible.

5. Inspiration

God's Spirit moves through and beyond our categories of biblical reading and understanding.

This claim is an acknowledgment that, in and through the text, God's wind blows through and past all our critical and confessional categories of reading and understanding. That powerful and enlivening force of God's wind, moreover, affects more than the text itself. It extends as well to the transmission and *interpretation* of the text.

6. Importance

Biblical interpretation is important.

Thinning the text to evade ambiguity is to give in to our culture and to make the Bible one-dimensional and trivial. What if liberals and conservatives put their energies to upholding the main truth against the main threat? Instead of fighting and struggling against one another, they might better spend time and energy together as stewards of the gospel of Jesus Christ to engage the culture and its false gospel. Chapters 5 and 6 will describe some of the issues in the struggle and how the church responds to being in the cultural caldron. The issues before the church are immense.

7. Scriptural Authority

Scriptural authority is to be taken seriously.

The Reformation lifted up the primacy of scriptural authority over the church. Each person can be his or her own priest; the only true authority is the Bible. The concept of *sola scriptura* was that the Bible is the sole measure of theology. Because the human factor enters in regard to translations, transmission, and interpretation of the text, the text must be approached humbly as well as seriously. The text should not be used as a weapon to proclaim that "I am right and you are wrong."

8. Passage of Time

The passage of time may lead to a growing consensus on particular issues of biblical interpretation.

Examples of the importance of the passage of time include:

The agreement reached in 1999 between the Lutheran World Federation and the Roman Catholic Church, which came 482 years after Luther's 95 Theses.

In regard to the structure and movements of the solar system, 359 years passed from the trial of Galileo to a papal expression of regret. (The trial was in 1633. In 1758, the general prohibition against heliocentrism was removed. On October 31, 1992, Pope John Paul II expressed regret for how the Galileo affair had been handled).

Though slavery no longer exists legally in the United States, the underlying roots of racism persist, even after a century and a half. Will it require another century and a half before the viral power of racism is eradicated? We will explore this further in the next chapter.

iAbolish has stated:

> Contrary to popular belief, slavery didn't end with Abraham Lincoln in 1863. Experts estimate that today there are *27 million people* enslaved around the world. It's happening in countries on all six inhabited continents. And yes, that includes the United States. The CIA estimates *14,500 to 17,000 victims* are trafficked into the "Land of the Free" every year.
>
> Why hasn't more been done to end a dehumanizing, universally condemned practice? One challenge is that slavery today takes on myriad, subtler forms than it did during the Atlantic Slave Trade — including sex trafficking, debt bondage, forced domestic or agricultural labor, and chattel slavery — making it tougher to identify and eradicate.[29]

The Nazi Holocaust and its practices of genocide ended in 1945. But genocide still persists in many parts of the world. We will also look further at this issue in the next chapter.

9. Culture

The prevailing culture affects biblical interpretation, as does taking into proper account the gospel's own cultural environment.

In the southern United States before the Civil War, interpretations of the Bible that made the most sense to the broadest public were those that incorporated the defining experiences of America into the hermeneutics used for interpreting what the infallible text actually meant.

---

29. This quotation was found on the Internet at www.iabolish.org/slavery_today/ primer/index.html.

The prevailing culture was what made the most sense to the broadest public. Because of this, those who, like James Henley Thornwell, defended the legitimacy of slavery in the Bible had the easiest task.

The church in Nazi Germany was eager to reacquire cultural prestige. The linchpin of the theology of the theologians who supported Hitler was the German *Volk,* or "people." The environmental culture of that time and place influenced and directed the biblical interpretation of the church.

A crucial precursor to removing Jews from Germany was the effort by theologians championing the Enlightenment to remove particular cultural baggage from the gospel, including the reality of Jesus' Jewishness. The surrounding culture was allowed to override and negate the gospel's own cultural environment. As Jason Byassee put it, "Ideas have consequences — something academics, of all people, sometimes forget."

Evolution of Hermeneutics (Biblical Interpretation)

We have observed in Chapter 2 that our understanding of stewardship has changed over the years and in Chapter 3 that we are learning the depths and meanings of "gospel." And so it is with hermeneutics. We must be very careful not to say or think that we have the "final word" in regard to any text. God's word is lively, and it can lead us to understandings and in directions that we might never anticipate ahead of time. That is exciting!

In the next chapter, we will look at some of the major issues confronting the church in the early twenty-first century. Our intent will be to look at these issues through biblical lenses, taking into account the nine principles of biblical interpretation mentioned above.

CHAPTER 5

Issues Confronting the Twenty-First-Century Church in North America

Shalom is the flower that
blooms only on the tree of justice,
planted near the waters of abundance,
warmed by the light of truth and faithfulness.

> Anthony Prete, closing plenary address, 2003 Friends
> General Conference Gathering in Johnstown, PA

We have delved into the meaning of stewardship, explored in depth the meaning of "gospel," and looked at criteria for biblical interpretation. We turn now to issues confronting the church in the twenty-first century. If our responsibility as stewards of the gospel indeed grows out of and is rooted in "thirst for God," and, therefore, a thirst for God's passion for justice, it necessarily follows that we must be aware of and care about the issues that burden and crush people.

Though the specific details of issues change over time, some issues, looked at in their broad strokes, seem always to be with us. In this chapter, we will look at a few of them as they appear in today's world. The ongoing task of the church is to examine, reexamine, and reflect on these issues through the lens of being stewards of the gospel and in the context of their times, places, and cultures. Even though we know that details of the issues will surely change over the coming years and decades, it is likely that their broad strokes will be an ongoing challenge to the church.

In this chapter, we will focus on these issues that plague and torment North America and the world, and confront the church:

- racism
- poverty and hunger
- war
- health
- science and faith
- the environment.

Racism

Slavery in America began long before there was a United States. In 1619, Virginia settlers took delivery of slaves from a Dutch man-of-war. Legalized slavery in the United States did not end until Lincoln's Emancipation Proclamation issued during the Civil War.

Now, in the twenty-first century, it is hard for many persons to realize fully the depths and depravity of the slavery system. Calvin O. Butts Jr. recounted an illustration of what it was like to be a slave:

> Let's go to Arkansas. . . . Let's make the year 1835. Let's make it August. Let's make it 3:00 p.m., when the sun is at its highest peak and at its hottest. No shade; the temperature is 120°. There's a black man and a black woman. They are enslaved people and they are in the field working. There's an overseer.
>
> The black man looks at his wife and then looks up at the overseer. He says, "Massa."
>
> "What you want, boy?"
>
> "My wife wants to step off the line."
>
> The overseer looks over at the woman and says, "All right, step off, girl."
>
> She says, "Massa, can I take my 13-year-old daughter with me?"
>
> "Take her home."
>
> So the woman and the 13-year-old walk maybe a thousand yards over the hill. They stop at a bush. The woman goes behind the bush, squats, and grunts one time. No pain, no crying, no tears. Just one

grunt and out comes a baby. By whatever method they have, they cut the umbilical cord and wrap the baby. She gives it to the 13-year-old, who goes back to the plantation. But where does the woman go? She goes back to the field and works alongside the man.[1]

By 1860, the year when Abraham Lincoln was elected to his first term as president of the United States, the nation had four million slaves. The Civil War started the following year. After the Civil War had ended, it was soon evident that slavery had been based on racism, not simply on economic factors buttressed by "proslavery biblical arguments."[2] A full hundred years passed between Lincoln's election in 1860 and the passage of the Civil Rights and Voting Rights Acts in 1960.

Post–Civil War Racism

Even after the Civil War had ended and slavery in the United States had been abolished,[3] the ugly face of racism reared its head. It soon became evident that slavery in the United States had indeed been based on more than economic advantages and "proslavery biblical arguments." A key question that had not generally been addressed by proslavery proponents was this: Could the general biblical sanction for slavery claimed by proslavery advocates be applied unambiguously to the *black-only form of slavery* that had existed in the United States?

In regard to the relation between race and slavery, Philip Schaff of the German Reformed seminary in Mercersburg, Pennsylvania, had concluded in 1861, *"the negro question . . . lies far deeper than the slavery question."*[4] Yet, overall, Schaff's article did not live up to that remarkable conclusion. Mark Noll commented on this disparity:

---

1. Calvin O. Butts III, "A New Heaven and a New Earth" (The Ministers and Missionaries Benefit Board of American Baptist Churches, 1999), pp. 9-10.

2. See William M. Swartley, *Slavery, Sabbath, War, and Women* (Scottsdale, PA: Herald Press, 1983), chap. 1, "The Bible and Slavery," pp. 31-64, for arguments presented by Christian statesmen and theologians for and against slavery from 1815 to 1865.

3. Modern slavery still exists in some parts of the world. Kevin Bales estimated that perhaps 27 million people are enslaved around the world, especially in South Asia and North Africa. Source: "Century Marks," *Christian Century*, 24 Apr.–1 May 2002, p. 6.

4. Philip Schaff, as cited by Mark A. Noll, *The Civil War as a Theological Crisis* (Chapel Hill: University of North Carolina Press, 2006), p. 51; Schaff's emphasis.

What Schaff saw when he defined "the negro question" and "the slavery question" as two distinct matters and what Schaff practiced in assuming that they could be treated as one problem constituted a theological crisis. The crisis created by an inability to distinguish the Bible on race from the Bible on slavery meant that when the Civil War was over and slavery was abolished, systemic racism continued unchecked as the great moral anomaly in a supposedly Christian America. This crisis reflected a greater difficulty than when a large Protestant population drew incommensurate theological conclusions from a commonly exalted sacred text that it approached with common hermeneutical principles.[5]

This theological crisis led to widely practiced racial segregation and discrimination, *de jure* in the South and *de facto* in the North. In the South, *de jure* laws that enforced racial segregation were known as Jim Crow laws.

Jim Crow Laws

The Jim Crow era in American history began in the late 1890s, when southern states began systematically to codify (or strengthen) legal provisions for the subordinate position of African Americans in society. Most of these legal steps were aimed at separating the races in public spaces (public schools, parks, accommodations, and transportation) and at preventing adult black males from exercising the right to vote. The system of legalized segregation and disfranchisement was fully in place in every state of the former Confederacy by 1910. This system of white supremacy cut across class boundaries and re-enforced a cult of "whiteness" that predated the Civil War.

According to Ronald L. F. Davis, the term "Jim Crow" is believed to have originated around 1830 when a white minstrel show performer, Thomas "Daddy" Rice, blackened his face with charcoal paste or burnt cork and danced a ridiculous jig while singing the lyrics to the song "Jump Jim Crow." Rice had created this character after seeing, while traveling in the South, a crippled, elderly black man, or perhaps a young black boy, dancing and singing the song:

5. Noll, *The Civil War as a Theological Crisis*, p. 52.

Weel about and turn about and do jis so,
Eb'ry time I weel about I jump Jim Crow.[6]

Jim Crow segregation laws gained significant impetus from U.S. Supreme Court rulings in the last two decades of the nineteenth century. In 1883, the Supreme Court ruled as unconstitutional the Civil Rights Act of 1875. The 1875 law had stipulated "That all persons . . . shall be entitled to full and equal enjoyment of the accommodations, advantages, facilities, and privileges of inns, public conveyances on land or water, theaters, and other places of public amusement." Not long after the Court's decision striking down the Civil Rights Act of 1875, southern states began enacting sweeping segregation legislation.

Growing up in Texas in the 1930s and early 1940s, I experienced firsthand and observed the effects of Jim Crow laws and the racism that lingered decades after the Civil War had ended slavery. I described some of these in an earlier book:

Though slavery was no longer allowed, Jim Crow laws were in full force and effect. For example, department stores had two kinds of drinking fountains (one for "colored" and one for "white") and there were four kinds of rest rooms (male and female for each of the two racial designations). Schools were segregated with the false claim that they were "separate but equal." Seating on buses and streetcars was segregated, with a movable sign indicating that "colored" people were to sit in the rear.

When I was 15 years old, I would often board buses and streetcars in Dallas and intentionally sit in the back. My boyhood fantasy was that I would be arrested for violating the Jim Crow laws and would then challenge those unjust laws all the way to the United States Supreme Court. I was never arrested, and no one ever said anything to me. Only later did I realize that the laws were not intended to keep me as a white person from sitting in the rear behind the movable signs; they were targeted at "colored" persons sitting in the front.

In the years afterward, I often wondered why I felt so strongly that justice was violated by the Jim Crow laws. No pastor or Sunday school teacher had ever said a word in my hearing about the injustice of racial segregation, nor had any family member or friend. I con-

6. Ronald L. F. Davis, "Creating Jim Crow: In-Depth Essay," Internet Site: www.jimcrowhistory.org/history/creating2.htm.

cluded that somehow the biblical texts and stories I heard and learned in church had gotten through to me, despite the fact that their human messengers had not communicated the message of God's passion for racial justice.

In later years, I recalled an African American woman whom I had met when I was about six or seven years of age. My mother's mother had died in 1913, when my mother was only 10 years old. Her father, a poor farmer in rural Lone Oak, Texas, was left with four young children to care for. I later met the woman whom he had engaged as a housekeeper, and she told me her story. As best as she could figure, she had been born about 1850, as a slave, and was about 15 years old when the Civil War ended and she was set free. She remembered her years as a slave and told me many of her experiences. I now believe that her story influenced me, primarily on a subconscious level, a few years later, when I began to sit "behind the signs" on buses and streetcars in Dallas. Her story reinforced and interacted with the story of justice that I heard in the gospel stories and accounts.[7]

The story of Rosa Parks is well known to most Americans. On a bus in Montgomery, Alabama, on Thursday, December 1, 1955, she refused to stand so that a white man could sit. She was arrested for violation of the segregation laws of Alabama. The usual explanation for her refusal to stand and move has been that she was a weary 42-year-old seamstress whose feet ached after working all day. She herself offered a different explanation to Jesse L. Jackson Sr. Here are his words:

> In her declining health, I would often visit Mrs. Parks, and once asked her the most basic question: Why did you do it? She said the inspiration for her Dignity Day in 1955 occurred three months prior, when African-American Emmett Till's murdered and disfigured body was publicly displayed for the world to see. "When I thought about Emmett Till," she told me, "I could not go to the back of the bus." Her feet never ached.[8]

L. E. "Ted" Siverns reported that her feet ached later: "In a Detroit gathering with Jesse Jackson, I heard Rosa Parks say, in relation to

---

7. Adapted from Ronald E. Vallet, *The Steward Living in Covenant: A New Perspective on Old Testament Stories* (Grand Rapids: Eerdmans, 2001), pp. 4-5.

8. Jesse L. Jackson Sr., "Appreciation," *Time*, 7 Nov. 2005, p. 23.

walking in support of the boycott, 'My feets was tired, but my soul was at rest.'"[9]

Her defiance led to a 381-day bus boycott, led by Martin Luther King Jr. Nine years later, the Civil Rights Act of 1964 was passed. Jackson continued: "Her righteous indignation literally changed the world."[10]

A lesser-known incident had happened in 1950. Thomas Edward Brooks, a 21-year-old black soldier who got on a bus in Montgomery, "made the mistake of entering through the front door instead of the back." For that, as authors Donnie Williams and Wayne Greenhaw related in *The Thunder of Angels,* a policeman bashed him on the head with a billy club and shot him dead. At least two other black men were similarly killed in the years leading up to Parks's act of civil disobedience.[11]

The primary leadership of the Civil Rights movement came from Martin Luther King Jr. (1929-1968). It is not my purpose to detail the storied ministry of King. That story has been chronicled in many writings over the years. I will include here only a few highlights. The impetus for his leadership of the movement came immediately after the arrest of Rosa Parks on December 1, 1955. King had been pastor of the Dexter Avenue Baptist Church in Montgomery since 1954.

King's selection on December 5 to lead the Montgomery Improvement Association (MIA), which guided the Montgomery bus boycott that focused national attention on racial segregation in the South, catapulted King into the national spotlight. Taylor Branch described the events of Monday evening, December 5, 1955, when King spoke in the Dexter Avenue Baptist Church, following Day One of the bus boycott:

> King paused. The church was quiet but it was humming. "My friends," he said slowly, "I want it to be known — that we're going to work with grim and bold determination — to gain justice on the buses in this city. And we are not wrong. We are not wrong in what we are doing." There was a muffled shout of anticipation, as the crowd sensed that King was moving closer to the heart of his cause. "If we are wrong — the Supreme Court of this nation is wrong," King sang out. . . . "If we are wrong — Jesus of Nazareth was merely a uto-

---

9. L. E. "Ted" Siverns in a private communication to the author, dated 5 May 2007.

10. Jackson Sr., "Appreciation," p. 23.

11. See Ellis Cose, "Transition: Rosa Parks, 1913-2005: A Legend's Soul Is Rested," *Newsweek,* 7 Nov. 2005, p. 53.

pian dreamer and never came down to earth! If we are wrong — justice is a lie." This was too much. He had to wait some time before delivering his soaring conclusion, in a flight of anger mixed with rapture: "And we are determined here in Montgomery — to work and fight until justice runs down like water, and righteousness like a mighty stream!" The audience all but smothered this passage from Amos, the lowly herdsman prophet of Israel who, along with the priestly Isaiah, was King's favorite biblical authority on justice.

"And I want to tell you this evening that it is not enough for us to talk about love," he said. "Love is one of the pinnacle parts of the Christian faith. There is another side called justice. And justice is really love in calculation. Justice is love correcting that which would work against love." He said that God was not just the God of love: "He is also the God that standeth before the nations and says, 'Be still and know that I am God — and if you don't obey Me I'm gonna break the backbone of your power — and cast you out of the arms of your international and national relationships.'" Shouts and claps continued at a steady rhythm as King's audacity overflowed. "Standing beside love is always justice," he said. "Not only are we using the tools of persuasion — but we've got to use the tools of coercion." He called again for unity. For working together. He appealed to history, summoning his listeners to behave so that sages of the future would look back at the Negroes of Montgomery and say they were "a people who had the moral courage to stand up for their rights." He said they could do that. "God grant that we will do it before it's too late."

The crowd retreated into stunned silence as he stepped away from the pulpit. The ending was so abrupt, so anticlimactic. The crowd had been waiting for him to reach for the heights a third time at his conclusion, following the rules of oratory. A few seconds passed before memory and spirit overtook disappointment. The applause continued as King made his way out of the church, with people reaching to touch him. Dexter members marveled, having never seen King get loose like that. Abernathy remained behind, reading negotiating demands from the pulpit. The boycott was on. King would work on his timing, but his oratory had just made him forever a public person. In the few short minutes of his first political address, a power of communion emerged from him that would speak inexorably to strangers who would both love and revile him, like all prophets. He was twenty-six, and had not quite twelve years and four months to live.[12]

A little less than eight years after the bus boycott, King's speech during the March on Washington on August 28, 1963, shook the nation. It is generally regarded as the highlight of King's ministry. Certainly it was the moment that brought him into national and international prominence. Estimates of the number of persons gathered that day vary, but a reasonable estimated figure is 250,000.

Earlier that year, in the spring and summer, events in Birmingham, Alabama, had inspired a wave of demonstrations in more than a hundred southern cities, resulting in over 20,000 arrests. On June 19, President John Kennedy had sent Congress a promised civil rights bill that offered federal protection to African Americans seeking to vote, to shop, to eat out, and to be educated on equal terms. Pressuring Congress to adopt this bill and to consolidate the protest activities brought together major civil rights, labor, and religious groups to organize a massive Washington demonstration.

Branch described the conclusion of King's memorable "I Have a Dream" speech in these words:

> The "Dream" sequence took him from Amos to Isaiah, ending "I have a dream that one day, every valley shall be exalted. . . ." Then he spoke a few sentences from the prepared conclusion, but within seconds he was off again, reciting the first stanza of "My Country 'Tis of Thee," ending, "from every mountainside let freedom ring." After an interlude of merely one sentence — "And if America is to be a great nation, this must become true" — he took it up again: "So let freedom ring." . . . As King tolled the freedom bells from New Hampshire to California and back across Mississippi, his solid square frame shook and his stateliness barely contained the push to an end that was old to King but new to the world: "And when this happens . . . we will be able to speed up that day when *all* God's children, black men and white men, Jews and Gentiles, Protestants and Catholics, will be able to join hands and sing in the words of the old Negro spiritual, 'Free at last! Free at last! Thank God almighty, we are free at last!'"[13]

12. Taylor Branch, *Parting the Waters: America in the King Years, 1954-63* (New York: Simon & Schuster Paperbacks, 1988), pp. 140-42.
13. Branch, *Parting the Waters,* pp. 882-83.

In the last years before his death, King was trying to build an inter-racial coalition to end the war in Vietnam and force major economic reforms, including guaranteed annual incomes for all. In April 1968, King went to Memphis, Tennessee, to march with striking garbage men. The march had degenerated into a riot. "We've got some difficult days ahead," King said the night before he was assassinated on Thursday, April 4. He was right.

Post–Jim Crow Racial Discrimination

Neither the ending of Jim Crow laws nor the assassination of King ended practices of racial discrimination in the United States. Note this jolting experience of Aidsand Wright-Riggins III when he took a religious studies course in 1970 at California State University, Fullerton:

> I was a Comparative Religions major in college. In a senior project, I sought to show how closely our racial images are wedded to our religious convictions. In front of a classroom of white students, I began a presentation about Albert Cleage's Black Jesus. As I spoke, I took a picture of the Black Christ out of my briefcase and slowly ripped it to shreds. Puzzled looks appeared on my classmates' faces as they watched and continued to listen to the presentation. A little while later, I reached into the same briefcase, pulled out a picture of a blonde-haired and blue-eyed Jesus and began to tear up this picture. Before I could make a quarter-inch rip, I was suddenly and violently knocked against the wall, thrown to the floor and kicked in the back and side by three or four members of the Campus Crusade for Christ.
>
> I thought that I was going to teach my colleagues something about the nature of religious and racial symbolism. I was the one who learned a very powerful lesson that day. Race and religion matter for people. Often, race matters most.[14]

The devastating effects of and responses to Hurricane Katrina on citizens of New Orleans in 2005 revealed that racism is still alive in the United States. Even as I write these words more than forty years after

---

14. Aidsand Wright-Riggins III, "The Segregated Hour," *Home Mission Today*, published by American Baptist National Ministries, Summer 1998, p. 2.

King's death, the ugly face of racism still confronts us. Even the election of an African-American man as president of the United States in 2008 did little to change this fact. In 2009 President Barack H. Obama was depicted as a Nazi by some opposed to his proposals for health care reform. Racism is deeply embedded in the American culture.

Immigration

Concern by some persons about so-called "illegal immigrants" is linked to racism. Issues related to immigration are much in the news in the early twenty-first century, though certainly not for the first time. In 2006, the Center for Immigration Studies reported that 35 million American residents were foreign-born, the most in American history. Many U.S.-born Americans complain, saying in effect that all the foreign-born should have stayed where they were before coming to the United States. Anna Quindlen found a quotation that summed up that attitude perfectly:

> "Today, instead of a well-knit homogenous citizenry, we have a body politic made up of all and every diverse element. Today, instead of a nation descended from generations of freemen bred to a knowledge of the principles and practices of self-government, of liberty under law, we have a heterogeneous population no small proportion of which is sprung from races, that, throughout the centuries, have known no liberty at all. . . . In other words, our capacity to maintain our cherished institutions stands diluted by a stream of alien blood."[15]

Quindlen then observed that the quotation was from circa 1927, the lament of an advocate of restrictive immigration. She continued:

> But there's never really anything new under the sun, or in the United States, and the notion that those who have been here awhile are inherently better than those who have just arrived still gets a lot of traction. It even holds sway among members of former immigrant groups reviled in their own time. The Irish and the Italians were the

15. Cited by Anna Quindlen, "The Last Word: Open to All: The Big Job," *Newsweek*, 9 Jan. 2006, p. 64.

Mexicans and Chinese of a hundred years ago. But now many of them have convenient immigration amnesia.[16]

As Quindlen observed in another column:

[T]his is not a new issue. The Founding Fathers started out with a glut of land and a deficit of warm bodies. But over its history, America's more-established residents have always found ways to demonize the newcomers to the nation needed to fill it and to till it. It was only human, the contempt for the different, the shock of the new.

Today, because so many immigrants have entered the country illegally or are living here on visas that expired long ago, the demagoguery has been amped up full throttle. Although the conventional wisdom is that immigrants are civic freeloaders, the woman with a sign that said I PAY TAXES was reflecting the truth. Millions of undocumented immigrants pay income taxes using a special identification number the IRS provides.[17]

The reality is that all Americans, except for Native Americans, are immigrants or descendants of immigrants. A column in *Christian Century* described how different Americans view such a statement:

That fact is often cited, and rightly so, by those in favor of providing immigrants who have been living and working in this country a straightforward path to citizenship. Those who want to clamp down on the illegal immigrants (as many as 12 million) complain that the immigrants are driving down wages and overwhelming American culture. The hardliners reveal signs of xenophobia or even racism. The concern that new immigrants stick to themselves, aren't learning English and are threatening American culture was voiced in earlier eras about the Irish, the Italians and the Jews — who at the time were considered members of a different race from Anglo-Saxon Americans.[18]

The column concluded with this admonition:

16. Quindlen, "The Last Word: Open to All: The Big Job," p. 64.
17. Anna Quindlen, "The Last Word: Undocumented, Indispensable," *Newsweek*, 15 May 2006, p. 78.
18. "Sojourners," *Christian Century*, 11 July 2006, p. 5.

Jews and Christians share this scripture: "You shall not wrong or oppress a resident alien, for you were aliens in the land of Egypt" (Exod. 22:21). Scripture says that God's people are to regard sojourners not with fear, indifference or loathing, but with love and respect. Movements to criminalize millions of individuals, break up families and destabilize industries are bad enough. The notion that the alien among us is anything other than beloved elicits some of scripture's strongest condemnations: "'Cursed be anyone who deprives the alien, the orphan, and the widow of justice.' All the people shall say, 'Amen!'" (Deut. 27:19).[19]

Having looked at issues related to racism, we now move to issues of poverty and hunger. As we shall see, these issues are also strongly tied to the issue of racism.

Poverty and Hunger

In 1964, President Lyndon B. Johnson, giving his first State of the Union address, put forth these words: "This administration, here and now, declares unconditional war on poverty in America." He added, "The richest nation on earth can afford to win it." That was true then, and it is true now. But the hard fact is that we have not won the war on poverty.

Almost forty years after Johnson declared war on poverty, historian Alice O'Connor said that her students laughed when she talked about how Lyndon B. Johnson declared a "war on poverty" in the 1960s. Apparently the idea struck them as quaint. O'Connor pointed out that the disparity between rich and poor today is greater than it was in the Depression or in the post–World War II years of affluence.[20]

In the early twenty-first century, it appears that things have gotten worse for the poor, not better. The same column in *Christian Century* offered these prophetic words:

We've moved from a political climate in which war can be declared on poverty to one in which war can be declared on the poor themselves — in the form of policies that favor the privileged. In the

19. "Sojourners," p. 5.
20. "Stiffing the Poor," *Christian Century*, 14 June 2003, p. 5.

[George W.] Bush administration's first tax cut in 2001, for instance, 40 percent of the benefits went to the richest 1 percent of taxpayers, while the bottom 20 percent of taxpayers received less than 1 percent of the benefits, according to Ichiro Kawachi and Bruce P. Kennedy in *The Health of Nations* (New Press). The more recent tax cut will only exacerbate the disparity between the very rich and very poor. . . .

When Jesus famously said, "The poor you have with you always," he was not prescribing how things ought to be, nor was he turning away from the needs of the poor. He was realistically describing the way things are. Further, Jesus was quoting from Deuteronomy 15:1-11, which included not just an assessment of the human community (there will always be someone in need), but also a goal (there should be no one in need) and a mandate (when there is someone in need, don't be tight-fisted). Indeed, Torah didn't just require benevolence toward the poor, but through the year of Jubilee and other measures, sought to address the systemic roots of poverty.[21]

Former president Jimmy Carter, in his Nobel Lecture when he received the Nobel Peace Prize in 2002, remarked on the growing gap between the rich and the poor:

At the beginning of this new millennium I was asked to discuss, here in Oslo, the greatest challenge that the world faces. Among all the possible choices, I decided that the most serious and universal problem is the growing chasm between the richest and poorest people on earth. Citizens of the ten wealthiest countries are now seventy-five times richer than those who live in the ten poorest ones, and *the separation is increasing every year, not only between nations but also within them.* The results of this disparity are root causes of most of the world's unresolved problems, including starvation, illiteracy, environmental degradation, violent conflict, and unnecessary illnesses that range from Guinea worm to HIV/AIDS.[22]

A 2004 report noted that, in the United States in 1973, 20 percent of the households accounted for 44 percent of total income, according to the Census Bureau. Their share jumped to 50 percent in 2002, while ev-

---

21. "Stiffing the Poor," p. 5.
22. Jimmy Carter, Nobel Lecture, Oslo, 10 Dec. 2002 (The Nobel Foundation, 2002); emphasis added.

eryone else's fell. For the bottom fifth, the share dropped from 4.2 percent to 3.5 percent.[23]

U2's lead singer Bono, addressing the 2006 National Prayer Breakfast as he urged the U.S. to double its foreign aid budget, said: "God is in the slums, in the cardboard boxes where the poor play house. God is in the silence of a mother who has infected her child with a virus that will end both their lives. God is in the cries heard under the rubble of war. God is in the debris of wasted opportunity and lives. And God is with us, if we are with them."[24]

The gap between rich and poor continues to widen. Clearly, poverty has been and continues to be a major issue that confronts the church and our responsibility to be stewards of the gospel.

War

In 2005, a man named Alfred Anderson died at age 109 in Newtyle, Scotland. He was the last surviving participant in the famous Christmas Truce of 1914, when British and German soldiers came out of their trenches along the Western Front near Ypres, Belgium, to exchange gifts and sing carols. The unofficial World War I truce spread to much of the Western Front and lasted for days in some areas. A year or so before his death, Anderson said of the truce, "I remember the eerie sound of silence."

World War I, or the Great War as it was known until World War II came a generation later, was billed for many years as the "war to end all wars." Tragically, the twentieth century saw many wars to follow, including, but not limited to, World War II, the Korean Conflict, the Vietnam War, and Middle East conflicts involving Israel and other countries.

The Nature of War

During the twentieth century, the nature of war shifted from being mostly clearly defined conflicts between or among nation states, with most of the violence affecting military personnel. The trend in warfare

23. "Disparity Growing Between People Who Have and Those Who Don't," *The [Syracuse, N.Y.] Post-Standard,* 17 Aug. 2004, p. A-3.

24. *Christian Century,* 21 Feb. 2006, p. 7.

was to conflicts that were movements and ideologies that were not clearly identified with nation states and whose violence was directed as much or more at civilian personnel as it was toward military units. In the twenty-first century, this trend seems to be intensifying.

As these words are written, the war that draws most of the world's attention is the War in Iraq. (More will be said about Iraq later in this chapter.) But other wars have also raged that have involved the loss of even more lives than the war in Iraq.

In Sudan, the word "genocide" has been used to describe the ongoing crisis in Sudan's Darfur region. In 2004, it was reported that government-backed militias drove roughly one million black villagers from their homes and land. Relief officials said that 300,000 or more of the victims could die within the next few months of hunger and disease. Haruun Ruun, executive secretary of the New Sudan Council of Churches, said, "The killings and rapes are still happening in Darfur."[25]

"For the past half century, human rights activists and legal experts have sought ways to prevent genocide," stated an editorial in *Christian Century*. The writer concluded:

> The signers of the Geneva Convention in 1948 (which include the U.S. and Sudan) declare that genocide is a "crime under international law," and they resolve to "prevent and punish" it. In the 1990s strong arguments were developed on behalf of "humanitarian interventions" in Bosnia and Kosovo. Actual preventive action, however, continues to depend on where in the world the genocide takes place, and on which nations have the capacity and will to act. After 50 years of noble, earnest efforts to make acts of genocide impossible to carry out, the nations have managed only to make them slightly more difficult.[26]

Kathleen Kern stated:

> Another war to which the world has paid scant attention is in the Congo. From 1996 to 2006, nearly four million people died in the Congo as a result of an international war, more than in any other country since World War II. Militias and armies from Uganda, Burundi, and Rwanda committed gruesome atrocities on Congolese

25. Haruum Ruun, as quoted in "Meanwhile in Darfur," *Christian Century*, 19 Oct. 2004, p. 5. See also "The Power of a Word," *Newsweek*, 12 July 2004, p. 30.
26. "Meanwhile in Darfur," *Christian Century*, 19 Oct. 2004, p. 5.

people and villages as they sought to claim land and mineral resources of the Congo.[27]

Siverns noted:

> [O]il and mineral rich nations are almost always high on the poverty
> and war list. Oil and minerals attract other nations, displace basic
> services such as farm production, and promote internal greed. To
> discover a new mineral or petroleum source leads nations to be rich
> today; poor tomorrow. It is almost like winning the lottery where
> such a person discovers that he/she has more "friends" than he pre-
> viously knew of and these "friends" have many schemes that will
> make that winner rich. The winner no longer needs a job or particu-
> lar skills, but instead follows the path recommended by his "helpful
> friends" that leads to debt, deterioration, and despair.[28]

Kathleen Kern also described how one of the weapons employed in
warfare is systematic rape: "Militia members rape women in front of
their husbands and children. Afterward the husbands or the husbands'
families drive the 'contaminated' women and their children from the
village."[29] Children born from the rapes are often killed, because caring
for these children is considered to be acquiescing to the assault. The
children of rape who survive are pariahs, and many end up as street
children in the cities.

In 2006, Peter Beinart observed that, a half-century before
George W. Bush took office as president, James Burham, a conservative
cold-war policy thinker of the early cold war, urged President Harry S.
Truman to embrace the doctrine of pre-emptive war. At that time, in
the years after World War II, the U.S. had a nuclear bomb and the Sovi-
ets were getting closer. Burnham urged the Truman administration to
launch a preventive war to protect America before it was too late. American leaders refused, deciding instead to pursue containment. Theologian Reinhold Niebuhr, whose writings influenced the Truman administration, argued: "The advocates of preventive war with Russia assume
that Russia will grow stronger and we will get weaker." Niebuhr continued, "Their calculations are not only strategically mistaken but morally
wrong." "NSC-68," which outlined the Truman administration's cold

27. See Kathleen Kern, "Victims as Pariahs," *Christian Century*, 24 Jan. 2006, p. 9.
28. Siverns, in a note to the author, July 2009.
29. Kern, "Victims as Pariahs," p. 9.

war strategy, predicted that it was Moscow that would eventually falter, because the "idea of freedom" is "peculiarly and intolerably subversive of slavery." Out of this patience came the Marshall Plan.[30]

In late 2002, shortly before the United States invaded Iraq, the U.N. inspectors did not find Saddam Hussein growing stronger. Beinhart drew this conclusion: "Had America not gone to war, containing Saddam would have been a diplomatic challenge for years to come. But if containment was taking its toll on the U.S., it was taking an even greater toll on Saddam."[31] The toll was even greater on the people, and especially the children, of Iraq.

The Costs of War

The costs of war can be measured in more ways than in dollars, though the economic impact is real and great. In a paragraph titled "Real Money," *Christian Century* estimated the eventual cost of the war in Iraq at $2 trillion. (This is a 2 followed by 12 zeros.) How else could this money have been used? "According to Nicholas D. Kristof (*New York Times,* October 24 [2006]), it is four times the amount of money needed to stabilize the Social Security system for the next 75 years, and it is four times the amount needed to provide health care insurance for all uninsured Americans for the next decade. Every minute we stay in Iraq costs another $380,000."[32]

A "box" titled "Up in Arms" listed the amount of military spending around the world in billions of dollars. The figures are for 2005, except for China and Russia, which are for 2004:

$522	United States
63	China
62	Russia
45	Japan
14	Adversaries (combined budgets of Cuba, Iran, North Korea, Syria, and Sudan)[33]

30. See Peter Beinart, "Let Your Enemies Crumble," *Time,* 5 June 2006, p. 80.
31. Beinart, "Let Your Enemies Crumble," p. 80.
32. "Century Marks," *Christian Century,* 28 Nov. 2006, p. 6.
33. International Institute for Strategic Studies, Department of Defense, as cited in *Christian Century,* 5 Sept. 2006, p. 7.

Another cost of war is the increasing use of torture. The cost is not only the pain, suffering, and sometimes death inflicted by one person upon another. There is also a moral cost of dehumanization to the persons inflicting the torture and to the authorities who sanction it or turn a blind eye to it.

In 2006, twenty-seven U.S. religious leaders endorsed a strong statement against the use of torture by American military and security forces, saying "the soul of our nation" is at stake. Their statement concluded, "Let America abolish torture now — without exceptions." Several evangelical leaders, including author-pastor Rick Warren, Ted Haggard of the National Association of Evangelicals, Fuller Seminary president Richard Mouw, and Roberta Hestenes, minister at large with World Vision, signed the statement that was released June 6 and appeared in an ad in the June 13 *New York Times*. Other signers included former president Jimmy Carter, Cardinal Theodore McCarrick of Washington, Greek Orthodox archbishop Demetrius of New York, emergent-church leader Bruce McLaren, Islamic Society of North America national director Sayyid M. Syeed, and Nobel laureate Elie Wiesel.[34]

Just War Theory

Just war theory has a long history, going back at least as far as Thomas Aquinas. In his *Summa Theologica,* he presented a general outline of what became just war theory. He discussed not only the justification of war, but also the kinds of activity that are permissible in war.

Just war theory has changed over the years. At its best, it is more than a simple checklist of criteria for evaluating a conflict. Daniel M. Bell Jr. noted that the just war tradition "developed as a form of Christian practical rationality. It was not a theory to be bantered about but a rigorous ecclesial practice which arose out of the church's day-to-day life and shaped that life." He continued, "just war as a form of Christian discipleship is first about forming the church and only derivatively about speaking to policy makers. Accordingly, it is deeply implicated in the character of our ecclesial communities." And, perhaps most importantly, he wrote, "The just war tradition makes theological sense as an

34. "Abolish Torture Now," *Christian Century,* 27 June 2006, pp. 14-15.

expression of the character of communities concerned daily with justice and with loving our near and distant neighbor."[35]

Two challenges face the church that seeks to embody the just war
tradition, according to Bell: (1) ignorance of the tradition and (2) the
emergence of "asymmetrical" or "fourth generation" warfare. He defined the latter as "conflicts that do not involve nation states (the war
on terrorism, for example, involves nonstate entities like al-Qaeda) or
involve them in 'low-intensity' or clandestine combat (like the U.S. involvement in guerilla warfare in Central America in the 1980s)."[36]

In response to arguments by many people that this new context of
war renders the just war tradition obsolete, Bell argued that "nothing
in the character of modern warfare . . . renders it incapable of being restrained by the disciples of the just war tradition."[37] Even though em-
bodying the just war tradition is more than memorizing a list of criteria, Bell argued, "knowing the criteria is a necessary part of being
formed by the tradition." Here is my summary of the criteria he listed:

- Legitimate authority. Authority over life and death belongs to
  God, who has shared this authority with the governing powers (cf.
  Rom. 13). "Thus, governing authorities may wage war. This delega-
  tion of authority, however, does not provide the ruler with carte
  blanche, for in the Christian tradition of just war, the determination of the justness of a war does not reside in the ruler's hands
  alone." Wise advisers are to be heeded.

    President George W. Bush led the U.S. to invade Iraq in 2003.
  Increasingly, during and after the invasion, questions were raised
  as to the validity of the rationale offered by the administration for
  the invasion. Many persons have contended that legitimate authority was not in place. James Madison, fourth president of the
  United States (1809-17), put it in these words: "In no part of the
  [U.S.] constitution is more wisdom to be found than in the clause
  which confides the question of war and peace to the legislative and
  not to the executive branch."
- Just cause. The modern, secular version of just war has effectively
  been reduced to self-defense against an unjust aggressor. "The

35. See Daniel M. Bell Jr., "In War and in Peace," *Christian Century*, 6 Sept. 2005,
p. 26.

36. Bell, "In War and in Peace," p. 26.

37. Bell, "In War and in Peace," p. 26.

Christian tradition understands just cause in a much more other-regarding manner. Christianity has consistently qualified . . . armed action principally on behalf of the neighbor — in the form of a government's defense of its people or a nation's intervention to aid an unjustly attacked neighbor." This challenge to risk ourselves for others leads us to face our sense of fear and inordinate sense of security. To proclaim the gospel is to remember "that Christ has defeated sin and death, that we need not be consumed by fear, that there are worse things than dying, that we are free to live in holy insecurity, free even to die in service to our neighbor."

- Right intention. This is more than a disavowal of revenge and a desire for peace. The desire must be for a peace that is truly just, and not merely self-serving. Even in warfare we are to love our enemy. Right intent entails "complete justice," which entails "looking forward (to how justice will be implemented) and backward (bringing the past before the bar of justice)."

James Hilton, in his novel, *Good-bye, Mr. Chips,* described a Sunday at Brookfield:

> On Sundays in Chapel it was he [Mr. Chips] who now read out the tragic list [of soldiers killed in the battles of World War I], and sometimes it was seen and heard that he was in tears over it. Well, why not, the School said; he was an old man; they might have despised anyone else for the weakness.
>
> One day he got a letter from Switzerland, from friends there; it was heavily censored, but conveyed some news. On the following Sunday, after names and biographies of old boys, he paused a moment and then added: —
>
> "Those few of you who were here before the War will remember Max Staeful, the German master. He was in Germany, visiting his home, when war broke out. He was popular while he was here, and made many friends. Those who knew him will be sorry to hear that he was killed last week, on the Western Front."
>
> He was a little pale when he sat down afterward, aware that he had done something unusual. He had consulted nobody about it, anyhow; no one else could be blamed. Later, outside the Chapel, he heard an argument: —
>
> "On the Western Front, Chips said. Does that mean he was fighting for the Germans?"

"I suppose it does."

"Seems funny then, to read his name out with all the others. After all, he was an *enemy*."

"Oh, just one of Chip's ideas, I expect. The old boy still has 'em."

Chips, in his room again, was not displeased by the comment. Yes, he still had 'em — those ideas of dignity and generosity that were becoming increasingly rare in a frantic world. And he thought: Brookfield will take them, too, from me; but it wouldn't from anyone else.[38]

- Last resort. The resort to arms is to come only "after other feasible means of addressing the injustice in question (such as mediation, negotiation, arbitration or referral to international tribunals — but not compromise or appeasement) have failed." The point at which this criterion is met is a judgment call that requires prudence and sound judgment.

Were there other alternatives to the invasion of Iraq? Jim Wallis maintained that there were other alternatives possible:

The war with Iraq was not a war of last or only resort, or the best way to deal with the real threats offered by Saddam Hussein. There were other alternatives possible — even some non-administration hawks thought that the "six-point plan" offered by some American religious leaders and released by *Sojourners* in March 2003 should have been tried — and they were simply not seriously considered by the Bush administration. And it is now undeniably true that this administration lied about the facts in Iraq and consistently manipulated intelligence to justify going to war.[39]

- Reasonable chance of success. "A just war is a limited war to address a particular, declared injustice. It is not a war to wipe out an ideology or to rid the world of evil."

Administrative preparations for the war in Iraq failed to plan for what would happen after the conflict. Fareed Zakaria used an analogy to point out the shortcoming:

38. James Hilton, *Good-bye, Mr. Chips* (Boston: Little Brown, 1934, 1962), pp. 101-2.
39. Jim Wallis, "If All You Have Is a Hammer . . . ," *Sojourners*, August 2006, p. 5.

Imagine if after the fall of apartheid in South Africa, the black majority had come to power and decided to dismantle the entire apparatus of the Afrikaner state. Let's say they disbanded the army, which had slaughtered them, and then fired all the whites in the civil service. The result would have been chaos, a dysfunctional state, and — in all probability — the rise of an Afrikaner insurgency. But they did none of that. On the contrary, the ANC was extraordinarily forgiving, reassuring white South Africans that they would have an important place in the new South Africa. As a result, South Africa has been more politically stable and economically successful than anyone would have predicted in 1994.

The contrast is obvious. The United States disbanded the Iraqi army and fired 40,000 bureaucrats after taking over Iraq, on the urging of some — though not all — Shia political leaders. We see the results. For two years now we have been attempting to reverse course. But to build a stable political order, it will take more than just an Iraqi military. It will take an Iraqi Mandela.[40]

- Noncombatant immunity/discrimination. "In a just war one has an obligation to distinguish combatants and minimize noncombatant deaths. . . . This is particularly the case in the era of fourth-generation warfare insofar as such warfare is increasingly conducted in the midst of civilian populations." Siverns wrote that in the small city of Kingston, Ontario, there is a fort outside the city that was built to protect citizens of Kingston during the war of 1812. He continued: "When I asked how the fort could protect citizens when it was so far away from the city, the answer was that any fighting would be outside the city so as to protect the civilian population."[41]
- Proportionality. This final criterion holds that "the means used in a war's prosecution must be proportional to the ends." This prohibits "overkill" and calls for prudence, not vengeance.

Consider this news item:

---

40. Fareed Zakaria, "How to Exploit the Opening," *Newsweek*, 19 June 2006, p. 39. Though the situation in South Africa was vastly improved after 1994, it is fair to say that violence, economic problems, and loss of leadership were still present to some degree.

41. Siverns in a note to the author, July 2009.

When two of Motti Tamam's brothers were killed by a Hezbollah rocket, the Israeli asked that his brothers' eyes be available for transplant. One of the recipients was an Arab, Nikola Elias, who was blind in one eye and had little vision in the other. The men met later, shook hands, and exchanged phone numbers.[42]

The church must teach these criteria and recognize that these criteria are important and helpful not only to soldiers, but to everyone. As Bell pointed out, "they are the same virtues necessary to navigate civilian and peacetime life faithfully." We are called to seek just peace for our neighbors as disciples of Jesus Christ.

Health

One of the ironies of the early twenty-first century is that even as remarkable progress continues to be made in medical science and the practice of medicine, the seeming difficulties in making health care available to everyone continues to elude many Americans and other people in most parts of the world. A few paragraphs in this chapter can scarcely begin to look at issues of health worldwide. We will note some highlights.

Worldwide, two million infants die each year within twenty-four hours of birth. In the United States, 0.5 percent of newborns die in their first month, the second highest infant mortality rate among industrialized nations, behind only Latvia.[43] Malaria kills two million African children a year. One obvious solution is to provide insecticide-treated bed nets, now engineered to last up to five years. The cost to manufacture, ship, and distribute each net is $10.[44]

The AIDS (Acquired Immune Deficiency Syndrome) epidemic is a case in point. The first known case in the U.S. was in 1981 in New York City. In 1984, scientists isolated the Human Immunodeficiency Virus (HIV) that causes AIDS. By 1985, the Centers for Disease Control estimated that one million people globally were HIV-positive. By 1994, AIDS was the leading cause of death in the U.S. for 25- to 44-year olds.

42. ABC News, 10 Aug. 2006, as cited by "Century Marks," *Christian Century*, 5 Sept. 2006, p. 6.

43. "Numbers," *Time*, 22 May 2006, p. 27.

44. Jeffrey D. Sachs, "The $10 Solution," *Time*, 15 Jan. 2007, p. 65.

Many people were saying, "Whoever gets AIDS deserves to have AIDS." In 1995, President Bill Clinton hosted the first White House Conference on HIV/AIDS. In 1997, U.S. AIDS-related deaths declined by more than 40 percent from 1996, largely due to the AIDS "Cocktail." In 2001, it was reported that more than 700,000 persons in the U.S. were HIV positive, and 450,000 had died since 1981. President George W. Bush, in 2003, initiated a $15 billion plan to address HIV/AIDS globally. In 2006, UNAIDS estimated that 40.3 million people worldwide were living with HIV and 25 million had died of AIDS.[45]

In a companion article, Claudia Kalb and Andrew Murr reported that AIDS now threatens tens of thousands of African Americans. They wrote:

> What's happening is an epidemic among black women, their husbands, boyfriends, brothers, sisters, sons and daughters. Twenty-five years after the virus was first documented in gay white men, HIV has increasingly become a disease of color, with blacks bearing the heaviest burden by far. African-Americans make up just 13 percent of the U.S. population but account for an astounding 51 percent of new HIV diagnoses. Black men are diagnosed at more than seven times the rate of white men, black females at 20 times the rate of white women.[46]

Part of the reason for this disparity may be traced to the mistrust of the medical establishment since the Tuskegee syphilis experiment launched in the 1930s. "[I]n a 2005 poll, 27 percent of black Americans said they thought 'AIDS was produced in a government laboratory.' Every day such wariness and misinformation breed new infections." Among African Americans, 63 percent say they personally know someone who has died of AIDS or is living with HIV.[47] Despite advances in treatment options for the treatment of AIDS/HIV, we are not winning the global war.

In the United States, the health care system has been described as a lottery. Jane Bryant Quinn used these chilling words:

45. The statistical data are from David Gerlach, "How AIDS Changed America," *Newsweek*, 15 May 2006, pp. 36-41.

46. Claudia Kalb and Andrew Murr, "Battling a Black Epidemic," *Newsweek*, 15 May 2006, pp. 43-44.

47. Kalb and Murr, "Battling a Black Epidemic," p. 45.

America's health-care "system" looks more like a lottery every year. The winners: the healthy and well insured, with good corporate coverage or Medicare. When they're ill, they get — as the cliché goes — "the best health care in the world." The losers: those who rely on shrinking public insurance, such as Medicaid (nearly 45 million of us), or go uninsured (46 million and rising).[48]

The false "debate" about health care reform in the United States in 2009 pointed once again to the chilling reality of Quinn's words.

The intertwining of issues of health and those of poverty is not uncommon. For example:

As Dr. Paul Farmer administers a spinal tap to a 13-year-old girl at his clinic in Cange, Haiti, the child begins shouting in Creole: *"Li fe-m mal, mwen grangou!"*

"Can you believe it?" exclaims Farmer. "She's crying, 'It hurts, I'm hungry.' Only in Haiti would a child cry out that she's hungry during a spinal tap."[49]

Science and Faith

"Why is the sky blue?" This was the question raised by Eric Cornell, 2001 winner of the Nobel Prize for physics, when he spoke on the occasion of his induction into the American Academy of Arts and Sciences in 2005. He offered two answers:

1) The sky is blue because of the wavelength dependence of Rayleigh scattering; 2) The sky is blue because blue is the color God wants it to be.

My scientific research has been in areas connected with optical phenomena, and I can tell you a lot about the Rayleigh-scattering answer. Neither I nor any other scientist, however, has anything scientific to say about answer No. 2, the God answer. This is not to say that the God answer is unscientific, just that the methods of science don't speak to that answer.

Before we understood Rayleigh scattering, there was no scientif-

48. Jane Bryant Quinn, "Health Care's New Lottery," *Newsweek*, 27 Feb. 2006, p. 47.
49. Debra Bendis, "Moving Mountains in Haiti: Dokte Paul," *Christian Century*, 2 Nov. 2004, p. 30.

ically satisfying explanation for the sky's blueness. The idea that the sky is blue because God wants it to be blue existed before scientists came to understand Rayleigh scattering, and it continues to exist today, not in the least undermined by our advance in scientific understanding. The religious explanation has been supplemented — but not supplanted — by advances in scientific knowledge. We now may, if we care to, think of Rayleigh scattering as the method God has chosen to implement his color scheme.[50]

Cornell's words speak volumes about the needless and useless conflicts that many persons create when dealing with issues that involve science and faith. George Bernard Shaw reminded us, "Science becomes dangerous only when it imagines that it has reached its goal."

Francis Collins said, "Faith is not the opposite of reason. Faith rests squarely upon reason, but with the added component of revelation." He added, "I am still able to accept and embrace the possibility that there are answers that science isn't able to provide about the natural world — the questions about why instead of the questions about how. I'm interested in the whys. I find many of those answers in the spiritual realm. That in no way compromises my ability to think rigorously as a scientist."[51] Theology is closer to poetry than it is to science. This is not to say, however, that science is not a gift from God.[52]

The Theory of Evolution

One conflict that has persisted for more than a century and a half has to do with the theory of evolution and principles of biblical interpreta-

50. Eric Cornell, "What Was God Thinking? Science Can't Tell," *Time*, 14 Nov. 2005, p. 100 (inside back cover).

51. Francis Collins, as cited by David Van Biema, "God vs. Science," *Time*, 13 Nov. 2006, p. 55.

52. Siverns argued: "I wouldn't want to take poetry away from science." John Dominic Crossan added: "A classic example by Russell Kirk records the delight of Albert Einstein as the poet St John Perse explained to him the importance of intuition in poetry. 'But it's the same thing for the man of science,' he said. 'The mechanics of discovery are neither logical nor intellectual. It's a sudden illumination, almost a rapture. Later, to be sure, intelligence analyzes and experiments confirm (or invalidate) the intuition. But initially there is a great forward leap of the imagination.'" John Dominic Crossan, *The Dark Interval* (Niles, IL: Argus Communications, 1975), p. 31.

tion. We have already discussed this earlier in Chapter 4, but the subject bears looking at in more depth here.

Charles Robert Darwin (1809-1882) had planned to enter the ministry. But instead he took a five-year voyage aboard *HMS Beagle* on a mission to chart the coast of South America. Darwin was a 22-year-old amateur naturalist when the ship set forth from Plymouth, England, in December 1831. The ship sailed up and down the coast of Argentina, through the Strait of Magellan, and into the Pacific, before returning home by way of Australia and Cape Town. At the remote archipelago of the Galapagos, Darwin began to formulate some of the ideas about evolution that would appear in 1859 in his book *The Origin of Species*. Since that time, the theory of evolution has sparked challenges rooted in religion. Here are some key dates and events compiled by the American Museum of Natural History:

1860 — Bishop Samuel Wilberforce led an attack on Darwin. Scientists Thomas Huxley and Joseph Hooker supported Darwin's work.

1882 — Darwin died and was buried in Westminster Abbey, a few feet from Sir Isaac Newton.

1925 — The "Monkey Trial" was held in Tennessee. Teacher John Scopes was convicted of violating a state law prohibiting the teaching of evolution.

1948 — The U.S. Supreme Court banned religious instruction in public schools, noting that the First Amendment requires the separation of church and state.[53]

1960s — The Supreme Court ruled that an Arkansas law prohibiting the teaching of evolution violates the First Amendment.

1981-82 — Arkansas passed the Balanced Treatment for Creation-Science and Evolution-Science act. The act was declared unconstitutional the following year.

1980s — Some U.S. proponents of creationism began to promote the idea that the complexity of living organisms shows that life was created by an "intelligent designer."

1996 — Pope John Paul II proclaimed there is no essential conflict between Darwin's theory and Catholicism.

53. Controversy about my views on the theory of evolution and biblical interpretation caused my ordination to be deferred from 1953 to 1955. See Chapter 4.

2000-2005 — Less than half of all Americans believed in evolution. In England, Darwin was honored with a portrait on the 10-pound note.[54]

Alan Padgett has reminded us that the current debate rests on two false assumptions: "The first is that evolution must imply that God does not exist. The second is that there is something wrong with the theory of evolution, so it must be defeated to promote theism." He added that both notions are "just plain wrong." "Christians need to get their thinking straight about natural science," said Padgett. "It doesn't tell us about God. It never has." "What do we mean when we say that the Bible is true?" asked Padgett. "Is it factual, literal events? We're going to get in a lot of trouble if we mean that. We need to think in a more open way about that. It doesn't always mean scientific, historical, factual truth."[55]

Evolution itself does not challenge the idea that a theistic God created the universe. In fact, Darwin himself wrote movingly of God. Saint Augustine criticized other Christians who "talk nonsense" about the laws of nature.

The most recent onslaught on the theory of evolution has come from advocates of "intelligent design" (ID). Intelligent design advocates contend that various forms of life began abruptly through an intelligent agency, with their distinctive features already intact: fish with fins and scales; birds with feathers, beaks, and wings; etc.

Jonathan Alter wrote:

> The most clever thing about intelligent design is that it doesn't sound like nonsense. It conjures up Cambridge, not Kansas. . . . The scholarly articles are often well written and provocative. But the science within these articles has been demolished over and over by other scientists. As [Stephen] Miller explains, science is perhaps the last true marketplace of ideas. After a decade in circulation, intelligent design has failed the market test. So now its backers are seeking the equivalent of a government bailout, by going around their scientific peers to red state politicians trying to slip religious dogma into the classroom.[56]

54. Jerry Alder, "Evolution of a Scientist," *Newsweek,* 28 Nov. 2005, pp. 49-58.
55. Alan Padgett, as quoted in "Theologians: No Need to Fight Evolution," *Vital Theology,* 30 Oct. 2005, Special Issue, p. 1.
56. Jonathan Alter, "Monkey See, Monkey Do," *Newsweek,* 15 Aug. 2005, p. 27.

In the fall of 2005, a U.S. federal trial in Harrisburg, Pennsylvania, ended. On December 20 of that year, Judge John E. Jones III issued a sweeping 139-page opinion. The results were reported in *Christian Century:* "Jones saw fit to excoriate the intelligent design movement and give evolutionary science the legal respect and status it deserves. It was the nation's first trial in regard to ID, and the ruling, though not binding nationwide, is expected to have an impact far beyond Dover [the Dover Area School District in Pennsylvania]."[57]

Perhaps, in regard to the theory of evolution, the pendulum in the United States is beginning to swing back toward a more balanced view of the relationship between science and faith.

Stem Cell Research

In more recent years, debate about the morality, or immorality, of the use of stem cells has broken out in the United States. An article in *Time* used this caption at the beginning of an article on stem cells: "The debate is so politically loaded that it's tough to tell who's being straight about the real areas of progress and how breakthroughs can be achieved."[58]

Stem cells have been described as nature's master cells, which are capable of generating every one of the many types of cells that make up the body. They have the ability to self-renew. They hold enormous promise as the basis for new treatments and even cures for diseases.

Despite this promise, stem-cell research has become controversial, especially when the stem cells are taken from human embryos. Stem-cell research has become as controversial in many circles as evolution and global warming. Nancy Gibbs put the controversy in these words:

> Back and forth it goes, the politics driving the science, the science pushing back. Stem-cell research has joined global warming and evolution science as fields in which *the very facts are put to a vote,* a public spectacle in which data wrestle dogma. Scientists who are having surprising success with adult stem cells find their progress being

57. "ID Ruling Expected to Impact Other States," *Christian Century,* 24 Jan. 2006, p. 12.

58. Nancy Gibbs, "Stem Cells: The Hope and the Hype," *Time,* 7 Aug. 2006, pp. 40-46.

used by activists to argue that embryo research is not just immoral but also unnecessary.

Controversies between science and faith have raged for centuries. Perhaps this section on science and faith can be summarized in this way: "Christians cannot give a free pass to everything presented by scientists. Sometimes scientists overstep the boundaries of their field and rule out religious belief as such — a move that simply begs for religious backlash — or link their findings to pernicious moral or social views."[59] Christians maintain that knowledge of God is not to be gained by looking only at nature. Knowledge of God's saving work through Jesus Messiah as revealed through scripture and guided by the Holy Spirit is part of the equation. We can say with the psalmist that "the heavens tell the glory of God." And that makes us "willing to learn about creation from scientists who may or may not profess belief in a Creator."[60]

The Environment

Global Warming

A jolting statistic: Americans constitute 4 percent of the world's population and produce 25 percent of the world's greenhouse gases. *Time* magazine, in a major article on global warming, stated, "Global warming, even most skeptics have concluded, is the real deal, and human activity has been causing it." The article continued, "What few people reckoned on was that global climate systems are booby-trapped with tipping points and feedback loops, thresholds past which the slow creep of environmental decay gives way to sudden and self-perpetuating collapse." The article also noted, "Even Evangelical Christians, once one of the most reliable columns in the conservative base, are demanding action, most notably in February [2006] when 86 Christian leaders formed the Evangelical Climate Initiative, demanding that Congress regulate greenhouse gases."[61] The success of Al Gore's movie and book, *An Inconvenient*

---

59. "Cosmic Design," *Christian Century*, 6 Sept. 2005, p. 5.
60. "Cosmic Design," p. 5.
61. Jeffrey Kluger, "By Any Measure, Earth Is at . . . the Tipping Point," *Time,* 3 Apr. 2006, p. 35.

Truth, has also helped turn the tide in the sentiments of most mainstream Americans.

In an ironic confluence of events, two major news items, each with major environmental implications, garnered headlines and major worldwide attention on the same date, Friday, February 2, 2007: (1) a report on global warming by the Intergovernmental Panel on Climate Change (IPCC) issued in Paris and (2) a report of record profits made by Exxon Mobil and other oil companies in 2006. The two reports reveal a marked contrast in perspective on environmental issues.

The IPCC Reports

The IPCC was established in 1988 to study climate change information. The group does not do independent research, but instead reviews scientific literature from around the world. IPCC is the United Nations-sanctioned group that was formed by the World Meteorological Organization and the U.N. Environment Program. The group's goal is to produce "a balanced reporting of existing viewpoints" on the causes of global warming, according to its website. In February 2007, the IPCC issued the first of four reports planned for 2007.

Cable News Network (CNN) commented on the first of these reports, "The debate is over: Global warming is here and humans are 'very likely' the blame, an international group of scientists meeting in Paris, France, announced Friday." "The evidence for warming having happened on the planet is unequivocal," stated U.S. government scientist Susan Solomon, who also is a member of IPCC. She added, "We can see that in rising air temperatures, we can see it in changes in snow cover in the Northern Hemisphere. We can see it in global sea rise. It's unequivocal," she said.

In its twenty-one-page report for policymakers, the group of climate experts unanimously linked — with "90 percent" certainty — the increase of average global temperatures since the mid-twentieth century to the increase of human-made greenhouse gases in the atmosphere.

It is well established that fossil fuels such as methane and carbon dioxide trap heat near the surface, a process known as the greenhouse effect. The greenhouse effect is a natural phenomenon, but human activities, like the burning of fossil fuels, can pour enormous volumes of these gases into the atmosphere, raising the planet's temperature and destabilizing the climate.

The report found that it is "likely" — "more likely than not" in some cases — that manmade greenhouse gases have contributed to hotter days and nights, and more of them, more killer heat waves than before, heavier rainfall more often, major droughts in more regions, stronger and more frequent cyclones, and "increased incidence" of extremely high sea levels.

Eleven of the previous twelve years ranked among the twelve warmest years on record, with the oceans absorbing more than 80 percent of the heat added to the climate system, the report noted. When the melt-off of glaciers and sea ice is added, sea levels are rising.

The IPCC predicted global temperature increases of 1.8 to 4 degrees Celsius (3.2 to 7.1 degrees Fahrenheit) by 2100 and sea levels to rise between 7 and 23 inches (18 and 58 centimeters) by the end of the century. "An additional 3.9-7.8 inches (10-20 centimeters) are possible if recent, surprising melting of polar ice sheets continues," the report stated.

In April 2007, the IPCC issued the second part of its four Assessment Report series, titled "Impacts, Adaptation and Vulnerability." This second report warned of widespread food shortages and starvation for humans and other animal species if steps are not taken immediately to combat the looming problem.

In an interview with the BBC, IPCC Working Group II Co-Chairman Dr. Martin Parry said that the areas hit hardest will be: "The arctic, where temperatures are rising fast and ice is melting; sub-Saharan Africa, where dry areas are forecast to get dryer; small islands, because of their inherent lack of capacity to adapt, and Asian mega-deltas, where billions of people will be at increased risk of flooding."

The report looked mostly at the impacts of climate change rather than the solutions. A later report will suggest ways to combat climate change such as carbon cap-and-trade systems, far more stringent energy efficiency and conservation, and rapid development of renewable energy.

The third installment of the IPCC climate assessment, issued in May 2007, indicated that it will take a lot of work to combat climate change, but it won't cost as much as many leaders have been claiming. The 120-nation IPCC said greenhouse gases, which have risen 70 percent since 1970, must be cut by 50 to 85 percent of year 2000 levels by 2050. Doing so, it said, would cost 3 percent or less of the global GDP, and some changes could even provide an economic boost; incentives such as carbon taxes will be a key part of the picture, the panel said.

An earlier IPCC report in 2001 had found that the 1990s were "very likely" the warmest decade on record. It also said that most of the observed warming over the last fifty years was "likely due to increases in greenhouse gas concentrations due to human activities."

Oil Company Profits

As noted above, news reports on the date of the first IPCC report, February 2, 2007, stated that Exxon Mobil posted the largest annual profit ever by a U.S. company — $39.5 billion. This record net income amounted to roughly $4.5 million an hour for Exxon Mobil, the world's largest publicly traded oil company. That compares to about $12 an hour for the average U.S. worker, according to the Labor Department.

Exxon Mobil's total revenue in 2006 also set an American corporate record, reaching $377.6 billion and surpassing the company's own record of $370.7 billion in 2005. But Exxon Mobil wasn't alone among oil and gas entities posting a huge profit in 2006. On February 1, three other companies — Royal Dutch Shell PLC, Marathon Oil Corp., and Valero Energy Corp. — also reported best-ever full-year profits. The four companies combined had earnings of $75.6 billion in 2006.

Exxon Mobil's profit didn't go unnoticed in Washington, D.C., on Capitol Hill, where Rep. Edward Markey, Democrat of Massachusetts, was among the critics. He called the earnings "the direct result of a [George W.] Bush energy policy that for seven years has used every lever of the American government to tilt the scales toward satisfying the special-interest demands of a single industry at the expense of the public interest." He noted, for example, that the oil companies haven't paid all royalties required of them for drilling on federal land.

Also reported in February 2007 was news that lingering crude from the largest U.S. oil spill to date had resisted weathering in some places *almost eighteen years* after the tanker *Exxon Valdez* ran aground and fouled hundreds of miles of Alaska shoreline, a federal study concluded. The *Exxon Valdez* ran aground March 24, 1989, emptying 11 million gallons of crude oil into Prince William Sound. The spill contaminated more than 1,200 miles of shoreline and killed hundreds of thousands of seabirds and marine animals. Exxon estimated it had paid $3 billion in cleanup costs, government settlements, fines and compensation, but it still had not paid an unresolved punitive damage judgment, originally set for $5 billion by a federal jury in 1994.

The estimated 85 tons — or more than 26,600 gallons — of oil remaining at Prince William Sound is declining by about 4 percent a year and likely even more slowly in the Gulf of Alaska, according to research chemist Jeffrey Short of the National Oceanic and Atmospheric Administration. At that rate of decline, oil could persist for decades below the surface of some beaches, Short and colleagues said in their report. The study was published in the February 15, 2007, edition of *Environmental Science & Technology,* the journal of the American Chemical Society.

There is evidence that the oil industry is trying to raise doubts about global warming. Paul Krugman alerted the public to this action of the American Petroleum Institute:

> A leaked memo from a 1998 meeting at the American Petroleum Institute, in which Exxon (which hadn't yet merged with Mobil) was a participant, describes a strategy of providing "logistical and moral support" to climate change dissenters, "thereby raising questions about and undercutting the 'prevailing scientific wisdom.'" And that's just what Exxon Mobil has done: lavish grants have supported a sort of alternative intellectual universe of global warming skeptics.[62]

On the other hand, there is some evidence of business being environmentally friendly. Takeo Fukui, CEO of Honda, is working to make Honda one of the first car companies to turn environmentalism into a competitive advantage. He has warned that if business continues as usual, "society will not let us exist."[63]

John Buchanan described a dialogue between Karl Barth and Emil Brunner several decades ago. It was a rancorous argument over natural theology:

> Barth's blunt response to Brunner's apologia for revelation in nature was "Nein." Later in their lives the antagonists began to talk to each other again, and near the end of his life Barth was saying that our final word should be one of gratitude, not only for God's revelation in Jesus Christ but also, I assume, for the blessings of life in God's world.
>
> William Sloane Coffin says we have "divorced nature from nature's God" and that we view nature essentially as a tool box. Coffin adds his voice to many others who understand that the environmen-

---

62. Paul Krugman, *The New York Times,* 17 Apr. 2006.
63. Bryan Walsh, "How Business Saw the Light," *Time,* 15 Jan. 2007, p. 56.

tal crisis is at least partially a theological crisis, and that one of the by-products of modernity is the desacralizing of nature. It's not enough to be smart ecologically so we don't exhaust natural resources. What we need beyond caution, Coffin says, is reverence.[64]

Summary

My own biblical studies over the years have convinced me that God's passion for justice runs throughout the fabric of Scripture. The Exodus event ("Let my people go"), for example, shows Yahweh's resolve to transform earthly power. Brueggemann used these words to convey the pervasiveness of God's passion for justice:

> In the context of Israel's completed testimony, it is difficult to overstate the pivotal importance of the rest of Israel's testimony of the Mosaic revolution and the commitment of Yahweh (and of Israel) to justice. If we consider in turn the prophetic, psalmist, sapiential, and apocalyptic texts, it seems evident that Israel, everywhere and without exhaustion, is preoccupied with the agenda of justice that is rooted in the character and resolve of Yahweh. This justice rooted in Yahweh, moreover, is to be enacted and implemented concretely in human practice.[65]

Though the specific details of issues change over time, some issues, looked at in their broad strokes, seem always to be with us. In this chapter, we have looked at them as they appear in today's world. The ongoing task of the church, of course, is to examine, reexamine, and reflect on these issues through the lens of being stewards of the gospel and in the context of the times, places, and cultural environments where the issues are present.

In a world with the seemingly overwhelming issues we have considered, and many more issues as well, some would say that our accustomed way of life is coming apart. Or, as the psalmist expressed it, "How could we sing the Lord's song in a foreign land?" (Ps. 137:4). In many ways, the church in North America in the twenty-first century is

64. John M. Buchanan, "Hymn to Creation," *Christian Century*, 30 Nov. 2004, p. 3.
65. Walter Brueggemann, *Theology of the Old Testament: Testimony, Dispute, Advocacy* (Minneapolis: Fortress Press, 1997), p. 736.

in exile — not in a foreign land, but immersed in a land in which dwells an alien culture.

The call of consumerism and materialistic values is to forsake the new covenant God has placed in the human heart and to turn to false gods of comfort, ease, and pleasure. In such a situation, God's desire for justice and equity may be thwarted, with the result that people suffer while an elite class rules and oppresses. Christians are called by God to form alternative communities based on a new covenant relationship. In alternative communities, we can live and demonstrate the way in which God's good creation can be enjoyed by all creatures. The alternative community put forth by God is called to be a community that relentlessly pursues God's vision of and intent for a justice that is specific and concrete, subversive and uncompromising. The implications for the Christian church are profound.

The church as a steward of the gospel needs to struggle with difficult questions, such as:

- When the church is tempted, does it succumb and become a market-driven church? (God waits, and the world waits, for the church to be an alternative community of stewards, who thirst for God and who seek to live in covenant with the living God.)
- How does the contemporary church in North America measure up as an alternative community?
- How can the church become an alternative community that answers God's call to faithful stewardship of the gospel?

In the next chapter, we will look at the culture — the caldron — in which the church is called to fulfill its responsibility as a steward of the gospel in the context of North American culture and its prevailing assumptions and issues.

CHAPTER 6

The Church in the Caldron

≈≈≈

Is not this the fast that I choose:
to loose the bonds of injustice,
to undo the thongs of the yoke,
to let the oppressed go free,
and to break every yoke?
Is it not to share your bread with the hungry,
and bring the homeless poor into your house;
when you see the naked, to cover them,
and not to hide yourself from your own kin?
Then your light shall break forth like the dawn,
and your healing shall spring up quickly;
your vindicator shall go before you,
the glory of the LORD shall be your rear guard.

Isaiah 58:6-8

There's a church in the valley by the wildwood,
No lovelier spot in the dale;
No place is so dear to my childhood,
As the little brown church in the vale.
Come to the church in the wildwood,
Oh, come to the church in the dale,
No spot is so dear to my childhood,
As the little brown church in the vale.

William S. Pitts, "The Little Brown Church in the Vale"

"Double, double, toil and trouble;
Fire burn and caldron bubble."

William Shakespeare, *Macbeth*, Act IV, scene 1

The Church in the Caldron

The words from Pitts and Shakespeare conjure in my mind contrasting images of the cultural context of the church in twenty-first-century America. Pitts's words, written in 1857, portray an image still clung to by many North American Christians: a beautiful church building nestled in a protected valley, safe and secure from the storms and onslaughts of the surrounding world. It is a place of refuge.

The image of the bubbling caldron as the culture in which the church is immersed is much less attractive. This is even truer when we remember that the church is the people who are called out by God to carry out God's mission in the world, that is, to be stewards of the gospel. The church is not called by God to escape from the caldron, but rather to minister *within* the caldron, adding salt and seeking transformation of the culture by the power of the Holy Spirit. (See Acts 2.)

The words of the prophet Isaiah paint an image of injustices in the culture and challenge persons of faith to respond with acts of justice. The response is to choose to minister within the caldron — "to loose the bonds of injustice."

My own ministry has taken me into many different dimensions of the caldron — both geographically and in terms of the responsibilities that I have had. I have lived in eight different American states, in diverse parts of the country. I have served as a pastor for twenty-nine years — twenty-six years full-time and three years part-time. God led me to be a denominational executive, on both state and national levels. I have served as an international, ecumenical staff officer. I had the joy and privilege of serving as an adjunct faculty member of a divinity college in Canada and teaching doctoral level courses in seminaries in both the United States and Canada. As I write these words, it is fifty-six years since my ordination. I rejoice that God has given me the opportunity to be a steward of the gospel in many different locales and, especially in the ecumenical church, to work with twenty-seven denominations in the United States and Canada. This diversity of experiences in different settings emboldens me to write this chapter about the church in the caldron.

God's Love for the World

God's love for the world is clearly expressed in Scripture — perhaps most clearly and succinctly in John 3:16: "For God so loved the world that he gave his only Son, so that everyone who believes in him may not perish but may have eternal life." Unfortunately, however, we often misconstrue the words to mean, "For God so loved the *church*." This interpretation is grossly misleading. The message is clear: "God so loved the *world*." The Bible is the story of God's love for and redemption of the world.

The human role in God's love of the world, as part of God's household in carrying out God's mission, is to be *stewards of the gospel*. As stewards of the gospel, as we noted in Chapter 3, we are to so thirst for God and respond to God's purposes that we become servants of Jesus Messiah to fulfill God's call to integrate the gospel of the Kingdom with the gospel of the cross, according to the Scriptures. It is also to remember and to acknowledge that the good news is for all of God's creation, not just for "me."

What is the household of God that is to carry out God's mission? Biblical texts remind us that the household of God is the church:

> So then you are no longer strangers and aliens, but you are citizens with the saints and also *members of the household of God,* built upon the foundation of the apostles and prophets, with Christ Jesus himself as the cornerstone. (Eph. 2:19-20)

> I hope to come to you soon, but I am writing these instructions to you so that, if I am delayed, you may know how one ought to behave in *the household of God, which is the church of the living God,* the pillar and bulwark of the truth. (1 Tim. 3:14-15)

God called the church, the household of God, into being to help carry out God's mission. Thus, it is fair to say, the church exists *for the sake* of God's passion for and mission to the world. God's mission is the plot. The church is a subplot. The work of the church as the household of

God — the economic work of God, as it were — is to redeem the world. Understood in this way, stewardship is a function of God's redemption of the world.

The Christian church as the household of God is the body called out by God to be stewards of the gospel of Jesus Christ. To be a faithful steward of the gospel is not only to thirst for God; it is to be part of *an alternative community* that relentlessly pursues God's vision of and intent for justice that is specific and concrete, subversive and uncompromising. The implications for the Christian church are profound. But we need also to consider the world — the culture — in which the church is called to be a steward of the gospel. In the words of Harold M. Daniels, "The church is a colony, an island of one culture in the middle of another. In baptism our citizenship is transferred from one dominion to another, and we become, in whatever culture we find ourselves, resident aliens."[1]

The Bubbling Caldron as a Metaphor

The caldron is a useful metaphor for the culture, the context in which the church exists in North America. "Caldron" has been defined as: (1) a large metal pot in which liquids are boiled and (2) a situation of great tension, unrest, and stress. Certainly the second definition is an apt description of the life of the church in North America in the twenty-first century. In that caldron, the church is tempted and often succumbs to being a market-driven church, instead of being a gospel-driven church. As a result of that seduction, the church may at times feel comfortable and at ease, but it may feel at other times as though it is immersed in a boiling liquid. In the latter case, the words of Shakespeare quoted above may seem especially relevant:

Double, double toil and trouble;
Fire burn, and caldron bubble.

Troubling questions then cry out for answers: How can/does/ should the church respond when the caldron is bubbling and double toil and trouble are all pervasive? How can our thirst for God rise above

1. Harold M. Daniels, *To God Alone Be Glory* (Louisville: Geneva Press, 2003), p. 132.

the heat and turmoil of the boiling caldron? How does the contemporary church in North America measure up as an alternative community? In this chapter, we will look at the cultural caldron in which the church is immersed and how the church can respond.

In Chapter 2, we noted God's love — God's passion — for the world, that caldron of human cultures. Hall's words are worth repeating here:

> This world, for all its pain and anguish of spirit, in spite of its injustice and cruelty, the deadly competition of the species and their never-wholly-successful struggle to survive — this world is the world for which God offered up "his only begotten Son." It was precisely the belief in a God crucified that gave Bonhoeffer the courage to go to his own death affirming the life of the world.[2]

John Buchanan reminded us that the Greeks taught that God is perfect. By that they meant that God is complete, that God has no needs, no hopes, no aspirations. As a result, the Greeks thought, God is isolated, unchanging, unfeeling. The Greek word for this was *apatheia*. "If God had feelings, became angry or happy, hated or loved, God would be as vulnerable as any human being — a preposterous idea, they thought."[3]

Buchanan described the idea that God loves, that God is love, as a new idea. God is "love with all the risk and vulnerability and heartbreak that go along with love."[4] He quoted Hall: "God is God only in relationship. God cares so deeply, loves so passionately that it hurts."

What is this caldron of cultures that God loves so much? What is it that the church is called to be "in," but not "of"? Why did God call the church into being to share God's love and passion? Can the church minister faithfully and effectively in a boiling caldron without itself becoming a part of the cultural stew, or trying to escape from and separate itself from the caldron?[5]

---

2. Douglas John Hall, *The Steward: A Biblical Symbol Come of Age* (New York: Friendship Press for Commission on Stewardship, National Council of the Churches of Christ in the U.S.A., 1982), p. 68.

3. John M. Buchanan, "Gift Wrapped," *Christian Century*, 12 Dec. 2006, p. 3. L. E. "Ted" Siverns, in a note to the author, observed, "I don't know how this squares with the pantheon of Greek (and Roman) gods."

4. Buchanan, "Gift Wrapped," p. 3.

5. H. Richard Niebuhr's 1951 work, *Christ and Culture*, is a classic that one must take into account when discussing the relationship between Christ and culture. In an introductory essay written by Niebuhr and never printed until the fiftieth anniversary, ex-

In a penetrating article, John Dart reminded us that the terms "kingdom of God" and "gospel" were not unique to the Christian faith. Others were called "the son of God" and also "Lord" and "Savior."[6] People in the Roman Empire were taught that Roman civilization brought stability and wealth. "[T]he people were urged to have 'faith' in their 'Lord,' the emperor, who would preserve peace and increase wealth." Dart quoted Richard A. Horsley: "In the Roman imperial world, the 'gospel' was the good news of Caesar's having established peace and security for the world."[7]

Christians gave a new meaning to secular words used by the empire. According to Horsley, even the Christmas passage in the Gospel of Luke has a *subversive* tone. Luke's text describes angels bringing "good news" to "all the people" because of the birth of a "Savior who is the Messiah, the Lord." A heavenly chorus joins the angels in proclaiming "peace on earth among those whom he favors." "For the Romans, peace was the militarily imposed *Pax Romana,* and it was already guaranteed by the Romans."[8]

Some church leaders lament that the United States in the twenty-first century has taken on some of the aspects of an empire. The United States is often referred to as a world superpower and sometimes as the world's only remaining superpower. I count myself as one of those who join in this lament. Whereas the early Christians used and reconceptualized the meaning of empire, current leaders in the United States in the early twenty-first century have used Christian language to support the American empire.

Dart reported that, in October 2004, about two hundred Christian ethicists issued a statement "about the erroneous use of Christian rhet-

---

panded edition of the book (H. Richard Niebuhr, *Christ and Culture* [San Francisco: HarperSanFrancisco, 2001], pp. xxxvii-lv), he discussed the typological method: "The main types of Christian ethics, from this theological point of view, are then (1) the new law, (2) the natural law, (3) the synthetic or architectonic, (4) the dualistic or oscillatory, and (5) the conversionist types" (p. xliii). While I prefer not to categorize myself or others, my own view probably aligns more closely with Niebuhr's conversionist type (Christ Transforming Culture) than it does with the others. In this type, "the function of the gospel is not conceived to be the establishing of a new society so much as the conversion of existent society. This conversion implies a radical revolution, ultimately metaphysical as well as moral in character" (p. lix).

6. John Dart, "Up Against Caesar," *Christian Century,* 8 Feb. 2005, pp. 20-24.

7. Dart, "Up Against Caesar," p. 20, quoting Richard A. Horsley in *Jesus and Empire.*

8. Richard Horsley, as cited by Dart, "Up Against Caesar," p. 20.

oric to support the policies of empire." The statement declared that "a time comes when silence is betrayal." The group added that the Christian call to peace-making is co-opted when "'a theology of war' is emanating from the highest circles of American government; the language of 'righteous empire' is employed . . . [and] the roles of God, church, and nation are confused by talk of an American 'mission' and 'divine appointment' to 'rid the world of evil.'"[9]

In a blurb for *Unveiling Empire*, Walter Brueggemann praised its authors, Wes Howard-Brook and Anthony Gwyther, for their critique of the "contemporary preoccupation with apocalyptic" themes. Brueggemann added that the writers "understand that the Book of Revelation is an exercise in eschatology. That is, how to be the Church in the face of a powerful and seductive empire."[10]

Tom Wright wrote that when Paul referred to the "gospel," "he was not talking about a scheme of soteriology. Nor was he offering people a new way of being what we would call 'religious.' . . . For Paul, 'the gospel' is the announcement that the crucified and risen Jesus of Nazareth is Israel's Messiah and the world's Lord. It is, in other words, the thoroughly Jewish . . . message which challenges the royal and imperial messages in Paul's world."[11]

Peasants in New Testament Palestine

The following description of Palestinian peasants is adapted from my sermon titled "Economic Dimensions of the Lord's Prayer," which includes material provided in a Bible study led by William Herzog II.[12] Consider the circumstances of the people — mostly Palestinian peasants — to whom Jesus ministered.

Who were the people who were taught the model prayer by Jesus? They were Palestinians who lived in the land where Jesus lived and min-

9. See Dart, "Up Against Caesar," pp. 20-21.

10. Walter Brueggemann, comment on the back cover of *Unveiling Empire* by Wes Howard-Brook and Anthony Gwyther (Maryknoll, NY: Orbis Books, 1999). Quoted in Dart, "Up Against Caesar," p. 21.

11. Tom Wright, "Paul's Gospel and Caesar's Empire," lecture at the Center of Theological Inquiry, Princeton. Quoted in Dart, "Up Against Caesar," p. 21.

12. See Ronald E. Vallet, *Congregations at the Crossroads: Remembering to Be Households of God* (Grand Rapids: Eerdmans, 1998), pp. 222-28.

istered; they were not wealthy or affluent, or even middle class. They were mostly peasants — men, women, and children who struggled from dawn to dark and from day to day to make ends meet and stay ahead of an oppressive regime, symbolized by the dreaded tax collector.

In his Bible study, Herzog offered these insights into the economic circumstances of the people whom Jesus taught:

> Most of the people farmed small plots of land that had been farmed by the same family for generations. Many grew crops of barley and some chickpeas, from which a wonderful paste was made. But there was just barely enough to get by.
>
> The landlord was always at the door, demanding more money for the rent. Herod's tax collectors and the Romans were everywhere, demanding more tribute. The rich, however, didn't pay taxes. Instead they took from the poor. The peasants did what they could to hide their crops and their herds. When they knew the tax collector was coming, they would run some of the sheep and goats up into the hills. They hid what they could, fought for every ounce of barley, and survived.
>
> In Jesus' model prayer, the words "give us this day our daily bread" were not part of an idle or inconsequential prayer. The words were real and grew out of a life-threatening concern.
>
> The struggle to keep from losing the land was a daily one. The landlord would even try to call in the loan before the agreed-on date. Neighbors often put money into a village fund to prevent the land from being lost to the landlord. If a man lost his land, he was out on the street — without a home and without a means of livelihood. After a few years of working hand to mouth and begging, death inevitably followed. It was Herod's contract with Galilee.
>
> In such an economy most persons barely had enough. Sometimes the landlord's steward would throw all of a family's possessions outside, pick through them, take what seemed to have value, and order the family out. The family would be left to pick up what they could carry and leave — many times without a good-bye because they did not want to put the village in danger. No one dared speak.
>
> Other times, villagers simply disappeared or were thrown into prison — often *debtor's* prison. The soldiers would show up, grab the villager, and cart him off. No explanation, no trial! Even when the prisons were full, the pattern continued.

That is why Jesus taught us to pray, "Forgive us our debts as we forgive our debtors." Not sins or transgressions, whatever they are. The debts were economic debts, with real consequences.

When we pray, "Forgive us our debts as we forgive our debtors," the prayer is dealing with real daily problems. Jesus was not speaking of some vague abstract notion of "sin." He was describing daily realities of economic life. It has to do with food and shelter.

"Rescue us from the evil one" were words that voiced concrete concern about the "evil empire" in which they were economic prisoners.

The words that Jesus taught were words of life for people in a society in which the rulers did not care what happened to the average person. It was a society of death in which the economy was stacked against the common people who desperately needed — and longed — to hear the words of good news. Jesus' words were practical, good news in an economy of death in which people were commonly dragged away and imprisoned.[13]

Another evidence of Jesus' taking a slap at Roman rule is found in Mark 5:1-20, when Jesus healed the demoniac whom no one had the strength to subdue. When Jesus asked the man's unclean spirit for its name, the man replied, "My name is Legion; for we are many." This was the Latin word for a large unit of Roman troops. Horsley believed that the symbolism is unmistakable: Jesus is taking control of the Roman forces who had brutalized people and is foretelling the army's demise.[14]

John Crossan summarized his conclusion: "The kingdom of God movement was Jesus' program of empowerment for a peasantry becoming more steadily hard-pressed . . . through insistent taxation, attendant indebtedness and eventual land expropriation, all within increasing commercialization in the booming colonial economy of a Roman empire under Augustan peace."[15] Crossan and co-author Jonathan L. Reed agreed that "kingdom of God" was a phrase that Jesus used to confront the divine Roman Empire.[16]

---

13. William R. Herzog II in Bible studies given in June 1995 at the Biennial Meeting of American Baptist Churches in the U.S.A., in Syracuse, New York.

14. See Dart, "Up Against Caesar," p. 22.

15. John Dominic Crossan, *Who Killed Jesus?* cited by Dart, "Up Against Caesar," p. 23.

16. Crossan and Jonathan L. Reed, quoted by Dart, "Up Against Caesar," p. 23.

The Twenty-First-Century Caldron

The boiling cultural caldron of the early twenty-first century resembles the culture of the first century under the Roman Empire more than it does the idealistic setting depicted in the 1857 hymn by William S. Pitts, "Little Brown Church in the Vale." Is it possible that many twenty-first-century American Christians dream more of the idealistic church set forth in the words of the old hymn than recognize the reality of the cultural caldron in which the church is called to minister today? The words of the hymn are appealing, but not realistic:

> There's a church in the valley by the wildwood,
> No lovelier spot in the dale;
> No place is so dear to my childhood,
> As the little brown church in the vale.

> *Refrain*

> *Come to the church in the wildwood,*
> *Oh, come to the church in the dale,*
> *No spot is so dear to my childhood,*
> *As the little brown church in the vale.*

The words of this old hymn stand in sharp contrast to the image brought forth by the phrase "the church in the caldron." The issues discussed in Chapter 5 are part of the cultural stew in the caldron. These issues confront the church and call for a response. To these six issues (racism, poverty and hunger, war, health, science and faith, and the environment), others (including human sexuality) could be added. It is not my intent in this chapter to deal with these other issues in detail. This is not to say that they are less important and therefore not deserving of our attention, but rather to say that some of them lie beyond my area of expertise, as well as beyond the range of issues needed to make the basic point of this chapter — namely, that *the church must be aware of and minister faithfully and meaningfully within the cultural environment in which it finds itself.* We are called to be stewards of the gospel, even (especially!) in the boiling caldron.

One danger for the church is that Christians may come to think that the culture will do the church's work. In 1954, when the phrase "under God" was added to the American Pledge of Allegiance, President Dwight D. Eisenhower observed: "Our government makes no sense unless it is founded on a deeply felt religious faith — and I don't care what faith it is."

Martin Copenhaver expressed the concern about the relationship between the church and the culture this way:

> Our culture's accommodation of Christianity was always rather thin, lulling us into the notion that the world would somehow do our work for us. When the culture-at-large tipped its hat to religion, we Christians became complacent. We assumed that the job of shaping Christians would be done in the world, rather than in the church. Of course, we should have been suspicious. When the gospel that Paul called "a stumbling block to Jews and folly to the gentiles" becomes widely and easily accepted by the culture-at-large, something is wrong.
>
> Today the secular culture makes no apology for defying or simply ignoring the challenges of the gospel. This should not surprise us. The world is once again acting like the world. This leaves the church with the challenge of acting like the church. We need to take up the job that was always ours, the job of becoming a community in which Christian lives can be formed.[17]

The specific nature of the issues in the cultural stew will change over time and from place to place. Thus, though I am writing about specific issues in the North American culture in the early twenty-first century, my larger purpose is to demonstrate that the role of the church is to minister faithfully as stewards of the gospel in whatever cultural stew exists at any particular time and place.

The Church and the Pangs of Childbirth

Edwin T. Dahlberg (1890-1986), an American Baptist minister, served as the president of the National Council of the Churches of Christ in the U.S.A. from 1957 to 1960. He was also president of American Baptist Churches in the U.S.A. from 1946 to 1947. The highest American Baptist award is the Edwin T. Dahlberg Peace Award. The first recipient was Martin Luther King Jr. in 1964. It was my privilege to know Dahlberg in

17. Martin B. Copenhaver, "Formed and Reformed," *Christian Century*, 14 Oct. 1998, p. 937.

the latter years of his life, and once to introduce him at a banquet where he was the featured speaker. I remember fondly one of his humorous comments about the benefits of growing older. He said, "As I get older and older, my memory gets better and better. I can now remember things that never even happened." The truth was that his memory was remarkably sharp that evening, and later as well.

Fred B. Craddock wrote about listening to Dahlberg talk about Walter Rauschenbusch.[18] Craddock relates what Dahlberg said:

> I was in his class one day, the morning following the bond issue in Rochester, New York, where he taught. Dr. Rauschenbusch had spent his time, apart from preparing and delivering lectures, working for this bond issue that would bring sewage and fresh water and cleanliness and sanitation to a large poor section of the city. The bond issue came to the voters. The next morning Dr. Rauschenbusch came into class. He had the newspaper under his arm. He opened up his notes. He looked again at the paper, held it up to the class — "Bond Issue Defeated." He started his lecture, Dr. Dahlberg said, "and then he put his head over on the desk. His shoulders shook and he cried like a baby." And I quit marking his book, because he groaned.[19]

Paul wrote that God groans: "In the same way, the Spirit helps us in our weakness. We do not know what we ought to pray for, but the Spirit himself intercedes for us with groans that words cannot express" (Rom. 8:26, NIV). Craddock interpreted this text as saying that God intercedes for us. "God is praying for us with groans too deep for words."[20]

John Calvin wrote of the church as mother who forms us in her womb:

> Let us learn from the simple title "mother," how useful, indeed how necessary, it is that we know her. For there is no other way to

---

18. Walter Rauschenbusch (1861-1918) lived in a time when mainline Protestant churches were largely allied with the social and political establishment and, in effect, supported the domination by robber barons that led to income disparity and the use of child labor. Most church leaders did not see a connection between these issues and their ministries and did not address the suffering. But Rauschenbusch saw it as his duty as a minister and student of Christ to act with love by trying to improve social conditions.

19. Fred B. Craddock, "What We Do Not Know," *Journal for Preachers*, Advent 1998, p. 35.

20. Craddock, "What We Do Not Know," p. 36.

enter into life unless this mother conceive us in her womb, give us birth, nourish us at her breast and lastly, unless she keep us under her care and guidance until, putting off mortal flesh, we become like the angels.[21]

When Jesus was curing a deaf man (Mark 7:31-37), he looked up to heaven, and then "he sighed and said to him, '*Ephphatha*,' that is, 'Be opened.'" Later, when the Pharisees came to Jesus demanding a sign from heaven, to test him (Mark 8:11-13), he "sighed deeply in his spirit and said, 'Why does this generation ask for a sign? Truly, I tell you, no sign will be given to this generation.'"

What is the significance of the deep sighing in the spirit — the groan? Craddock had this comment:

> There is at the center of reality a groan. And the closer to the center you live, the more you will hear it and the more you will share in it: the center of creation, the center of the church, the center of ministry, the center of those things that belong to the people of God, and the center of the human race. The closer you move there, the more you will hear the groan — the more you will share the groan. And you will recognize it. In the meantime, please don't add groaning to the curriculum. Under church administration: how to orchestrate the groanings of the local congregation. Under worship: liturgical groaning. Don't have any groaning retreats. After all, by the time you work on that, the groan may be obsolete. Because, you see, Paul says that the groan in creation, in us, in God, is a groan not of death, not the death throes, but a groan of childbirth. God is giving birth to something new. God is doing something fresh. God is creating new heaven, new earth, and by the time I have mastered the groan, I will have to exchange it — for a WOW![22]

The Local Congregation

We turn now to look at the role, the life, the struggles, and the ministry of the local congregation in the boiling caldron. In 1982, the World Council of Churches declared: "*A vital instrument for the fulfillment of the*

21. John Calvin, *Institutes,* 4.1.4.
22. Craddock, "What We Do Not Know," p. 36.

missionary vocation of the Church is the local congregation."23 Some go a step farther to say that the local congregation is *the* basic unit of Christian mission or witness. Darrell L. Guder reminded us: "'Local' implies 'place,' a 'particular, identifiable place.'"24 Characteristics of the congregational experience include particular places where members can gather for worship and work, mutual contact and supportive relationships, struggling and growing together in the faith.

Built into such an understanding are the actuality and, hopefully, the realization that the shape of the local congregation will vary from culture to culture, place to place, and time to time. Guder observed, for example, that in tribal and clan societies, the local congregation can be large and numerous. In cultures where the family is the dominant social form, the local congregation will often function as an extended family. In the geographical parish mode of Christendom, the congregation brought together everyone within walking or reasonable riding distance. In the industrialized West, the dominant form of organization became the "voluntary society," in which the congregation is made up of people who have made a choice to come together in a particular local congregation.25

Because there are dimensions of the American culture that are hostile to the gospel, or, conversely, that feel threatened by the gospel, *the congregation must be guided by the church's mission, and not guided by the culture.* This results in cultural hostility. Sometimes the church has responded by a reductionism that turns away from the gospel mission. One way this happens is when the values and assumptions of the competitive market take over the church and make it into a business. When this happens and the life and ministry of the congregation are based on a business model, a crisis of faith and spirit results. This crisis cannot be solved simply by reorganization. This missional challenge, according to Guder, "will be met only through conversion, the continuing conversion of the church." He added: *"The continual conversion of the church happens as the congregation hears, responds to, and obeys the gospel of Jesus Christ in ever new and more comprehensive ways."*26

23. World Council of Churches, *Mission and Evangelism: An Ecumenical Affirmation* (Geneva: WCC, 1982), ¶25; emphasis in the original.

24. Darrell L. Guder, *The Continuing Conversion of the Church* (Grand Rapids: Eerdmans, 2000), p. 170.

25. Guder, *The Continuing Conversion of the Church*, p. 146.

26. Guder, *The Continuing Conversion of the Church*, p. 150; emphasis in the original.

Large or Small?

A fundamental question confronts the church: Is the primary role of the congregation to grow larger, with the numbers of people in attendance filling the pews, thus requiring additional pews and/or added worship services? Is it to have overflowing offering plates and oversubscribed budgets? Is it to have programming for every segment of potential participants in terms of age, marital status, vocational interests, avocational interests, and more?

Cardinal Joseph Ratzinger, now Pope Benedict XVI, said:

> We might have to part with the notion of a popular Church. It is possible that we are on the verge of a new era in the history of the Church, perhaps very different from those we have faced in the past, when Christianity will resemble the mustard seed [Matt. 13:31], that is, will continue only in the form of small and seemingly insignificant groups, which yet will oppose evil with all their strength and bring Good into this world.[27]

Ratzinger added, "Christianity might diminish into a barely discernible presence."

Consider this account. Daniel Harrell wrote about attending a gathering of large-church pastors and how he enjoyed meeting colleagues whose situations were similar to his own:

> It was helpful to hear how they struggle with the same problems — how to create community among crowds, how to provide sufficient leadership training, recruit volunteers and run programs effectively. However, I confess that at times, instead of sounding like ministers, we sounded like managers of religious shopping malls who generate goods and services for the betterment of the customers who walk through our doors. This isn't necessarily bad, but it isn't necessarily Christian either.
>
> By contrast, when I attended a gathering of pastors from much smaller churches, nickel-and-dime operations with meager attendance on Sundays, barely able to support their pastors, I did not hear

27. Christopher Dickey and Melinda Henneberger, "The Vision of Benedict XVI," *Newsweek*, 2 May 2005, p. 43, quoting interviews published in a 1996 book titled *Salt of the Earth*.

the pastors talk about improving their facilities or putting together a smoother operation for Jesus. All these pastors could talk about was how they were going to bring revival to Boston and turn the city upside down. They were gong to halt violence, redress economic injustice, and preach peace and forgiveness to every neighborhood. I can also be cynical about planned revival, but this sounded like Christ-directed ministry to me. When God does show up in the ways these small churches expect, we'll know it is definitely God, for they cannot accomplish these things by their own power.[28]

Pastor Rick Warren of Saddleback Church in California has gained fame and following for his book *The Purpose Driven Life*. Four hundred thousand pastors have been trained in the art of being purpose-driven. More than 20,000 persons come to hear him preach on Sundays. But recently, he has come under increasing criticism. Are people tiring of megachurches? The numbers do not support this. According to Lisa Miller, there are twice as many megachurches in America today as there were five years ago.[29]

In a *Sightings* article, "Ups and Downs Across the World," Martin E. Marty quoted from an article in the September 2006 issue of Germany's *Spiegel Special*. The article was titled "The Power of Faith: How Religion Impacts Our World." Marty described the article in these words: "It's a stunning issue published in a nation stunned by evidences of vital religion almost everywhere in the world except Western Europe and, closest to home, Germany itself. Half the issue is given to "World Religions" and half to "Faith and Values" and "Christianity."

Marty included this paragraph about the article:

In the section on the United States, the editors unsurprisingly turn to the eye-catching. The headline "Karaoke for the Lord" sets readers up for pages treating megachurches — "feel-good temples providing entertainment," with ministers delivering "weekly jeremiads excoriating homosexuality, feminism and abortion." But take note of the observation that "particularly younger evangelists are now using the pulpit to preach about Africa and the environment." Two other notable lines: "Liberals are warning that the United States could become a theocracy"; and "even evangelical foot soldiers are edging

---

28. Daniel Harrell, "Power Source," *Christian Century*, 27 June 2006, p. 17.
29. See Lisa Miller, "Beliefwatch: On Purpose," *Newsweek*, 23 Oct. 2006, p. 9.

away from the GOP camp." One can't complain about the newsworthiness of that. One can, however, wonder whether it fairly points to the real varieties of religious strength in America. But again, is this how "others see us"?[30]

However, a comment such as was made by Joel Osteen, pastor of Lakewood Church in Houston, reportedly the largest church in the United States, stands in sharp contrast and does not give one a sense of confidence: "I talk about things for everyday life. I don't get deep and theological."[31]

An amazing example of the way God can do great works from small beginnings shows up in the history of Koinonia Farm and the beginning of Habitat for Humanity International. Koinonia Farm in Americus, Georgia, was established in 1942 by Clarence Jordan as an interracial community founded on the principles of non-violence and sharing that changed the lives of thousands of people. The community had a radical commitment to embody the teachings of Jesus in the Sermon on the Mount. The Koinonia partners bound themselves to the equality of all persons, rejection of violence, ecological stewardship, and common ownership of possessions. For several years the residents of Koinonia lived in relative peace alongside their Sumter County neighbors. But as the civil rights movement progressed, white citizens of the area increasingly perceived Koinonia, with its commitment to racial equality, as a threat. In the 1950s and early 1960s, Koinonia became the target of an economic boycott and repeated violence. When Jordan sought help from President Dwight D. Eisenhower, the federal government refused to intervene, instead referring the matter to the governor of Georgia. The governor, a staunch supporter of racial segregation, responded by ordering the Georgia Bureau of Investigation to investigate Koinonia's partners and supporters for purported communist ties.

In 1958, there were fifty-eight people at Koinonia. In 1963, only four adults remained on the farm. In December 1965, Millard Fuller and his wife stopped for a visit, intending to stay for only two hours. They were so captivated by Jordan that they remained for a month. Returning in 1968, they worked with Clarence and Florence Jordan to create a minis-

30. Martin Marty, *Sightings*, 12 Feb. 2007, and the Martin Marty Center at the University of Chicago Divinity School.

31. *Christian Century*, 9 Aug. 2005, p. 7.

try called Koinonia Partners. Part of Koinonia Partners ministry was "partnership housing." Fuller described those years in these words:

> It was there, in 1968, that my wife, Linda, and I worked with Clarence and Florence Jordan to create a ministry called Koinonia Partners. A part of that Koinonia Partners ministry was "partnership housing." We actually started the first house at Koinonia in the fall of 1969. While that house was under construction, Clarence Jordan died suddenly of a heart attack while preparing a sermon in his study out in the field behind the community at Koinonia. So, he never lived to see the first house completed. Linda and I, along with others, continued the vision and kept building houses in Koinonia until 1973 when . . . we moved to Zaire to work with the Church of Christ of Zaire to build houses patterned on the partnership housing program of Koinonia.[32]

From those visits came the founding of Habitat for Humanity International in 1976.

One of the most perceptive and penetrating articles I have read that accounts for the growing number of both megachurches and small churches was written by Mark Chaves. In a carefully researched and documented article, he came to these conclusions: "Churches are subject to Baumol's cost disease. Like schools, universities, theater companies and symphony orchestras, churches face ever-rising costs with no significant opportunities to reduce these costs by becoming more efficient. The only options in such a situation are to sacrifice quality or increase revenue."[33] Chaves continued:

> When cost increases outpace revenue increases, churches cut corners and reduce quality by deferring maintenance, declining to replace youth ministers when they leave, replacing retiring full-time ministers with half-time pastors, and so on. In short, churches find it difficult to maintain the same level of programming and quality they had before. And this will be true even if the church loses no mem-

---

32. See the DVD *Briars in the Cottonpatch: The Story of Koinonia Farm*, A Cottonpatch Production. See also the interview with Millard Fuller in the December 1995 issue of *Christian Ethics Today*, found on the website www.christianethicstoday.com/Issue/004/ An%20Interview%20With%20Millard%20Fuller_004_6_.htm.

33. Mark Chaves, "Analyzing the Trend Toward Larger Churches: Supersized," *Christian Century*, 28 Nov. 2006, p. 24.

bers. If costs rise faster than revenues, a 200-person church will be unable to produce the same level of programming and quality it produced before, even if it remains a 200-person church. Moreover, the minimum size at which a church can be economically viable will increase. The result is that people will be pushed out of smaller churches that no longer meet their minimum standards and into larger churches that still do.

Scholars and journalists who have written about megachurches have focused almost exclusively on the attractions of large churches. The rising-cost explanation calls attention to forces that are pushing people out of smaller churches as well as the factors pulling them into large churches. Since newly large churches are populated mainly with people who previously attended smaller churches, understanding increasing religious concentration means understanding what is behind the flow of people from smaller to larger churches.

The cost-increasing explanation for increasing religious concentration remains speculative, but the concentration trend itself seems incontrovertible. Like it or not, we are in the midst of a significant change in the social organization of churches, one whose causes and consequences we do not fully grasp.[34]

Chaves's *description* of the trend toward concentration into megachurches appears solid. It seems true that for many years the trend has been "that people will be pushed out of smaller churches that no longer meet their minimum standards and into larger churches that still do."

On the other hand, however, I believe his statement that the minimum size at which a church can be economically viable is based on certain unfounded assumptions. Chaves is correct in this regard only if we assume that the small church must operate in the same manner and with the same purpose and goals that it has traditionally done. But where is it written in stone that the church should or must operate year after year in the same manner and with the same purpose and goals? Nor is it written in stone that the same dollar level (in constant dollars adjusted for inflation) is required for a small church to have a faithful and effective ministry. It is too easy to fall into the trap of trying to replicate the past rather than venture into a new and different future.

When Chaves wrote that people will be pushed out of smaller churches that no longer meet their minimum standards, he assumed

34. Chaves, "Analyzing the Trend Toward Larger Churches: Supersized," p. 25.

that their minimum standards are unchangeable. Perhaps the currently prevailing minimum standards are not appropriate. The underlying assumption is that the members and participants are religious consumers who demand such a *minimum standard.* What if they think of themselves first as *disciples of Jesus Messiah and stewards of the gospel?* I believe that more and more Christian disciples are tired of being religious consumers, or being thought of and treated as religious consumers.

L. E. Siverns noted that Baumol's cost disease, referred to above, appears also to take its toll on television ministries that start with a sincerity of purpose that sometimes then moves to "stunt ministries" coupled with more and more appeals for money. It appears to be like a merry-go-round that starts off slowly but goes faster and faster until the riders are dizzy or have fallen off the ride.[35]

Disciples of Jesus Messiah and Stewards of the Gospel

Let us explore what it means to be a disciple of Jesus Messiah, God's anointed One, and a steward of the gospel.

Vine and Branches

The metaphor used by Jesus in John 15:5 is helpful in reminding us that a disciple of Jesus is essentially and vitally connected to Jesus and to other disciples: "I am the vine, you are the branches."

> I am the true vine, and my Father is the vine grower. He takes away every branch in me that does not bear fruit, and everyone that does he prunes so that it bears more fruit. You are already pruned because of the word that I spoke to you. Remain in me, as I remain in you. Just as a branch cannot bear fruit on its own unless it remains on the vine, so neither can you unless you remain in me. I am the vine, you are the branches. Whoever remains in me and I in him will bear much fruit, because without me you can do nothing. (John 15:1-5, NAB)

The metaphor of the vine and the branches shows that the relationship between Jesus and his disciples is one of interrelationship,

35. Siverns in a note to the author.

mutuality, and indwelling. All of the branches connect to the vine, and their fruitfulness depends on their relationship to the vine. The branches are also vitally connected to one another through the vine.

Stan Wilson described a 2005 visit to his church by Kingsley Perera, general secretary of the Baptist Sangamaya (Union) of Sri Lanka. Sri Lanka, Wilson noted, has been mostly Buddhist for 2,500 years. Christians came 500 years ago, bringing colonial rule and religious persecution with them, but since 1947 there has been general religious freedom. More recently, aggressive Christian missionaries have stirred up angry resistance. Hundreds of churches have been burned, and there have been attempts to outlaw Christian conversion. Wilson continued:

> Every time he [Kingsley Perera] told the story, somebody asked him what his church would do if Christian conversion were outlawed, and he always replied, "Suffer. Our people are prepared to suffer." Kingsley actually believes that it might be necessary for his people to suffer, that this might contribute somehow to the healing of their land, and he is prepared for it. "We believe that if we are persecuted, the church will only grow. Some nominal members might be pruned away, but that will only make us stronger. Study history, and you will see that the church always grows under persecution."
>
> I have read that the key to church growth is parking, not pruning, but Jesus has another vision of church growth: "Unless a grain of wheat falls into the ground and dies, it remains a single grain; but if it dies it bears much fruit" (John 12:24).[36]

This description resonates with Tertullian's words, "The blood of the martyrs is the seed of the church."

Salty Disciples of Jesus

Jesus also used the metaphor of salt to describe the relationship between his disciples and the culture:

> You are the salt of the earth, but if salt has lost its taste, how can its saltiness be restored? It is no longer good for anything, but is thrown out and trampled under foot. (Matt. 5:13)

36. Stan Wilson, "On the Vine," *Christian Century*, 2 May 2006, p. 19.

Throughout human history, salt has been a precious commodity. During baptismal ceremonies, the Romans placed a few grains of salt on the child's tongue. The early Chinese used coins of salt and in Europe some Mediterranean people used cakes of salt as currency. Roman soldiers were sometimes paid in salt. The word "salary" comes from *sal*, the Latin word for salt. The main sources of salt in ancient times were dry coastal areas near the Mediterranean. Early trade routes centered on Spain, Italy, Greece and Egypt. Many of the caravan trade routes were developed to transport salt, and Genoa, Pisa and Venice emerged as centers for the salt trade.

Wars have been fought over salt, or lost for the lack of it. During the American Revolutionary War, Benjamin Franklin made a secret pact with Bermuda to supply salt to the American forces. In 1783, after the Revolutionary War was won, salt works were set up along the Atlantic Coast. Major salt deposits found near Syracuse, New York, provided one of the main reasons for the construction of the Erie Canal, which opened in 1825.

One of the historic struggles for human rights showed the importance of salt. The British enacted the Salt Act in 1882, giving the British a royal monopoly on the manufacture of salt in India. Because of heavy taxation, most Indians were already at a starvation level. The Salt Act made it illegal to sell or produce salt. Since salt is necessary in everyone's daily diet, everyone in India was affected.

The Salt Act made it illegal for workers to freely collect their own salt from the coasts of India, forcing them to buy salt they couldn't really afford. The penal sections of the 1882 Salt Act included these provisions:

- any person convicted of an offence under section 9, shall be punished with imprisonment for a term which may extend to six months
- all contraband salt, and every vessel, animal or conveyance used in carrying contraband salt shall be liable to confiscation
- any salt-revenue officer guilty of cowardice shall on conviction before a magistrate be punished with imprisonment which may extend to three months.

In 1930, Mahatma Gandhi was looking for a subject that could unite the independence movement. On February 15, the Congress

Working Committee authorized Gandhi and his associates to launch civil disobedience "as and when they desire and to the extent they decide." Gandhi's response, in order to help free India from British control, was to propose a *nonviolent* march protesting the British salt tax and continuing Gandhi's pleas for civil disobedience.

Before embarking on the 240-mile journey from Sabarmati to Dandi, Gandhi sent a letter on March 2 to the Viceroy, forewarning him of their plans of civil disobedience. The letter included these words:

> If my letter makes no appeal to your heart, on the eleventh day of this month I shall proceed with such co-workers of the Ashram as I can take, to disregard the provisions of the Salt Laws. I regard this tax to be the most iniquitous of all from the poor man's standpoint. As the Independence movement is essentially for the poorest in the land, the beginning will be made with this evil.

The letter was delivered by a British co-worker and Quaker, Reginald Reynolds, to signal that this was not merely a struggle between the Indians and the British.

As promised, on March 12, 1930, Gandhi and seventy-eight male satyagrahis (activists of truth and resolution) started their twenty-three-day-long journey.

On April 5, 1930, Gandhi and his satyagrahis reached the coast. After prayers were offered, Gandhi spoke to the large crowd. He picked up a tiny lump of salt, breaking the law. Within moments, the satyagrahis followed Gandhi's passive defiance, picking up salt everywhere along the coast. A month later, Gandhi was arrested and thrown into prison, already full with fellow protestors.

An Associated Press article, dateline Jalapur, India, April 6, 1930, began: "Mahatma Gandhi manufactured salt from sea water at Dandi, this morning, thereby breaking the British law establishing a monopoly on salt manufacture." The world embraced Gandhi and his followers and their non-violence, eventually enabling India to gain their freedom from Britain.[37]

When Jesus called his disciples "the salt of the earth," this was a profound statement. Just as salt is critical for human physical life and well-being, Jesus' disciples are critical to the human race in terms of the

---

37. Information about the 1930 Salt March in India was found on the Internet at http://www.algonet.se/jviklund/gandhi/ENG.MKG.salt.html.

"issues" in the cultural stew. Just as salt makes food more flavorful and enjoyable, so Jesus' disciples can bring flavor and zest to the world. Salt is also known for its preservative qualities and for its medicinal qualities. It is essential for life. The world needs "salty disciples" of Jesus Christ.[38]

Martin Luther King Jr. was certainly a "salty disciple" of Jesus Christ. While a student at Crozer Theological Seminary in Chester, Pennsylvania (1948-51), he became acquainted with Mahatma Gandhi's philosophy of nonviolent social protest. On a trip to India in 1959, King met with followers of Gandhi. During these discussions, he became more convinced than ever that *nonviolent* resistance was the most potent weapon available to oppressed people in their struggle for freedom. Gandhi had ended British rule over his native India without striking a single blow.

In 1963, while imprisoned in a Birmingham jail, King was criticized by eight white religious leaders of the South who called his present activities "unwise and untimely." In his prison cell, King penned an eloquent response, known as "Letter from Birmingham Jail," dated April 16, 1963. He began the letter on the margins of the newspaper in which the critical statement appeared. The letter was continued on scraps of writing paper supplied by a friendly trustee, and concluded on a pad his attorneys were eventually allowed to leave him.

His letter listed four basic steps in any nonviolent campaign: "collection of the facts to determine whether injustices are alive, negotiation, self-purification, and direct action." He noted that he and his colleagues had gone through all these steps in Birmingham. But still the criticism continued. Their acts were called untimely; they were asked to "wait." He wrote:

> We know through painful experience that freedom is never voluntarily given by the oppressor; it must be demanded by the oppressed. Frankly, I have yet to engage in a direct-action campaign that was "well timed" in the view of those who have not suffered unduly from the disease of segregation. For years now I have heard the word "Wait!" It rings in the ear of every Negro with piercing familiarity.

38. Siverns noted that in Mark Kurlansky, *Salt: A World History* (New York: Penguin, 2002), Kurlansky indirectly pointed out the difficulty in sustaining the metaphor by noting that salt is so cheap now that it is thrown on roads and sidewalks to melt ice. Nonetheless, I think that it is a powerful metaphor that needs to be retained.

This "Wait" has almost always meant "Never." We must come to see, with one of our distinguished jurists, that "justice too long delayed is justice denied."

We have waited for more than 340 years for our constitutional and God-given rights.[39]

King's letter noted that even as nations in Asia and Africa were gaining political independence, "we still creep at a horse-and-buggy pace toward the gaining of a cup of coffee at a lunch counter." He went on to distinguish between laws that are just and laws that are unjust. He agreed with St. Augustine that "an unjust law is no law at all" and with St. Thomas Aquinas that "an unjust law is a human law that is not rooted in eternal and natural law." He gave biblical examples such as Shadrach, Meshach, and Abednego, who refused to obey the laws of Nebuchadnezzar because a higher moral law was involved. Early Christians were willing to face hungry lions and the pain of chopping blocks before submitting to the unjust laws of the Roman Empire. He asked if Jesus was not an extremist in love, Amos an extremist for justice, and Paul an extremist for the gospel of Jesus Christ.

The early church, he wrote, "was not merely a thermometer that recorded the ideas and principles of popular opinion; it was the thermostat that transformed the mores of society." In every century, a disciple of Jesus is called not to be a simple thermometer, but a herald of God seeking to be a thermostat.

Light of the World

Jesus also said to his disciples, "You are the light of the world" (Matt. 5:14). As Jesus' disciples, we are called to be light for the world. Just as God's love is for the *world,* so our love as disciples of Jesus is to be for the whole world — not only for our own ethnic or racial or religious group.

The metaphor of light is used other places in the Bible. The prophet Isaiah summoned Israel:

Arise, shine; for your light has come,
and the glory of the Lord has risen upon you . . .

39. Martin Luther King Jr., "Letter from a Birmingham Jail," was found on the Internet at http://www.africa.upenn.edu/Articles_Gen/Letter_Birmingham.html.

Nations shall come to your light,
and kings to the brightness of your dawn.

(Isa. 60:1, 3)

The people who walked in darkness have seen a great light;
those who lived in a land of deep darkness —
on them light has shined.

(Isa. 9:2)

Jesus said, "I am the light of the world. Whoever follows me will never walk in darkness, but will have the light of life" (John 8:12).

Paul exhorted the Christians in Philippi "to be blameless and innocent in the midst of a crooked and perverse generation, among whom you shine as light in the world" (Phil. 2:15).

To be a steward of the gospel is to be a light to the world, working to bring justice to all.

Is not this the fast that I choose:
to loose the bonds of injustice,
to undo the thongs of the yoke,
to let the oppressed go free,
and to break every yoke?
Is it not to share your bread with the hungry,
and bring the homeless poor into your house;
when you see the naked, to cover them,
and not to hide yourself from your own kin?
Then your light shall break forth like the dawn,
and your healing shall spring up quickly;
your vindicator shall go before you,
the glory of the LORD shall be your rear guard.

(Isa. 58:6-8)

Church Membership

Is there a model for a church — a congregation — that is small, faithful, and vital? I believe there is. What would a small, faithful, and vital congregation look like?

In the Western tradition of Christianity, Christian identity is usually defined as church "membership." Probably the underlying reason for the widespread use of the term "membership" relates to Paul's use of the term "member," in 1 Corinthians, especially in 12:27: "Now you are the body of Christ and individually members of it."

Christian "reductionism," Guder argued, has led us far from Paul's dynamic and incarnational understanding of membership:

> As the church focused more on the benefits of salvation enjoyed by the individual Christian, membership came to mean "saved." In the same way, as the church redefined itself as the institution that administers salvation, its membership was understood as the rights and privileges of those who were receiving the benefits of that salvation. Baptism came to be understood as the event that put the person into the status of "saved," which was then maintained within the disciplines of the church. Following the passage called confirmation, admission to the Lord's Supper was then primarily admission to the main source for the continuing grace of salvation. As a communicant, one was a full member of the church. Nonmembership meant "unsaved": *extra ecclesiam nullus salus* — "outside the church there is no salvation" (Cyprian). Excommunication was a very serious thing, because it put one's salvation in jeopardy.[40]

The Christian community — the church — is to find its model and mandate in Jesus himself. The church of the twenty-first century, as well as the first-century church, is to be rooted in and continue the ministry of Jesus.

The church, if it is truly the church, will be treated as Jesus was treated — even being hated as Jesus was hated. Despite the pressures of voluntarism that plague the local congregation (for example, attracting new members, keeping old ones, motivating people to participate), the church is different than other social groups. Because it has a divine origin, the church discovers its reason for being not in its apparent successes or failures, nor in its growth or influence, but in the call and commission of Christ.

Yet the truth is that the church has had a minimal understanding of membership over the entire history of Western Christianity. Guder and others have referred to this as "nominal" Christianity, "that is, people who 'name' themselves Christian, who maintain a minimal level of faith commitment and practice, but for whom the vocation to serve

---

40. Guder, *The Continuing Conversion of the Church*, p. 170.

Christ does not define their lives."[41] Some have used the term "cultural Christian" to describe this minimal understanding of membership.

In the Reformation period, many churches tried to deal with the issue of nominal Christianity by translating the Bible into vernacular languages, formulating catechisms, establishing parish schools to train the laity. Also, from the sixteenth century onward, "believers' churches" have provided an alternative to the major Reformation traditions.

Despite varied efforts over the centuries, "nominal" membership is now deeply rooted in American culture, so deeply rooted that it is difficult for many Americans to separate their patriotic fervor from religious zeal. Guder identified some of the factors that have led to this:

> When membership is defined in terms of the church as a voluntary society, it becomes almost entirely a matter of an individual's decision. It is an organizational matter. People choose their church membership in ways that parallel other memberships they opt for. There is, for many, little of the sense of mission and Christian interdependence that were at the heart of Paul's teaching about membership. At the beginning of the American experiment, there was some rigor attached to church membership, at least in the New England colonies. But over time, these practices have become less demanding. American revivalism in the nineteenth century, with its emphasis on personal salvation and the benefits of religion, contributed to the dilution of membership as a discipline. As a result, most mainline churches maintain what is, interestingly, called a "low threshold" to church membership. It is more difficult to become a member of many service clubs than to join most Protestant congregations.[42]

This low threshold to church membership is reminiscent of a statement attributed to Groucho Marx: "I wouldn't belong to any club that would have me as a member."

For the past several years, my own thoughts have questioned whether the category of church "membership" is a relic that does a great disservice to the church and to those persons and communities of faith who seek to be stewards of the gospel. Surprisingly, or perhaps not so surprisingly, I have found that this questioning resonated in my conversations with many pastors, lay leaders, and denominational lead-

---

41. See Guder, *The Continuing Conversion of the Church*, p. 170.
42. Guder, *The Continuing Conversion of the Church*, p. 172.

ers. Unfortunately, the term "membership" has become more of a legal than a relational term. L. E. "Ted" Siverns noted that is especially so in the Presbyterian Church in Canada, where "voting for or against union to join with Methodists and Congregationalists required membership. From that time it has been stressed that voting on significant issues requires membership and people are encouraged to 'join the church.'"[43]

Jesus and His Disciples as "Aliens"

The "Resurrected Jesus" was an "alien." The story of the appearance to the two disciples on the road to Emmaus (Luke 24:13-49; Mark 16:12-13) is one of the most developed and beautiful of the accounts of the risen Jesus. The two disciples failed to recognize their fellow traveler. The suspense built until the moment when the two recognized the risen Lord and he disappeared from their presence. As the story begins, we, the readers, know something that the two travelers do not know: it is Jesus who joins them.

The two travelers began to share with Jesus the account of the crucifixion and resurrection. They asked Jesus, "Are you the only *stranger* in Jerusalem, who does not know . . . ?" The Greek word used here *(paroikos)* can be translated as alien, stranger, exile. Notice the root *oikos,* which means household. *Paroikos* means to be outside the household. How was it that Jesus was mistaken for an alien? Actually, it was a fitting term for Jesus. His ancestors in the faith — Abraham, Jacob, Jeremiah — had all lived as aliens at one time or another. Jesus himself was in exile in Egypt as a young child. In a more important sense, Jesus was not of this world. He came from above, and for this reason he was an alien in his own country. Jesus was not bound by any one culture or region. So, in a real sense, those who are disciples of Jesus are strangers, even aliens, in the boiling cultural caldron.

The Gift of God's Grace

Even though we are "aliens" and "strangers," God gives us the gift of God's grace. A look at two of Jesus' parables provides insights about

43. Siverns, in a note to the author, July 2009.

this gift. The parable of the vineyard and the laborers (Matt. 20:1-16) was told to the disciples — the insiders. It was not addressed to the crowds. The parable describes two sets of relationships.

The first relationship is that between the owner of the vineyard and the laborers who work all day. Consider the apparent unfairness of the owner. What would happen if the world really functioned this way! People would sleep late and come to work only in the late afternoon, knowing that they would get paid for a full day. The owner's actions upset the whole scheme of things.

The first dimension of grace that Jesus was telling us about is that God's grace does not rest on the merit system. As a result, we who are "insiders" are prone to grumble. We fear that God's grace will undermine the reasons for being good and for living justly. We tend to second-guess a God who breaches the system and equalizes the pay like this.

I remember a woman who was an active member and leader in one of the churches I served as pastor. After a worship service when I had preached on this parable and tried to interpret God's grace that we can never earn or deserve, she spoke to me. She was upset, even flabbergasted. She asked, "How could God be like the owner of the vineyard?" The word she used a number of times in our conversation was "unfair." How could God be so "unfair" and "irresponsible"? At one level, she was correct. If our standard of measurement is economic or cultural, rather than by grace, God is unfair. We remained good friends, though I am not sure she ever accepted what I had said about the parable and God's grace that day.

But there is a second set of relationships in the parable, which goes even more deeply into the offensive nature of grace: the relationship between the laborers who worked all day and the laborers who came later in the day. The "early" group griped. They were angry and envious of the generosity shown to those who came to work later in the day. *A second dimension of God's grace is that the grumblers were not against grace so much as they were against grace shown to others and what that might imply.*

Let's add another dynamic. What if those who were invited to work later in the day are different than we are? What if they are members of an ethnic minority or from the so-called lower class? Does that make it even worse in our eyes? We like to say that we believe in God's grace, but sometimes we grumble when God appears to show more grace to others than to us.

Jonah pouted when God showed grace to the city of Nineveh. The

145

older brother thought his father was a fool when the father invited him to join the celebration at the return of his younger brother. The Pharisee at prayer thanked God that he was not like the sinful publican. God's grace is a great equalizer that rips away our assumed privilege and puts all recipients on a par.

A third dimension of God's grace is that it is not cheap. It is costly. The parable of the wicked tenants, which appears in all three synoptic Gospels (Matt. 21:33-44; Mark 12:1-9; and Luke 20:9-16), tells of a son who is killed by the tenants. The wicked tenants reasoned that, if they eliminated the son, they would be able to take control of the vineyard. So the tenants seized the son, threw him out of the garden, and killed him.

Jesus asked the religious authorities, "Now when the owner of the vineyard comes and discovers what has happened, what will he do to those tenants?" They answered, "He will put those wretches to a miserable death, and lease the vineyard to other tenants who will give him the produce at the harvest time."

The religious authorities didn't get the point and unknowingly condemned themselves by their answer. Then Jesus quoted Psalm 118:22-23: "The stone that the builders rejected has become the chief cornerstone. This is the Lord's doing; it is marvelous in our eyes." Jesus continued, "Therefore I tell you, the kingdom of God will be taken away from you and given to a people that produces the fruits of the kingdom."

Suddenly, the religious authorities realized that Jesus was talking about *them*. The parable brings us face-to-face with the exclusive demands of God. We are pushed to examine ourselves and not to rest easily. God's grace is not cheap grace.

Worship

The word "worship" comes from the old Anglo-Saxon *worth-ship*. To worship is to see and to respond to the true worth of something, to recognize and to adore the value of another.

Public worship is central to the life of the local congregation. The ancient practice of proclaiming a gospel text every Sunday keeps the congregation centered and focused on the gospel of which its members are stewards. Over the centuries, the Christian church has developed liturgical seasons, with the liturgical year in the Western church beginning on the First Sunday of Advent, which falls each year on the

Sunday nearest to St. Andrew's Day, November 30. The last Sunday of the liturgical year is Christ the King Sunday, which is the Sunday preceding the First Sunday of Advent in the following calendar year. Thus Christ the King Sunday falls on whichever day from November 20 through 26, inclusive, is a Sunday in a given year. In connection with the liturgy, a lectionary, which consists of a three-year cycle of selected biblical texts to be used on given days throughout the liturgical year, has evolved over the years.

In the tradition of many churches, the liturgical calendar and the lectionary are followed without variation; in some other traditions, the use of the liturgical calendar and the lectionary is optional; in still other traditions, the liturgical calendar and the lectionary are largely unknown and unused.

At the same time, the American culture has developed its own "liturgical calendar," which sometimes mimics and distorts the church's liturgy. L. Gregory Jones wrote a provocative article about the season of "HallowThanksMas." His words lead us to reflect not only on the period from the last week of October to Christmas Day, but also on how the American culture impacts the church throughout the year:

> We are coming to the close of the season of HallowThanksMas. It begins the last week of October and extends until Christmas Day. At the end of October the children are loaded up on sugar that doesn't seem to leave their systems until early January. Shopping centers have Christmas decorations up in mid-October, and then the materialistic press to buy more and more sets in. Throughout this season, adults become frenetic, anxious and — all too often — depressed. Such depression is particularly acute for those people whose calendars are not filled and who feel more acutely than ever the absence of places to go, of loved ones with whom to celebrate.
>
> I have never liked HallowThanksMas. In the past, I went along with a grudging acceptance that it was something we — and particularly those of us with children — just had to endure. I have found ways to resist the excessive sugar and the materialism of the season. This year, however, I reflected on the ways in which the frenetic pace of HallowThanksMas may be a microcosm of our culture throughout the year — including especially my own life.[44]

44. L. Gregory Jones, "Faith Matters: HallowThanksMas," *Christian Century*, 22-29 Dec. 1999, p. 1258.

My own sense is that the season of HallowThanksMas is a symptom of a much larger problem — we might even call it a virus that has infected the church. One by one, over the decades, the cultural virus has attacked, invaded, and enculturated much of the church's life. Seasons that once held a sacred meaning have become carriers of secular and materialistic values. An inevitable byproduct of this process has been the thinning and watering down of the worship life of the church.

Worship Wars

For the past generation, worship wars have marred the worship life of many churches in the North American culture. "Years ago," wrote Peter W. Marty, "it would have been unthinkable that two adjectives, *contemporary* and *traditional* would so thoroughly captivate the imagination of the church. It would have seemed strange that these simple words could govern the views of those who plot the church's worship. But captivate and govern they do."[45] He noted that:

> When Bill Moyers was researching a television series on creativity, an artist told him, "If you know what you are looking for, you will never see what you do not expect to find." Every genuine exercise of faith entails some openness to the unexpected, some eagerness to encounter the surprise of grace. It's in the nature of discipleship. When worship gets packaged in narrow boxes marked *contemporary* and *traditional* an inevitable predictability sets in. Mystery gets shortchanged. Preconceived biases get confirmed. Worshipers arrive expecting only that their preferred style will be in place. Ever so subtly, our minds begin to conceptualize God as one who might be reducible to a size that fits neatly into our preferences for worship.
>
> The gospel, of course, doesn't permit this kind of grasp of God. Jesus turns things inside out everywhere he moves, eluding the clutch of those who would manipulate him. As J. P. Sanders once said regarding biblical interpretation, "Anytime we read scripture and find ourselves right away on Jesus' side, we have probably misread the passage." Translate this overconfidence to worship, and the praise of God becomes a pitiable idol that serves our own interests.[46]

45. Peter W. Marty, "Beyond the Polarization: Grace and Surprise in Worship," *Christian Century*, 18-25 March 1998, p. 284.

46. Marty, "Beyond the Polarization," pp. 286-87.

The danger is that sometimes our overwhelming preference, or even demand, for a particular form or structure of worship will so dominate our thinking and reinforce our prejudgments to the extent that our worship of the living God is obscured or even made impossible.

Music

Cultural infections such as observing the season of HallowThanksMas and engaging in worship wars stand in marked contrast to the experience of Jones when he visited Estonia:

> Our hosts in Estonia were somberly describing the challenges they faced in maintaining a Christian presence throughout the Soviet era. One Methodist district superintendent had been deported to Siberia during the Stalin era and then executed. The KGB was regularly present at their church gatherings, watching suspiciously to see what was going on.
>
> Then one older leader of the church, a minister, smiled. "Let me tell you how little they understood us, and how little they could understand people's deep longings for God's love." He described how the church people would often disguise their time for Christian education with the children, fearing that the KGB would use their catechesis as an excuse to arrest church members. "Yet," he added, "they just didn't get it. We couldn't disguise the children's love for singing songs about their faith. We were afraid of their reaction. But one of the officers came over to me and asked: 'Why are the children singing?'"[47]

"Why are they singing?" the KGB officer asked. Jones's answer to this question was that even good habits are hard to break. "Oppressors can take away physical freedom or material goods, but they can't take away people's music. In the midst of Nazi Germany, a guard commented that the disruptive singing led by a priest came not only from people but seemed to be 'in the bricks.'"[48]

This observation resonates with the music created and sung by slaves in the Southern United States. African American spirituals rose

47. L. Gregory Jones, "Faith Matters: Why Are They Singing?" *Christian Century*, 8-15 Sept. 1999, p. 864.
48. Jones, "Faith Matters: Why Are They Singing?" p. 864.

from the songs the slaves sang while working in plantation fields. In the fields, the slaves developed a musical combination of "call and response" that became a characteristic of gospel singing. Many of the early spirituals provided practical functions for the slaves, serving as a means of communication or a map to freedom in the North. The music, especially, was a cry for freedom and salvation. The messages were coded in such a way that the slaveholders did not grasp the underlying messages.

In response to the statement "the church is about the only setting left in our culture in which people sing together," John Bell agreed and pointed out: "The church should be proud of being countercultural; we believe that music is a community activity and that all God's children can and should sing."[49]

A closing word on worship in the life of the local congregation: John Buchanan wrote about a trip Barbara Wheeler, president of Auburn Theological Seminary, made from New York to California one December to speak at Fuller Theological Seminary. She used three of her valuable upgrade coupons to secure a seat in first-class so she could work on her speech during the flight. Just before takeoff, the seat next to her was taken by a mother with a baby — one "small enough to be carried in her lap, big enough to resist being restrained." When Wheeler took out her computer and papers to go to work, the baby batted her computer and grabbed her papers. When Wheeler put her papers away, the baby kicked and screamed. Other passengers, who were also trying to work, glared at the mother and baby. Finally, the flight attendant placed the mother and baby in an empty seat in coach. Wheeler said, "We all went back to work, they no doubt to projects related to mammon, I to writing about God."

Here is Buchanan's description of the rest of the story:

> When she arrived at Fuller, seminary president Richard Mouw began the meeting with a brief homily. It was Christmastime, and he read the familiar story in Luke 2. Then he talked about the carol "Away in a Manger," which is attributed to Martin Luther. "A great hymn," he said, "but one line is just wrong. 'Little Lord Jesus, no crying he makes.' Not so. He cried. He cried for us. He died for us."

---

49. John Bell in an interview, "Sing a New Song," *Christian Century*, 25 July 2006, p. 20.

Wheeler said she was cut to the quick, and felt terrible all week-
end. She knew that the Holy Spirit had arranged for her to be re-
buked for her self-importance and intolerance.

Of course he cried. He was a baby, a totally human baby. That's
the point. That is the incredible claim Christians make at Christmas:
a claim about the soul-stirring, heart-warming, intellectually challenging notion of incarnation. Emmanuel, God with us, God among
us in the birth, the child, the man Jesus — God living among us, God
teaching us, God showing us what it means to be human in his humanity, God speaking the final word about us and to us about our
death. Of course, he cried.[50]

In worship the word of God can cut through our pretensions and
feelings of self-importance. In worship we come to the Holy One and
see ourselves as we really are. In so doing we are open to becoming more
faithful stewards of the gospel.

Money and Possessions

For the past quarter century and a little more, since 1983, my ministry
has focused on stewardship. Most people on hearing this fact have concluded that I am primarily a fundraiser for the Christian church. This
is far from portraying an accurate picture of the meaning of stewardship and what my ministry involves. I have consistently said and written that while Christian stewardship involves our attitudes about
wealth and possessions, it is not primarily about money. Jesuit Theologian John Haughey wrote: "We read the Gospel as if we had no money,
and we spend our money as if we know nothing of the Gospel."[51]

Tragically, this attitude is far too often found in the church. Sometimes, the church goes to such an extreme that it makes the mistake of
linking church membership with financial support, saying in effect:
"The greater the level of financial support, the better and more dedicated member you are." Such an attitude has sometimes led to the trag-
edy of some members receiving more favorable treatment or advantages
than those who cannot or do not give as much as others. Sometimes, an

50. John M. Buchanan, "A Good Cry," *Christian Century*, 27 Dec. 2005, p. 3.
51. Jesuit theologian John Haughey, as cited by Ched Myers, *The Biblical Vision of Sabbath Economics* (Washington, DC: The Church of the Saviour, 2001), p. 5.

extreme is reached in which one's financial support becomes the equivalent of membership dues or the price of admission. Sometimes those who provide greater financial support receive choice leadership positions in the church, or have greater influence and sway over decision making than others who might actually be farther along on their faith journeys. Siverns reported that "recently at a meeting of leaders in a congregation, I asked about the couple who sought to have their child baptized: 'What is their level of participation? Are they involved?' The answer was, 'He dropped $300 onto the collection plate on Sunday.'"[52]

Clarence Jordan used to say that a parable from Jesus is like a Trojan horse. "You let it in, and bam! It's got you." Jesus' familiar parable of the talents, found in Matthew 25:14-30, is often used in connection with financial stewardship campaigns to remind people that our talents and gifts belong to God and are to be invested wisely for the sake of God's kingdom. The line goes something like this: "God has blessed you; don't be like the wicked servant; pledge to us; it's an investment in the kingdom."

Jesus' parable about the talents (Matt. 25:14-30) is one that hasn't quite "gotten" most people, in the "bam" sense. Preaching from this parable to talk about money and financial commitments and one's talents is hazardous. This parable *is* about stewardship. It is far too easy, however, to let the congregation come away with the implied, or even expressed, notion that the essence of stewardship is to make a sacrificial pledge to the church. This notion may boost the budget a bit, for a while, but unfortunately it downgrades stewardship as Jesus taught it and it avoids the hard message of the parable.

Here is an example of such avoidance: On November 4 and 5, 2000, Denny Bellesi, pastor of Coast Hills Community Church in Aliso Viejo, California, asked for 100 volunteers and handed each one a crisp $100 bill. There were three requirements:

1. The $100 belongs to God.
2. You must invest it in God's work.
3. Report the results in ninety days.

The results were startling: people made money hand over fist to contribute to the church. It was covered by NBC's *Dateline*. We may ask,

52. Siverns in a communication to the author dated 6 May 2007.

"What's wrong with that?" If the goal of Christian stewardship is fund-raising, such a program might make sense. But this understanding is not the fullness of Christian stewardship.

Look again at Jesus' parable of the talents. The word "talents" is an unfortunate translation of the Greek word *talanta*.[53] The word is not about a special ability that an individual may have, nor one's passion in life, nor letting "this little light of mine" shine. It is not a mere $100. Jesus was not even saying, "Use what is in you and invest what you have for the kingdom." The word *talanton* describes the largest denomination of currency in the world economic system of that time.

The word *talanton* could be understood as "a huge bucket full of solid gold," or a "corporate chief executive officer's mega bonus," or "winning a state's multimillion dollar lottery." Only a physically strong person could pick up a *talanton,* which might weigh fifty or seventy-five pounds. Each was worth around 6,000 denarii (which is probably more than I have earned in fifty years of ministry) or twenty of the flasks of nard that Mary used on the feet of Jesus. In short, a *talanton* was a staggering amount. For the average person, it was uncharted territory.

What then was Jesus teaching in the parable that we call the parable of the talents? Get ready for the Trojan horse, "bam" description that Clarence Jordan ascribed to Jesus' parables. If I were presenting this information as a sermon, I would issue a warning at the beginning: "Fasten your seat belts; it's going to be a bumpy ride." It would not be a sermon on "using your talents" or "investing your money wisely."

In a remarkable book, Ched Myers presented an "upsetting" understanding of Jesus' parable of the talents — upsetting in that it turns upside down our traditional understanding of this parable.[54] Myers wrote:

53. The English word "talent" is the most common translation of the Greek word *talanton* (plural, *talanta*), which appears in Matthew 25. *The Oxford English Reference Dictionary,* in its fourth-level definition, lists "talent" as "an ancient weight and unit of currency, esp. among the Greeks." Most of the cultures of the ancient eastern Mediterranean world had a measurement of weight known as a "talent." Large sums of currency were measured in "talents" of gold or silver. Eventually, the word came to be used as a sum of money more often than as a measure of weight. Around A.D. 1450, the word "talent" began to develop a meaning of "power or ability of mind or body viewed as something divinely entrusted to a person for use and improvement." Today, the word's etymology is largely forgotten and is not something English speakers think of when they use or hear the word "talent." It has become a "dead metaphor."

54. Myers, *The Biblical Vision of Sabbath Economics,* chap. 5, pp. 38-45.

The parables of Jesus as preserved in the synoptic gospels represent the very oldest traditions in the New Testament. Despite this (or perhaps because of it), our churches still handle these stories timidly, and often not at all. Perhaps we intuit that there is something so wild and subversive about these tales that they are better kept safely at the margins of our consciousness.[55]

He continued by noting that stories are "lifted out of their social and historical context and reshaped into theological or moralistic fables bereft of any political or economic edge — or consequence." As a consequence, "we inevitably recontextualize the story in terms of our own unconscious political assumptions."[56]

William Herzog posed the problem of how to understand Jesus' parables in a series of questions:

What if the parables of Jesus were neither theological nor moral stories but political and economic ones? What if the concern of the parables was not the reign of God but the reigning systems of oppression that dominated Palestine in the time of Jesus? What if the stories they presented were not stories about how God works in the world but codifications about how exploitation worked in Palestine? . . . What if the parables are exposing exploitation rather than revealing justification? What would all this mean for a reading of the parables?[57]

The parable that immediately precedes the parable of the talents is the story of the bridesmaids (Matt. 25:1-13). The story sounds the traditional gospel exhortation to "stay awake." Then comes the parable of the talents. *Remember, "Stay awake."*

Earlier in this chapter, we referred to Herzog's description of the life of peasants in Palestine at the time of Jesus. Their plight was real:

The vast majority of the population, about 70 percent, were peasants who worked the land and lived in the towns and villages that dotted the countryside. Peasants provided the labor that generated the wealth on which agrarian societies were based. The peasants were attached to the land they worked, perhaps claiming it as their patri-

55. Myers, *The Biblical Vision of Sabbath Economics*, p. 38.
56. Myers, *The Biblical Vision of Sabbath Economics*, p. 39.
57. William R. Herzog II, *Parables as Subversive Speech: Jesus as Pedagogue of the Oppressed* (Louisville: Westminster/John Knox Press, 1994), p. 7.

mony, but they labored for the urban-based aristocracy who controlled the land and its usufruct. The primary issue in most agrarian societies was not who owned the land but who controlled its use and could extract its usufruct. Thus ownership was a moot point, at least until the forces of commercialization made ownership a more profitable venture than control of the land.

Theoretically, the land belonged to the ruler, who could — and often did — dispose of it as he saw fit. Most elite families owed their landed status to the beneficence of an agrarian ruler, although they tried to convert that donation into a hereditary right. Peasants simply went with the land and were regarded as little more than animals whose energy was needed to produce the wealth that the land generated. . . . [T]he goal of the aristocracy was to push exploitation to the limit in order to maximize their yield. Because the limit beyond which they could not go was the extinction of the peasants themselves, urban elites learned how to extract everything but the "barest minimum needed for subsistence. . . ." *At times the burden of tribute was so great that it entailed the deaths of the older and more infirm members of peasant households.*[58]

A great household in Palestine during the time of Jesus, according to Myers, was the closest thing in antiquity to a modern corporation. The powerful patriarch — the master — was often away for long periods of time on economic or political business. His affairs were handled by slaves who often rose to prominent positions as "stewards" (Matt. 25:14). The sums that were dealt with by these stewards were enormous, as we saw above in the description of a *talanton*.

This is not a kingdom parable. In this parable, Jesus said the master of the household entrusted *talanta* to three of his servants — five to the first, two to the second, and one to the third — before he set off on his journey. The first two servants engaged in trading and doubled their master's investment. The master praised and rewarded them. "Well done, good and faithful servant," the master said to each of the first two servants. It appears from the evidence presented by Herzog and Myers that to double one's investment was the acceptable *minimum* expected by the master. Anything above that 100 percent return on investment was "gravy" that could be kept by the servants who had doubled the master's investment.

---

58. Herzog, *Parables as Subversive Speech*, pp. 63-64; emphasis added.

But this feat of the first two servants would have drawn disgust from Jesus' first-century audience. (Today we have nothing but praise for them.) The operations of this household were less than exemplary. Myers wrote: "Greed was widely believed to characterize the rich, who exhorted and defrauded other members of the community." He continued, "The biblically literate, moreover, would recall the warning against stored surplus in Exodus 16:16-20, the prohibition against usury and profiteering off the poor in Leviticus 25:36f, or Isaiah's condemnation of those who 'join house to house and field to field' in their real estate dealings (Isaiah 5:8)." That is what this parable is dealing with.

The third servant was the *hero* — the one who did the dirty work! He explained to the master his action of burying in the field the *talanton* that was entrusted to him: "I knew you were a harsh man, reaping where you did not sow, and gathering where you did not scatter seed so I was afraid, and I went and hid your talent in the ground. Here you have what is yours."

In 1837, Danish author Hans Christian Andersen wrote a fairy tale that he titled "The Emperor's New Clothes." It is the story of the emperor of a distant land who was so enamored of his appearance and clothing that he had a different suit made for every hour of the day.

One day two swindlers arrived in town, claiming to be gifted weavers. They convinced the emperor that they could weave the most wonderful cloth, which had a magical property. But, they told him, "The clothes are only visible to those who are completely pure in heart and spirit."

The Emperor was impressed and ordered the weavers to begin work immediately. The rogues, who had a deep understanding of human nature, feigned their work on empty looms.

Members of the emperor's court went to view the new clothes. All of them came back extolling the beauty of the cloth on the looms, even though none of them could see a thing.

Finally a grand procession was planned for the emperor to display his new finery. When the emperor went to view his clothes he was shocked to see absolutely nothing. But he pretended to admire the fabulous cloth, inspected the clothes with awe, and, after disrobing, went through the motions of carefully putting on the new garments.

Under a royal canopy, the emperor appeared to the admiring throng of his people. All of them cheered and clapped, because they all knew the rogue weavers' claim and they did not want to be seen as less than pure of heart.

But the bubble burst when a young child loudly exclaimed for the whole kingdom to hear, *"But he has nothing on!"* The emperor had no clothes. This was whispered from person to person, until everyone in the crowd was shouting that the emperor had nothing on. The emperor heard it and felt that they were correct, but he held his head high and finished the procession.

Frequently, this story has been used to describe a situation in which the overwhelming majority of observers (usually *unempowered*) willingly share in a *collective* ignorance of an obvious fact, even though *individually* they recognize its absurdity. The young child had spoken in innocence, simply telling others what he had seen. The crowd was afraid to tell the truth to the emperor — to speak truth to power.

In Jesus' parable, the third slave, with the words he spoke, became a "whistleblower." He *knowingly* spoke truth to power, knowing the risk that he was taking. The master's retaliation followed swiftly:

> You wicked and lazy slave! You knew, did you, that I reap where I did not sow, and gather where I did not scatter? Then you ought to have invested my money with the bankers, and on my return I would have received what was my own with interest. So take the talent from him, and give it to the one with ten talents. For to all those who have, more will be given, and they will have an abundance; but from those who have nothing, even what they have will be taken away. As for this worthless slave, throw him into the outer darkness, where there will be weeping and gnashing of teeth. (Matt. 25:26-30)

The master had wanted appreciation — 100 percent return — on his capital, so he made an example of the third slave. The master dispossessed the third slave — the whistleblower — and the one talent that had been entrusted to him was turned over to his *obedient* colleague. The master showed the third slave how the *real* world worked.

The place of outer darkness has usually been understood as referring to hell. And perhaps it does — "that is, the hell on earth experienced by those rejected by the dominant culture."[59] Myers tied this parable of the "talents" to the judgment story that follows in Matthew:

> This singular judgment story in the Gospels suggests that we meet Christ mysteriously by feeding the hungry, giving drink to the

59. Myers, *The Biblical Vision of Sabbath Economics*, p. 45.

thirsty, welcoming the stranger, clothing the naked, and visiting the imprisoned (25:35-40). In other words, in places of pain and marginality — the "outer darkness." The whistleblower's punishment kicks him out of the rich man's system, but brings him closer to the True Lord, who dwells with the poor.[60]

This brings us once again to the image of the church as countercultural — the salt in the boiling caldron. The overall risks are great both for individuals and for congregations, including threats and risks to money and possessions.

What risks are we willing to take with our money and possessions — even our livelihood? What risks are we willing to take in the realm of social justice? During a three-and-a-half-year, part-time pastorate that I completed recently at Fredonia Baptist Church in New York State, I became aware that Spanish-speaking children and youth in the neighboring city school district were not receiving the education that they needed, deserved, and were entitled to receive under New York State law. Even though 40 percent of the students in the district were Hispanic, no bilingual educational program was available in the district.

Shortly after learning this, several members of the church and I recruited some others to join with us to form an interfaith network of persons who were concerned about this injustice. Monthly meetings began, with these as the initial goals:

- get acquainted with one another
- gather and share information about the educational requirements of state law and how they are being fulfilled in the school district
- determine what additional information is needed
- identify others who may want to be part of our group
- plan next steps.

Some of the persons participating did so at risk to their means of livelihood and reputations in the community. The network has been in existence for over four years, as I write these words, and now has a Hispanic pastor as its chair. Changes have occurred in the school district, including the resignation of the district superintendent. Much has been accomplished; much remains to be done.

60. Myers, *The Biblical Vision of Sabbath Economics,* p. 45.

Jesus taught: "For those who want to save their life will lose it, and those who lose their life for my sake, and for the sake of the gospel, will save it. For what will it profit them to gain the whole world and forfeit their life?" (Mark 8:35-36).

We are called to be stewards of the gospel!

Church Buildings

Among the greatest drains on local congregations in terms of finances and time and energy is the erection and maintenance of church buildings. In fact, the buildings in which Christians gather to worship, learn, and fellowship with one another are most commonly referred to as the "church." For example, we may say, "The meeting will be at the church." "I go to church every Sunday."

When Moses and the Israelites were in the wilderness (Num. 21:4-9), there was a problem: Israel had left the "fleshpots" of Egypt to go to a new, "promised" land. But as they moved farther away from Egypt, the more the people engaged in nostalgia for the old *brick-demanding empire*. It was as though amnesia had set in. These former slaves did not remember the burden of abuse in the Egyptian empire. They only remembered the guaranteed food supply that an empire always gives to cheap labor. They quarreled with one another, charged God with infidelity, and accused Moses of failed leadership.

I would argue that many North American Christians are so enamored with church buildings that their ardor for the church edifice overshadows the call to be the people of God who are faithful stewards of the gospel. My own experience has shown many times over that the easiest dollars to "raise" are those that are to be used for major capital projects or the maintenance of existing buildings. Sometimes I have made a bad joke by calling it an "edifice complex." Like the Israelites who longed for a brick-demanding empire, Christians sometimes respond more favorably to a brick-demanding church than to God's call to discipleship.

Consider what can happen when a local congregation does not make a church building its first priority. William H. Willimon wrote about a church that met in a school cafeteria and had just given away its entire hard-earned building fund to a family with six adopted foster children with severe developmental needs. Members of the church said to the family: "God wouldn't want us to build him a house before we built you one." Willimon concluded, "Jesus has some odd notions of success."[61]

Leadership: Lay and Ordained

Leadership in the life and ministry of the church is crucial. Let me state clearly at the outset of this section that I do not mean only ordained or so-called "professional" leadership. The church includes all persons of faith who have heard and accepted God's call to be stewards of the gospel of Jesus Christ. God calls each one to provide leadership based on God-given abilities and opportunities to serve in the household of God — the church — as it ministers to the larger world, symbolized by the boiling caldron.

Deuteronomy 18:15-20 is part of a section of Scripture that is sometimes known as the "Torah of Moses." Moses authorized a number of leadership roles: judge, king, and priest, as well as prophet and elder. These leaders were to guide and guard Israel, when it came to the land that God had promised, so that the community of faith would maintain its identity and vocation as Yahweh's people in the face of powerful cultural seduction. There were two issues regarding leadership: valid *authorization* and the threat of seductive *idolatry*.

When Holocaust survivor Elie Wiesel was asked, "Do you have a favorite Bible hero?" he replied, "Moses was the greatest legislator and the commander in chief of perhaps the first liberation army. He was a prophet, God's representative to the people and the people's representative to God. And he never had a good day in his life. Either the people were against him, or God was against him."[62] Leadership is not an easy task. What can modern leaders learn from Moses' example? Humility. Everyone needs it, but especially leaders because of the power that God entrusts to them.

Preaching

A key leadership role in the church is that of prophet — the preacher who is the bearer and speaker of God's word. Though the church is to

---

61. William H. Willimon, "Dispatch from Birmingham: First Year Bishop," *Christian Century*, 20 Sept. 2005, p. 31.

62. "10 Questions for Elie Wiesel," *Time*, 30 Jan. 2006, p. 8.

be led by the transcendent purpose of God, provision is made for human leaders who are called to make known in concrete and specific ways how the transcendent purpose of God is to be implemented in that time and place. They may be ordained or non-ordained. There are two important provisos for the prophetic voice:

On the one hand, the prophet bears authority and must be taken seriously and honored. The prophets were usually an unwelcome voice in Israel. They were commonly not heeded; they were disregarded, ignored, and treated with hostility.

On the other hand, even as the people were warned if they did not heed, so the prophet was also warned. The prophet is to witness to the living God and to resist the temptation to tone down the word, which in effect is to compromise Yahweh and to scuttle Yahweh's covenant. The counterpart to resistance by the people is the seduction of the prophet. Seduction may yield a false message that bears witness to other gods who are more palatable to the people and less demanding.

Leaders in the North American church in the twenty-first century must remember and learn from the words about prophets of Israel. (1) To be a leader in the household of God does not usually lead to popularity in the larger world. (2) Nor does being a leader necessarily lead to widespread acclaim within the household of God.

Let me state again clearly that these words about leaders do not apply only to ordained men and women. More and more, leaders of the church will be women and men who are not ordained and who are not considered to be "professional" church leaders. For many reasons, both theological and economic, not every local congregation will be able to have, or needs to have, a pastor who serves full time and who has what has traditionally been considered the standard theological education: a four-year undergraduate degree and a three-year M.Div. degree (or the equivalent) from an accredited theological school.

Perhaps bi-vocational ministry will be an answer in many situations. Or perhaps the model set by Paul's tent-making ministry, in which the leader does not rely at all on the local congregation for his or her livelihood, may be an answer that comes to the fore. My own opinion is that such possible solutions, and others as well, may actually strengthen local congregations as more Christians actively see themselves and their fellow congregants as stewards of the gospel.

In my latest pastorate (2003-06), at Fredonia Baptist Church, which was part-time, we created a Pastoral Ministry Team to provide major leadership in all of the worship services, and to preach on the two Sundays a month that I was not able to be present. The team consisted of nine members, most of whom had never preached before. Meeting once or twice a month, we engaged in prayer and Bible study, looking particularly at the lectionary texts for the Sundays when I would not be present. We explored together the question "What is the gospel?" as we did earlier in this book. In the exploration, the question that once seemed so simple to answer took on profound depth and meaning. It was marvelous to witness the growth and joyful responses of the team's members. As I write these words, it has been almost a year since my pastorate there concluded. The team continues to be active and has not expressed any desire to go back to the older pattern. It should also be noted that the whole congregation has welcomed and embraced the team as its members lead in worship and proclaim the Word.

Let me hasten to add, however, that such possibilities should in no way lessen our appreciation of and need for schools of theological education. The implications of these possibilities are far-reaching, both for local congregations and for schools of theological education.

Often popular opinion about the "prophet," the one who preaches, is that he or she lives and preaches in an ivory tower — not knowing reality or in touch with the people. The preacher needs a good dose of reality, it is sometimes said. In *Grapes of Wrath*, Tom Joad, talking about Jim Casey who had been a lay preacher but had given it up, said of him, "That Casey! He might have been a preacher, but he seen things clear."[63] Perhaps the truth is that it is the preacher, who is a faithful steward of the gospel, is the one who sees things clearly. The implication of Tom Joad's remark is that if one sees things clearly, one will not want to become or remain a preacher. To be a preacher is not necessarily to be popular.

Have you ever received a telephone solicitation asking for a pledge to support a charitable organization? Certainly most of us have. Ofttimes a question such as this is asked, "Are you comfortable making a pledge of $50.00?" The language of psychotherapy uses the "comfort" question, such as, "Are you comfortable talking about your mother?" Gordon Marino recounted an experience when he visited a church in a neighboring town: "After the service, I exchanged greetings and small talk with the pastor. A sentence or two into our conversation the minister remarked, 'I

---

63. John Steinbeck, *The Grapes of Wrath* (New York: Viking Press, 1939).

hope you were comfortable with the sermon.' Not uplifted — comfortable."[64] To offer comfort is not the prime purpose of preaching.

Nor is the prime purpose of preaching to give answers to questions in a way that has been described as "answerizing." L. Gregory Jones described "answerizing" as "a tendency that is polarizing people and crippling our capacity for meaningful discourse: the belief that we know what the right answer is, regardless of the question that has been asked or the issue being addressed."[65] Jones described "answerizing" in this way:

> "Answerizing" . . . grows out of the conviction that the only right way to handle any question is to offer The One Correct Answer. In a lecture titled, "Who Owns the West? Ten Wrong Answers," [David James] Duncan describes answerizing as "an activity that stands in relationship to truly Answering as the ability to memorize the phone book stands in relationship to the ability to love every preposterous flesh and blood person whose mere name the phone book happens to contain."
>
> Duncan goes on to note: "Questions that tap into our mortality, our pain, our selfishness, our basic needs, questions that arise from the immeasurable darkness, lightness or mystery of our lives, require more than mere Answerization." Such questions require sustained conversation, a willingness to listen and speak with one another in ways that can acknowledge the complexity of our lives; Christians believe such complexity involves the God whom we worship.
>
> Job's friends were experts at answerizing. They were unable to tolerate the inexplicable complexity and mystery of Job's suffering, and were sure there must obviously be One Correct Answer to his predicament. Job refuses their answers by insisting that his suffering remains a mystery. We know with whom God sides in that story.[66]

Walter Brueggemann reminded us that we preach to a world that no longer makes reference to God: "the most important thing about preaching in the contemporary US church is that proclamation of the gospel is no longer a privileged claim." His reference is to the recogni-

---

64. Gordon Marino, "Beyond the Comfort Level," *Christian Century*, 13 May 1998, p. 492.

65. L. Gregory Jones, "Answerizing," *Christian Century*, 18-25 Nov. 1998, p. 1121.

66. Jones, "Answerizing," p. 1121.

tion that "we must face that construal of the world *without reference to God* is intellectually credible and socially acceptable as it has never been before in Euro-American culture. . . . The upshot of that changed intellectual, social climate is that preaching has to start 'farther back,' because nothing is conceded by the listening assembly at the outset."[67]

Role of the Pastor

In 2002, when I accepted a call at the age of 73 to serve part-time as pastor of Fredonia Baptist Church, which I had previously served full-time for nine years in the 1960s, I shared with the church my vision about what I hoped the church would strive to be "If I Were a Pastor Again." The following is adapted from that statement:

> If I were a pastor again, this is my vision of what I hope the church would be:
>
> Together, the church and I would view ourselves as a household of God, seeking to remember who we are and whose we are. We would seek to be a vital, faithful church.
>
> Our goal would be to be faithful to God's call for the church to be a steward of the gospel of Jesus Christ. The church is *ekklesia,* that is, those who are "called out" by God for a purpose. To be faithful is to participate in God's mission, which grows out of God's love — God's passion — for the world. God calls the church to enable people to live by the logic of the gospel of Jesus Christ, rather than by the logic of the prevailing culture.
>
> To be vital is to be alive. For the church this means to have a sense of joy as it participates in God's mission and to be open to growth and change. It is important to define growth carefully, because not all growth is good. In the human body, the growth of a cancerous tumor, for example, is not good. In fact, such growth is harmful and may be lethal. It is important to define what is good growth in the church and what is not good growth. Size is at best a secondary issue.
>
> A vital church will be based and built on the resurrection of Jesus Christ. It will be built around the table. When we pray the prayer that Jesus taught us, we will remember that Jesus was mindful of

67. Walter Brueggemann, "Life-or-Death, De-privileged Communication," *Journal for Preachers,* Lent 1998, p. 22.

those who were — and are — poor. The debts of which he spoke were real economic debts, not some amorphous trespasses or sins. Mission — outreach — will be the heartbeat of the church. Our sense of mission will include what has been described as God's "preferential option for the poor."

The worship of God will be central and will convey to all who participate the purpose of the church. Participants in worship will sense mystery in the wonders of God. Guests at worship will experience the hospitality of the members of the church. Worship will be creative and will include music and drama on a regular basis. A festival sense of joy will be apparent and a connection to mission both near and far will be an integral part of worship.

The pastor will be seen by him/herself and the congregation primarily as a *theologian in residence,* rather than in the traditional roles of therapist/counselor (internal role) or the CEO/administrator (external role). Lay members of the church will be seen as full members of the church, not second-class citizens whose responsibility is limited to "temporal" matters. Together, pastor and people are entrusted with stewardship of the gospel at that time and place.

Giving to and participation in mission outreach will be generous. A long-range financial goal of giving 50 percent of income to mission outreach will be accepted, with a system in place to move consistently toward that goal year-by-year. Tithing will be a standard, with the expectation that everyone will give a tithe of his/her income, or make a commitment to move toward the tithe on a consistent basis. Gifts will be seen as offerings to God, not simply as a means of supporting budgets or programs. Together, and individually, we will see ourselves as stewards of the gospel.

Theological categories, such as conservative and liberal, will not be emphasized. They will be seen as relatively meaningless, inadequate labels fastened on persons in modernity that do more to divide people of faith than to solve real problems. We will seek to learn more about God and God's plan for us without trying to encase God in our preconceived notions. In faith, we will be open to the future toward which God is leading us.

We will not present the Christian faith as easy and painless. We will neither proclaim nor practice any version of self-serving redemptionism. We will not present the gospel simplistically, as though to say: "All you have to do is believe."

Our life together will encompass a life style that includes Bible study, theological reflections, and prayer.

One of the dangers for those who serve as pastor is to become caught up in the authority and influence that a pastor may yield, even feeling that such authority and influence come with the position. Many times that feeling is aided and abetted by the positive aura in which some lay persons view the position of pastor. The temptation, then, is that the pastor may feel invincible and beyond criticism. Pride replaces humility and an attitude of servanthood.

Henri Nouwen reminded us that in our faith journeys, we are called to be "wounded healers." Felipe N. Martinez described the change in the way people perceived him as their pastor when they saw him in pain. The turning point in his ministry came a couple of years after he accepted his first position as minister, as pastor of a church in St. Anne, Illinois. His parents had come from Mexico for a visit. During their stay his father, who had recently turned 80, suffered a minor stroke that paralyzed the left side of his body. Martinez took his father to a local hospital. For a week, Pastor Martinez's mother refused to leave her husband's bedside, and the intensive care unit made arrangements so she could stay with him. Martinez described what happened next:

> The week is a blur in my mind, but I know that every day I went to the hospital to support Dad and Mom. He was able to regain a good deal of his prestroke mobility by the time he was released from the hospital but was still too weak to travel back home. That Sunday, as I led the congregation in the first hymn, I looked up and saw my family making a late entrance. Dad walked slowly down the sanctuary's center aisle, assisted by my wife on one side and my mom on the other.
>
> Seeing Dad looking so frail brought up all the emotions that had been bottled up through the week, and my tears flowed so freely that I could not continue singing. My ministry in that church, which lasted ten years, hit a pivotal moment that Sunday. When the members of the congregation saw me in pain, they ministered to me — not from a distance, but as fellow travelers on the same patch of winding road. They comforted me, and through their actions they taught me how to give direction to a lost traveler looking for a town called Hope.[68]

68. Felipe N. Martinez, "Are We There Yet?" *Christian Century*, 31 May 2005, p. 21.

As he said, that was a pivotal moment in his ministry. The people saw his humanity and vulnerability, and made his ministry with and to them more faithful and meaningful.

Women as Leaders

It is probably obvious to the reader that I think both men and women are called by God to be active in ministry as leaders, as stewards of the gospel. One of the tragic factors in the life of the church is that too often women are shut out of ministry, or relegated to a second-class status.

John 20:1-18 tells the story of Mary Magdalene going to the tomb where Jesus had been buried and discovering that the stone had been removed and that his body was gone. She was the first person to see the risen Jesus. Jesus told her to go to his brothers and tell them, "I am ascending to my Father and our Father, to my God and your God." Mary went as directed by Jesus — an obedient response to Jesus' command — and reported what had happened. Her words included, "I have seen the Lord." She — a woman — was the first person to bear witness to Jesus' resurrection!

Anna Quindlen, a Roman Catholic, wrote an article, "Separate, Not Equal at All," in which she explained why she remains a Catholic, even though women are not allowed to be ordained in the Catholic Church. She noted that the Anglicans worship God with female priests and married clergy; the Archbishop of Canterbury once brought his wife and their four children to meet Pope John Paul II. She observed that Judaism now has female rabbis. She continued:

> The argument in orthodoxy is that women are separate but equal, an argument that made racial segregation — and flagrant inequality — possible for many years in the United States. Power is not relinquished easily; fear of the other is an enduring human handicap. "What orthodoxy is partly about is fear," says Rabbi Joy Levitt. "The world is moving very fast, and not all of it is positive." But ultimately many faiths came to the conclusion that strictures on women were the product of outdated norms and entrenched prejudice, not sacred texts.

Quindlen concluded the article:

For all those who ask why we [Roman Catholic women] stay, I say: because it is our church. Literalists like to harp on the gender of Jesus himself. What they overlook is that in clear violation of the norms of his own time, the founder of the faith surrounded himself with women. In seeking the counsel, opinions, and advice of female Catholics, church leaders would not be conforming to modernity, but modeling Christ. They argue that they cannot tailor church bedrock to suit social fashion. The truth is that they have tailored its bedrock to suit their blind spots. "Woman," the new pope might ask, "why are you crying?"[69]

I offer a final word here about women in ministry. With tongue in cheek and yet making a valid point, *Christian Century* listed "Ten Reasons for NOT Ordaining Men":

10. A man's place is in the army.
9. Men with children might be distracted by their parental responsibilities.
8. Ministry is unnatural for men since their physical build suits them better for chopping wood.
7. Man, having been created before woman, is an experiment, not the crowning achievement of creation.
6. Men are too emotional; see how they respond at sporting events.
5. Handsome men will distract female worshipers.
4. Pastoring is a nurturing role; historically women have been the nurturers.
3. Men are too prone to violence and would be dangerously unstable in conflict situations.
2. Men can still be involved in church work without having to become pastors.
1. Jesus was betrayed by a man, whose lack of faith and subsequent punishment symbolizes the subordinate position all men should assume.[70]

69. Anna Quindlen, "The Last Word: Separate, Not Equal at All," *Newsweek,* 2 May 2005, p. 74.
70. "Ten Reasons for NOT Ordaining Men," *Christian Century,* 18 Apr. 2006, p. 7.

The Church as an Alternative Community

What does it mean to be an *alternative* community? What new thing is God calling the church to be and to do? To be a faithful steward of the gospel is not only to thirst for God as an individual; it is to be part of an alternative community that relentlessly pursues God's vision of and intent for justice that is specific and concrete, subversive and uncompromising.

One of the most difficult challenges facing the church in becoming an alternative community is to heed Jesus' stunning moral demand, actually given as a command, that we *love our enemies:* "But I say to you that listen, Love your enemies, do good to those who hate you, bless those who curse you, pray for those who abuse you" (Luke 6:27-28). Loving our enemies may mean to clench our fists, grit our teeth, and, in an act of daring love, show our determination to love them no matter what. How is this possible? It is when we realize that even though we were enemies of God, God in Christ loves us. God not only puts up with us, but also comes to us and embraces us.

The role of the preaching office in an alternative community is critical. Brueggemann made this point with these words:

> The preaching office is an office of an alternative truth that makes its bid for assent. It does so, moreover, in the face of the empire that wants to stop talk of *miracles, promises, and neighbors,* because such talk runs against the grain of imperial, ruthless self-sufficiency. And thus soon or late — as every preacher knows — agents of the status quo will move in to halt the countertruth. They may be friendly or hard, open or covert. But they will try. Against such a risk, the sender says, "fear not."[71]

To become an alternative community is fearful. The very idea of change is fearful, even when we know that something better would result. Consider the standard keyboard, formerly on typewriters and now found on computers. The most commonly used keys are placed as far apart as possible. Why? Originally the purpose of this arrangement was to *slow down* typing speed! The keys on machines of the 1800s would jam if the typist went too fast.

About fifty years ago, a keyboard called the Dvorak Simplified Key-

71. Brueggemann, "Life-or-Death, De-privileged Communication," p. 27.

board was invented. On this keyboard, the keys used most frequently are in the home row and the right hand does most of the work. Tests have shown that typists using this keyboard can type up to five times faster with no increase in errors. But we prefer the inefficient keyboard. We don't want to change.

God calls the church to change: to become an alternative community — the salt in the cultural stew in the caldron. The questions for the church are: Are we willing to change in the ways that God calls and intends for us to change? Are we willing to take the risks involved?

Brueggemann used the metaphors of "script" to represent the prevailing culture and "counterscript" to represent the Bible as providing the alternative for a faith community. He wrote of "the ways in which *the Bible is a critical alternative to the enmeshments in which we find ourselves in the church and in society*" (emphasis added). His nineteen theses about the Bible in the church are summarized below (direct quotations are in quotation marks):

1. "Everybody has a script. People live their lives by a script that is sometimes explicit but often implicit." Not only individuals but also communities are organized by a script. The local congregation lives by a script. As the household of God, the church should look to the Bible as the source of its script.
2. "We are scripted by a process of nurture, formation and socialization that might go under the rubric of liturgy." Brueggemann mentioned Mark Douglas's observation that "regular table prayers of thanksgiving are a primal way in which to challenge the market view of the supply and movement of valuable goods."[72]
3. "The dominant script of both selves and communities in our society, for both liberals and conservatives, is the script of therapeutic, technological, consumerist militarism that permeates every dimension of our common life." *Therapeutic* refers to the assumption that "there is a product or a treatment or a process to counteract every ache and pain and discomfort and trouble, so that life may be lived without inconvenience." *Technological* refers to "the assumption that everything can be fixed and made right through human ingenuity." *Consumerist* indicates that "we live in a culture that believes that the

---

72. See Walter Brueggemann, "Living with the Elusive God: Counterscript," *Christian Century*, 29 Nov. 2005, pp. 22-28.

whole world and all its resources are available to us without regard to the neighbor." *Militarism* pervades our society and "exists to protect and maintain the system and to deliver and guarantee all that is needed for therapeutic technological consumerism."

4. "This script — enacted through advertising, propaganda and ideology, especially in the several liturgies of television — promises to make us safe and happy." This script gives us an illusion of safety and happiness and "invites life in a bubble that is absent of critical reflection."

5. "That script has failed." Its failure is indicated by the reality that we are not safe and we are not happy.

6. "Health depends, for society and for its members, on disengaging from and relinquishing the failed script." This is difficult to utter and to imagine. We are ambivalent about disengaging and relinquishing.

7. "It is the task of the church and its ministry to detach us from that powerful script." This is the work set forth in the biblical tradition, as in Moses indicating that brickyard quotas were not the true destiny of Israelite community and Jesus delineating a regime change in Mark 1:14-15.

8. "The task of descripting, relinquishment and disengagement is undertaken through the steady, patient, intentional articulation of an alternative script that we testify will indeed make us safe and joyous." We have become jaded and have forgotten what God entrusted to us. We have become a household of amnesia, rather than a household of God.[73]

9. "The alternative script is rooted in the Bible and enacted through the tradition of the church. . . . [W]hat we find there [in the Bible] is an alternative world, an alternative network of symbols and signs that stitched together yield a coherence that subverts dominant scripts, a world in which newness keeps welling up."

10. "The defining factor of the alternative script is the God of the Bible, who, fleshed in Jesus, is variously Lord and Savior of Israel and Creator of heaven and earth, and whom we name as Father, Son and Holy Spirit. . . . [T]he alternative script is about God, about a particular God whose name we know, whose story we tell."

73. See Mark Douglas, *Confessing Christ in the Twenty-first Century* (Boulder, CO: Rowman & Littlefield, 2005).

11. "The script of this God of power and life is not monolithic, one-dimensional or seamless, and we should not pretend that we have such an easy case to make in telling about this God." God, the key character, is elusive. "God is, as Job found out, irascible in freedom and pathos-filled in sovereignty, one who traffics in hiddenness and violence."

12. "The ragged, disjunctive quality of the counterscript to which we testify cannot be smoothed out." The script of the culture is "all about privilege, certitude and entitlement. But the script of the church and its ministry is not about privilege, certitude or entitlement."

13. "The ragged, disputatious character of the counterscript to which we testify is so disputed and polyvalent that its adherents are always tempted to quarrel among themselves." Polyvalence — the fact that in the Bible God speaks in different voices — "invites us to choose the part we happen to like." This leads to quarrels, which may become vicious. They also detract us from the main claims of the text.

14. "The entry point into the counterscript is baptism." Baptism is a bold counteract that "means entry into a stream of promise that is free but not cheap." The ancient liturgy asked. "Do you renounce Satan and all his works?" By inference, in baptism, we ask, "Do you renounce the dominant script?"

15. "The nurture, formation and socialization into the counterscript with this elusive, irascible God at its center constitute the work of ministry." Many ministers are in despair, exhausted and cynical, having confused means with the ends. The ends are nurture (the embracing of a new script); formation (the receiving and living into an alternate reality); and socialization (the entering into another world that comes by "switching stories").

16. "Ministry is conducted in the awareness that most of us are deeply ambivalent about the alternative script." We do not want to choose decisively between the dominant script and God's counterscript.

17. "The good news is that our ambivalence as we stand between scripts is precisely the primal venue for the work of God's Spirit." In our ambivalence, "the Spirit in us can be stirred and we can be opened to new possibilities." When we minister so as to name the deep ambiguity within us, we create a place for waiting for God's Spirit to bring newness among us. Then, even liberals and conser-

vatives may find common ground amidst our shrillness, our passions, and loudness.

18. "Ministry and mission entail managing that inescapable ambivalence that is the human predicament in faithful, generative ways." To manage ambivalence is not to manipulate toward our preferred ends. "It is management for truth telling, waiting and receiving newness."

19. "The work of ministry is indispensable." Ministry is not done so that the church may prosper. Ministry is that "the world may live (and not die) and rejoice (and not cower)."[74]

Summary

The image of the bubbling caldron as the culture in which the church is immersed is not an attractive image. To many in the church, the image may be frightening, especially when we remember that the church is not called by God to escape from the caldron, but rather to minister *within* the caldron by being the salt that seeks to transform the culture by the power of the Holy Spirit.

When Jesus called his disciples "the salt of the earth," this was a profound statement. Just as salt is critical for human physical life and well-being, Jesus' disciples are critical to the human race in terms of the "issues" in the cultural stew. The world needs "salty disciples" of Jesus Christ.

The church — the household of God — is called out by God to be a faithful steward of the gospel of Jesus Christ. To be a faithful steward of the gospel is not only to thirst for God; it is to be *an alternative community* that relentlessly pursues God's vision of and intent for justice that is specific and concrete, subversive and uncompromising.

The church's minimal understanding of membership over the entire history of Western Christianity has led to a "nominal" Christianity — people who name themselves Christian, but whose level of faith commitment and practice is minimal.

Such a minimalist level of faith and commitment on the part of Christian disciples leads to being seduced by the culture so that the disciples feel comfortable and at ease as residents of the culture. Con-

---

74. See Vallet, *Congregations at the Crossroads.*

trast this with Jesus' experience on the road to Emmaus when two travelers asked Jesus, "Are you the only *stranger* in Jerusalem, who does not know . . . ?" Jesus was taken to be a stranger, an alien. In a real sense also, those who are disciples of Jesus are strangers, even aliens, in the boiling cultural caldron.

Yet, even if and when we are seduced by the culture, God gives us a gift — a gift of grace that is not based on a merit system. It is freely given. Despite this we humans often grumble when God's grace is shown to someone else. We do not grumble when we are the recipients of God's grace. God's free gift of grace does not mean that God's grace is cheap, however. The death of Jesus was the price paid by God.

In worship, the word of God can cut through our pretensions and feelings of self-importance. In worship, we come to the Holy One and see ourselves as we really are. In so doing, we are open and vulnerable to becoming more faithful stewards of the gospel.

In the twenty-first-century church in North America, many congregations have found themselves struggling financially. Questions abound: How can we get enough offerings and pledges to meet next year's budget? Can we still "afford" to have a full-time pastor? Can our church even survive? For many, it is difficult to imagine a church that is radically different from the church they have known in the twentieth century. Or, if they can imagine it, they see the prospect as threatening and frightening — something to be avoided. Financial stewardship, however, is not the essence of being a steward of the gospel.

Leadership in the life and ministry of the church is crucial. This includes both women and men, whether ordained or not ordained. The church includes all persons of faith who have heard and accepted God's call to be stewards of the gospel of Jesus Christ. God calls each one to provide leadership based on God-given abilities and opportunities to serve in the household of God — the church — as it ministers to the larger world, symbolized by the boiling caldron. The office of pastor is one of the leadership roles.

Ideally, the church and the pastor would view themselves as a household of God, seeking to remember who they are and whose they are. They would seek to be a vital, faithful church, whose goal would be to be faithful to God's call for the church to be a steward of the gospel of Jesus Christ.

God calls the church to change: to become an alternative community — the salt in the cultural stew in the caldron. The questions for the church are: Are we willing to change in the ways that God calls and intends for us to change? Are we willing to take the risks involved?

The image of the church in the caldron lifted up in this chapter is frightening and challenging. The cultural caldron promises safety and happiness, even as it boils and leads to death. God's vision for the church as salt in the caldron can be fulfilled as God's Spirit works through human leaders. God calls men and women of faith to lead the church of the twenty-first century to become an alternative community.

Then the words of old will come to fruition:

Then your light shall break forth like the dawn,
and your healing shall spring up quickly;
your vindicator shall go before you,
the glory of the LORD shall be your rear guard.

(Isa. 58:8)

In the next chapter, we will ask and seek answers to questions about the role of theological education in enabling the church to become an alternative community that ministers as a steward of the gospel. Our primary question will be: What is the role of theological education in equipping men and women to be the leaders of such an alternative community?

CHAPTER 7

Theological Education in the Twenty-First Century

> Theological schools are unique environments. While they
> share much in common, they are deeply different in very par-
> ticular ways.
>
> Daniel O. Aleshire, *Earthen Vessels*

These words of Aleshire make it clear that the task of reforming theological education is not an easy one. The road is difficult and long. Yet,
the preparation of leaders — lay and ordained — in the life and ministry
of the church is crucial. Leadership does not refer only to ordained or
so-called "professional" leadership. The church includes all persons of
faith who have heard and accepted God's call to be stewards of the gospel of Jesus Christ. God calls each one to provide leadership based on
God-given abilities and opportunities to serve in the household of God
— the church — as it ministers to the larger world, symbolized by the
boiling caldron.

A key *leadership role* in the church is that of *prophet* — the preacher
who is the bearer and speaker of God's word. Though the church is to
be led by the transcendent purpose of God, provision is made for human leaders who are called to make known in concrete and specific
ways how the transcendent purpose of God is to be implemented in
that time and place. They may be ordained or non-ordained.

A key *office* in the life of the congregation is that of *pastor*. In the life
and work of the congregation, pastor and people are called to share to-

gether a vision of what the church should be. My vision is that people and pastor view the congregation as a household of God, seeking to remember who we are and whose we are. We would seek to be a vital, faithful church with a goal of being faithful to God's call for the church to be a steward of the gospel of Jesus Christ.

In such a congregation, it is recognized and acknowledged that both men and women are called by God to be active in ministry as leaders, as stewards of the gospel. One of the tragic factors in the life of the church is that too often women are shut out of ministry, or relegated to a second-class status.

The church of Jesus Christ is composed of congregations in which each congregation is called to be an *alternative community*. What does it mean to be an alternative community? What new thing is God calling the church to be and to do? To be a faithful steward of the gospel is not only to thirst for God as an individual; it is to be part of an alternative community that relentlessly pursues God's vision of and intent for justice that is specific and concrete, subversive and uncompromising.

One of the most difficult challenges facing the church in becoming an alternative community is to heed Jesus' stunning moral demand, actually given as a command, that we *love our enemies:* "But I tell you who hear me: Love your enemies, do good to those who hate you, bless those who curse you, pray for those who mistreat you" (Luke 6:27-28). Loving our enemies may mean to clench our fists, grit our teeth, and, in an act of daring love, show our determination to love them no matter what. How is this possible? It is when we realize that even though we were enemies of God, God in Christ loves us. God not only puts up with us but also comes to us and embraces us.

Kosuke Koyama, a Japanese theologian internationally known for using arresting metaphors drawn from his experience as a missionary to convey an influential vision of Christianity as compatible with Asian traditions, died in the spring of 2009 at age 79 in Springfield, Massachusetts. Koyama was born on December 10, 1929, in Tokyo. In 1945, as American bombs rained down on Tokyo, he was baptized as a Christian at the age of 15. He was struck by the courageous words of the presiding pastor, who told him that God called on him to love everybody, "even the Americans." Love your enemies.

The image of the bubbling caldron as the culture in which the church is immersed is not attractive. The image is frightening, especially when we remember that the church is not called by God to escape from the caldron, but rather to minister *within* the caldron by being the salt that seeks to transform the culture by the power of the Holy Spirit.

The church needs leaders who are willing to be salt in the boiling caldron and who will point by word and example to what it means to be a steward of the gospel.

The Role of Theological Education

How does the church secure such leaders? We now look at the role of theological education in enabling the church to become an alternative community that ministers as a steward of the gospel. The primary question is: What is the role of theological education in equipping men and women whom God calls to be the leaders of such a community?

As noted in Chapter 1, in 2001 I formulated a proposal that the metaphor of "steward" become the organizing principle for the core curriculum of theological education in the twenty-first century. The remainder of this chapter will look at this proposal, as revised and seen through the lens of the material appearing earlier in this book.

The proposal began with these words: "The work of the pastor is to help people understand the life-giving logic of the gospel in the totality of their lives."

The proposed thesis was:

The object of theological education is to develop Christian stewards who, in turn, can provide leadership for the development of Christian stewards in Christian congregations, denominations, and in the church at large.

The proposal said that to advance this proposed thesis we will:

(1) Put forth an understanding of Christian stewardship that is radically different than the prevailing view [this understanding has been stated in this book, especially in Chapter 2];

(2) Look briefly at the roots and practices of theological education in North America [see below];

(3) Explore how the concept of "steward" can bring a unifying purpose and focus to the several dimensions of theological education and the traditions of *paideia* and *Wissenschaft* [see below].

To say that the church of Jesus Christ is called to be a steward of the gospel can mark the beginning of a new understanding. Then, when we realize that our participation in mission grows out of our identity as Christian stewards, we will be adequately motivated to participate in the mission.

Individual Christians and the church collectively are called to be stewards. The identity of the Christian (and the church) as steward is a fundamental category. To be a steward of the gospel is the essence of God's call to God's people and the church. Our *identity* is "steward." Mission is what God calls us to *do* because we are stewards. The task to which God calls us is "mission." When that understanding takes hold, funding the mission will no longer be a major concern or problem.

As I have explored the dimensions of what it means to be a Christian steward, I have become increasingly convinced that *to envision one's primary identity as a steward of the gospel can represent a summing up of the Christian life.* As John Westerhoff wrote:

> Stewardship is nothing less than a complete life-style, a total accountability and responsibility before God. Stewardship is what we do after we say we believe, that is, after we give our love, loyalty, and trust to God, from whom each and every aspect of our lives comes as a gift. As members of God's household, we are subject to God's economy or stewardship, that is, God's plan to reconcile the whole world and bring creation to its proper end.[1]

Both Individuals and Congregations Are Called to Be Stewards of the Gospel

The desire for "more" causes fears and anxieties that lurk in the minds of pastor and people, both consciously and subconsciously. These fears and anxieties are largely unrecognized and unsuspected. They relate to the reality that money has power. And because money has power, the temptation to worship in its great temples and to bow before its idols is powerful and alluring. It is the theology of "more." It becomes a crisis of faith when money, or our love of and desire for money, becomes more powerful than our thirst for God — our love of and desire for God.

---

1. John Westerhoff, *Building God's People in a Materialistic Society* (New York: Seabury Press, 1983), p. 15.

The typical congregation in North America stands in sore need of a divine reversal, or, to use Guder's word, "conversion." Though divine reversals vary widely in their scope and type, they share certain characteristics:

- Divine reversals unsettle the status quo. Because of this, reversals are usually resisted and are hard to come by.
- The rate of change of divine reversals is not predictable. Reversals may come quickly or slowly.
- Short-term reversals are often not enough. The long term is important. Long-term reversals have far-reaching consequences.

At its best and truest, the church, as a household of God, is a resurrection people who are called to be countercultural stewards of the gospel. This is to say that God calls the church to live by the logic of the gospel and not by the logic of the prevailing culture. Unfortunately, during most of North American history, the church has related to its culture so closely that it was hard to tell the two apart. Mainline Christian churches often have been so closely tied to the culture that to criticize one was viewed as criticizing the other.

When the church is a household of God, it will not allow itself to be subordinated to, or tamed or seduced by, the political order — especially in "self-interested pursuit of material comforts." To be able to claim free exercise of religion at the cost of making religion private and subordinate is a price not to be paid. Whenever nationalism takes precedence over our faith in the living God, our faith is diminished.

Jesus was not condemned and executed because he saw religion as private and subservient to the ruling authorities. He was seen as a threat. The authorities did not dismiss him as a harmless crank who went about the countryside preaching the "pop psychology" of his time.

When the church truly becomes an alternative, countercultural community — the salt of the earth and a light to a culture living in the shadows — many will rejoice. Those who are poor and oppressed will welcome an alternative to a culture that tramples the downtrodden. Such a countercultural community will be a household of life, not of death.

The alternative community put forth by God will be a community that relentlessly pursues God's vision of and intent for a justice that is specific and concrete, subversive and uncompromising.

Context of the Contemporary Church in North America

A Hindu fable tells about a motherless tiger cub who was adopted by goats and brought up by them to speak their language, emulate their ways, eat their food, and, in general, believe he was a goat himself. Then one day a king tiger came along. After others scattered, the young tiger bleated nervously and nibbled grass.

Human beings as they usually exist in this world are not what they were created to be. The goat is not really a goat at all — he is really a tiger — except that he does not know who he is. We were created in the image of God, but something has gone awry. As a result humans search for self-identity.

There is enough of the tiger in us to make us discontented with our goathood. We eat grass, but it never really fills us. We bleat well enough, but deep down there is the suspicion that we were really made for roaring. All the most succulent grass in the world will not fill the emptiness within us. Our television, our busy schedules cannot solve the problem. The Christian steward is one who has seen the Tiger. For the Christian, Christ is the Tiger. The question is: Has the church in North America seen the Tiger? Or has the church mistaken the culture for the Tiger? There is strong evidence that the church has confused the two.

To move beyond being market-driven and member-driven is to be ministry-driven. It happens when the church is driven by the imperatives of the gospel, rather than by market surveys or member needs. It will happen when the church and its pastors and members are stewards of the gospel, not consumers trying to satisfy a market that is never satisfied. It will happen when the church remembers that it is called to be an alternative community living in covenant with God.

A Brief Look at the Roots and Practices of Theological Education in North America

A Snapshot of Ancient Greek Philosophy

In the fifth century B.C., various streams of Greek thought and art converged and Athens reached the peak of its cultural creativity and political influence in Greece. In that setting, the Sophists were the teachers who carried major influence. Their teachings were characterized by the rationalism and naturalism that had preceded them. But, with the Sophists, an element of skeptical pragmatism entered Greek thought. The Sophists taught that

> man was the measure of all things, and his own individual judgments concerning everyday life should form the basis of his personal beliefs and conduct — not naive conformity to traditional religion nor indulgence in far-flung abstract speculation. Truth was relative, not absolute, and differed from culture to culture, from person to person, and from situation to situation. Claims to the contrary, whether religious or philosophical, could not stand up to critical argument. The ultimate value of any belief or opinion could be judged only by its practical utility in serving an individual's needs in life.[2]

The Sophists' radical skepticism toward all values led some to advocate an explicitly amoral opportunism. As a result, the political and ethical situation in Athens moved toward crisis. Daily life saw ethical standards violated — especially in the way that male Athenians exploited women, slaves, and foreigners. "[T]he whole development of reason now seemed to have undercut its own basis, with the human mind denying itself the capacity for human knowledge of the world."[3]

In this cultural climate, Socrates began his philosophical search. In his search, he sought answers to questions not asked before. The Sophists believed that words such as goodness, justice, courage, piety, and beauty are only words — names for human conventions. Socrates came to believe that such words could point to a precious, invisible mystery, to something genuine and enduring. The philosopher's task is to find one's way to that reality. In this view, philosophy was a process, a discipline, a lifelong quest. Socrates is reported to have said, "The unexamined life is not worth living."[4] In Socrates, a desire to seek philosophical truth combined with a life that modeled that search for truth and ultimate reality. His philosophy was a direct expression of his personality. His ideas came from the core of his personal character.

---

2. Richard Tarnas, *The Passion of the Western Mind: Understanding the Ideas That Have Shaped Our World View* (New York: Ballantine Books, 1991), p. 27.

3. Tarnas, *The Passion of the Western Mind*, p. 31.

4. Socrates (Greek philosopher in Athens, 469-399 BCE), in Plato, *Dialogues, Apology*.

"Athens" and "Berlin"

David H. Kelsey has used "Athens" and "Berlin" as metaphors for two types, or strands, of theological education. He described the "Athens" strand in these words:

> Because it was the picture of schooling celebrated in the culture of ancient Greece, we will let "Athens" stand for a type of schooling for which *paideia* is the heart of education. In Greek *paideia* meant a process of "culturing" the soul, schooling as "character formation." It is the oldest picture of education to be found in Christianity and has been powerfully retrieved in the current debate about theological education. By the end of the first century, Christians in a Hellenistic culture had already unselfconsciously come to think of Christianity as a kind of *paideia*. This model exercised a very long hegemony over Christian understandings of both Christianity and education. Toward the end of *Early Christianity and Greek Paideia*, Werner Jaeger, the foremost historian of *paideia*, claims that this model of education "can be pursued through the Middle Ages; and from the Renaissance the line leads straight back to the Christian humanism of the fathers of the fourth century A.D." At this end of the historical line, this model was introjected into the debate about theological education by the book that can fairly be said to have started the current discussion, Edward Farley's *Theologia*, "which," in its own words, "purports to promote a Christian *paideia*."[5]

The characteristics of *paideia* are:

1. The excellence of the soul. It is to know the Good.
2. The Good is the highest principle of the universe; it is the divine.
3. The goal of *paideia* cannot be taught directly, as, for example, by simply conveying information. It comes through contemplation — intuitive insight.
4. Insightful knowledge of the Good requires a conversion — a turning from appearances to focus on reality, on the Good.

---

5. David H. Kelsey, *Between Athens and Berlin: The Theological Education Debate* (Grand Rapids: Eerdmans, 1993), pp. 6-7. Kelsey cited Werner Jaeger, *Early Christianity and Greek Paideia* (Cambridge, MA: Harvard University Press, 1961), p. 100, for the first internal quotation and Edward Farley, *Theologia: The Fragmentation and Unity of Theological Education* (Philadelphia: Fortress Press, 1983), p. xi, for the second internal quotation.

Kelsey added this observation:

Clement of Alexandria and his brilliant student Origen were self-consciously affirming, not that Christianity was *like paideia*, not that it could simply make use of received *paideia*, but that Christianity *is paideia*, given by God in Jesus Christ, turning on a radical conversion possible only by the Holy Spirit's help, and taught only indirectly by study of divinely inspired Scriptures in the social context of the church understood to be in some ways a school. Thus, very early in the history of Christianity, *paideia* was simply built into the very way in which Christianity was understood by Christians themselves.

That is the historical reason why Christian theological education in North America is so deeply committed to "Athens" as a normative type of education. If Christianity is seen as a *paideia*, as it has been in its most ancient traditions, then it is simply a theological education whose goal is knowledge of God and, correlatively, forming persons' souls to be holy. However else theological education may come to be conceived — say, more narrowly as the education of clergy — it nonetheless will simply be a mode or variation of the *paideia* that Christianity itself more broadly is.[6]

The "Berlin" strand can be traced to the founding of the University of Berlin in 1810. After much controversy, a faculty of theology was included to create a new type of theological education. This education was bipolar: it stressed both (1) *Wissenschaft*, orderly, disciplined critical research and (2) "professional education" for ministry.

The university was designed to be a "research university" and was part of a movement throughout Europe to reshape education along Enlightenment principles. The overarching goal was research and inquiry that sought to master the truth.

Kelsey added:

Theological education of the "Athens" type is inherently communal. The learning is in one way "individualistic," in that each must do it for herself or himself. Yet, by definition it cannot be solitary. Teachers and learners together constitute a community sharing the common goal of personally appropriating revealed wisdom. It is, then, a community ordered to the same end, a community under or-

6. Kelsey, *Between Athens and Berlin*, p. 11.

ders. Some members of the community, presumably the teachers, have been engaged in this common quest longer than others, presumably the learners; but it is a shared quest.[7]

The "Berlin" model stands in contrast, however:

> According to the "Berlin" model, theological education is a movement from data to theory to application of theory to practice. This movement correlates with its bipolar structure: *Wissenschaft* for critical rigor in theorizing; "professional" education for rigorous study of the application of theory in practice.[8]

Historically, North American Christian theological education came to be tied to *both* "Berlin" and "Athens." With the founding in 1876 of Johns Hopkins University, the Berlin model became decisive for American higher education. Its subsequent influence on theological education was indirect and subtle.

In more recent years, however, shifts have occurred in some schools. "I believe that teaching and scholarship at Wesley [Theological Seminary] have become less driven by the concerns of *Wissenschaft* and are moving in more of a direction in keeping with *paideia*, although the present reality is somewhere in between," wrote Bruce C. Birch.[9] Based on what I heard at the six conferences we held in 2007-08, the concerns of *Wissenschaft* are likely to be more controlling in university-based and schools of theological education that focus on research.

Birch continued:

> The engagement of many of our faculty, myself included, in the wide discussions that are broadening the scope of stewardship in the life of the church, have had an impact less on the formal shape of curriculum than on the way things are taught. There is less concern of a body of knowledge as an end in itself and a greater concern for teaching that informs ministry. It is here that the influence of the concept of steward can be found, for ministry itself is a stewarding role. Ministry itself is an enterprise in which men and women are entrusted by God — for

7. Kelsey, *Between Athens and Berlin*, p. 21.
8. Kelsey, *Between Athens and Berlin*, p. 22.
9. Bruce C. Birch, "The Bible, Stewards, and Ministry," paper prepared for a planned 2003 conference at McMaster Divinity College in Hamilton, Ontario, that did not take place.

God's Word, for God's people, for the mission of the church in the world. Ministry itself becomes an issue of stewardship.[10]

A Brief Look at the History of
Theological Education in North America

The history of theological education in North America does not go back a long way. For example, the first Protestant seminary in the United States opened in 1808 in Andover, Massachusetts. Before that, the pattern was "reading divinity." A student or apprentice sat under the jurisdiction of one person. The student sat in the pastor's study and read. What the student read was subject to the limits of the pastor's library. If the pastor had one hundred books, a large library in that day, that became the limit of the reading.[11]

The second reform in theological education, after the first reform in 1808, came in the middle decade of the nineteenth century as an import from Germany. This reform was known as the fourfold theological encyclopedia, meaning simply that theological education was organized into four divisions: (1) Bible, (2) theology, (3) history, and (4) practical or pastoral theology. This reform considerably lessened the chaos that had been there and was regarded as a significant step forward.

The third reform, at the end of the nineteenth century, maintained the four divisions of the second reform, but added the dimension of field preparation or field education. This was an attempt to center on practice upon which the student would reflect. The student became a reflective practitioner.

A New Reform?

Is a fourth reform beginning? The answer is not yet clear.

David H. Kelsey understood the classic fourfold model of theologi-

10. Birch, "The Bible, Stewards, and Ministry."

11. This brief description of the first reform of theological education in 1808 and the description of the second and third reforms that followed in 1850 and at the end of the nineteenth century are adapted from presentations made by Robert Wood Lynn at a Colloquy for Theological Educators held in Waterloo, Ontario, in July 1992.

cal education as functioning theoretically in a linear way: the truth (Bible) is explicated; it is then organized systematically (theology); clarified and understood from out of the past (history); and then applied to today (practice). In contemporary curricula, this has led to a clutch of courses. What is now in place is a movement from theory to practice that *lacks integration*.[12]

This leads to the question: What is the primary purpose or goal of theological education? Kelsey resisted the "theory to practice" thinking referred to above and answered the question "What's theological about a theological school?" with two foundational insights: its goal is to understand God more truly; and it is a community of persons trying to understand God more truly.

> What distinguishes a theological school is that the subject it seeks to understand truly is *theos*, God. However, God cannot be studied directly, as though God were immediately given like the page of a text. Nor can God be studied by controlled indirection the way, for example, subatomic particles, which are not immediately given, can be studied under the conditions of controlled manipulation in the laboratory. Therefore, it is more accurate to say that what distinguishes a theological school is that it is a community that studies those matters which are believed to *lead* to true understanding of God.[13]

The Traditional Fourfold Division

The traditional fourfold division of theological education — biblical, theological, history, and pastoral or practical theology — fosters a sharp (I would contend *too* sharp) distinction between "theoretical" and "practical." Most usually, theological education has viewed the "practical" as flowing from and dependent upon the "theoretical." This one-way movement, in my view, is inadequate, and theology that is based on use of this formula is inadequate.

Charles Wood maintained that it is not sufficient to merely possess a theology: "it is not the mere possession of 'a theology' that is the measure of a theological education; it is rather one's ability to form, re-

---

12. See David H. Kelsey, *To Understand God Truly: What's Theological about a Theological School* (Louisville: Westminster/John Knox Press, 1992), pp. 96-97, 231-32.

13. Kelsey, *To Understand God Truly*, p. 31.

vise, and employ theological judgments that counts. Vision and discernment are exhibited in practice."[14] Wood added: "Hence the overarching goal that will unify theological schooling is the goal of helping people to acquire 'that complex set of intellectual and personal qualities which go to make up what we might still call the theological *habitus*' — that is, to make sound theological judgments."[15]

Theological *habitus*, in this understanding, is the ability to make theological judgments based on theological inquiry. Thus the *questions* that guide teaching and learning in the realm of theological education are critical. Kelsey elaborated:

> The leading question in every course dealing with any subject matter must be this: How does this subject matter (be it "logic, or Mexican-American history, or the sociology of religion") contribute to assessing the validity of Christian witness? When this question expresses the dominant interest governing the inquiry, then it can subsume the interests that define the several academic disciplines. The student is helped to acquire the aptitudes needed in order to do history or philosophy or a social science *as* aptitudes needed to inquire critically into the validity of Christian witness.[16]

James Packer, writing about his own self-understanding as a biblical theologian, described himself as "the believer, theologian, and preacher that I am."[17] This can serve as a model for theological education today in a threefold pattern: "to walk with God, to interpret God's Word, and to lead God's people."[18]

How does all this relate to the "Athens" and "Berlin" models? Perhaps a modification of the two is needed so that a *third way* is found — a shift from "Berlin" toward "Athens." In this third way, the acquiring of "concepts" would be understood as grasping concepts in a way that requires a capacity to understand *oneself* by them, that is, one's identity is

14. Charles M. Wood, *Vision and Discernment* (Atlanta: Scholars Press, 1985), p. 82.
15. Wood, *Vision and Discernment*, p. 79.
16. Kelsey, *Between Athens and Berlin*, p. 213.
17. James Packer, "In Quest of Canonical Interpretation," in *The Use of the Bible in Theology: Evangelical Options*, ed. Robert K. Johnston (Atlanta: John Knox Press, 1985), p. 40, as cited by Robert K. Johnston, "Reclaiming Theology for the Church," *Theology, News and Notes*, October 1993, p. 9.
18. Covenant Seminary, mission statement, as cited by Johnston, "Reclaiming Theology for the Church," p. 9.

shaped by the concepts, and one understands oneself critically. "To be rigorously critical in inquiry 'is more like a "character-trait" than like a skill.'"[19]

Pastoral Ministry:
The Dream, the Preparation, and the Reality

Pastors, when asked how they *actually* spend their time, give an answer quite different than the answer they give when they are asked how they *should* spend their time. The answer is often different again if they are asked how they *wish* they could spend their time. A typical pastor of a mainline church might describe the dilemma in these words:

> *What I expected ministry to be when I entered seminary bears scant resemblance to what it has turned out to be since I left seminary. As a matter of fact, what seminary prepared me to do is not what I had anticipated, nor is it closely related to what I have ended up doing. Before seminary, I had a dream of preparing sermons that would transform people. I expected people to be eager to learn about the Bible and what it means to be a disciple of Jesus. But it hasn't happened that way. On the whole, I'm not sure that seminary prepared me for what I have faced in pastoral ministry.*
>
> *The people in my church are not really in agreement about what they want me to spend my time doing. Some think I should spend most of my time in counseling and calling on the sick and shut-in members. In short, they want me to be a chaplain. Others, not as many, want me to focus on pulpit ministry and preach sermons "that make them feel good." Others, even fewer in number, want me to make sure that the organization runs smoothly, that money is available to pay all the bills, and that all the elected and appointed positions described in the bylaws are filled. Members say they want the church to grow, but deep down I think they are afraid that new people coming into the church could mean that the new members will take power away from those who have been around forever. I suspect what they really want are new members to give money to support the church budget so they — the older members — won't have to increase their giving to the church.*
>
> *I obviously can't do all these things and give a high priority to each one. Sometimes, it is very frustrating. What the church wants is a knight in shining*

19. Kelsey, *Between Athens and Berlin*, p. 216; citing Wood, *Vision and Discernment*, p. 88, in the internal quotation.

armor — a pastor-messiah — who can defeat every enemy and rescue the church from all problems and distress. I feel like I've been put into an impossible situation.

The dream and the reality are far apart. Almost unanimously, pastors, lay leaders, and observers in general agree that how they feel a pastor should spend his or her time does not match reality. On the other hand, there is not general agreement about what the "should" should be.

Pastoral Ministry: More Than Two Choices?

M. Douglas Meeks noted that most pastors, once they have been in the pastorate for a few years, nearly always move toward one of two tasks. These two models, or paradigms, said Meeks, have been a disaster for stewardship, that is, stewardship as it should be as the household of Jesus Christ. The two models are:

(1) The external: focusing on the organization. In this model, the pastor's main task is managerial, serving as the chief executive officer (CEO) of the institution. The external model uses principles of organizational development and management as its guide.
(2) The internal: focusing on individuals and the inner life. In the internal model, the pastor is a counselor/therapist and psychological principles are the guide.[20]

Many pastors consider that the preparation and delivery of a sermon is the most important part of their ministry. Yet, as important as it is, sermon preparation is a small portion of the work of the gospel — and the pastor. The work of the pastor is to help people understand the life-giving logic of the gospel in the totality of their lives. The totality of life includes relationships in the home, how people make decisions politically, how people make decisions economically, and more. The gospel is meant for the totality of life.

A look in more detail at the two models for pastoral ministry mentioned above will be helpful.

20. M. Douglas Meeks, in presentations made at an Educational Event for Stewardship Leaders in July 1993 at Bolton, Ontario.

External Model

The external model is followed by a much smaller number of pastors than the number of pastors who adopt the internal model. Those who follow the external model, and do it well, are viewed as very successful pastors. The external model is more likely to appear in larger-sized congregations in which the pastor's main task is seen as being the chief executive officer of the congregation's organizational structure and life. Because these congregations tend to be larger, pastors who follow the external model have greater visibility in the community and in denominational circles. They are sought out to participate in leadership roles in the community and denomination. Administrative skills are especially sought and valued, both by the congregation and by the pastor. Within the congregation, the criteria by which the pastor is evaluated are balanced budgets, boards and committees that function efficiently and effectively, and a staff that knows its job and does it well. The phrase "senior minister" is often used for the title of the pastor. A feeling of hierarchy pervades the organization.

Because the spotlight is so keenly focused on the organization and its chief executive officer, the life and welfare of the organization take on paramount importance. When this happens, the life-giving logic of the gospel may be clouded or even forgotten inside a household of amnesia.

Internal Model

The use of the internal model is much more widespread in the North American church. In fact, a principal danger in the North American church is that the gospel has become limited to internal questions of purpose and meaning in life. That represents a theology that has been given over to the assumptions of modernity — in the arenas of a consumer society, science, politics, etc. — and has kept for itself only the questions related to the meaning and interpretation of life. The gospel is meant to claim the totality of our being and, as such, is a full-time job. For the pastor, it is more than just a sermon to work on, although that's very important. It is helping the congregation understand that the gospel is about the life-giving promises and commands of God that are meant for all of life.

The inner, therapeutic model of pastoral ministry has other dangers as well. In recent years, the issue of clergy sexual misconduct has come to the fore in virtually every denomination. One denominational official wrote that in every case of clergy sexual misconduct he had investigated, the origin and the opportunity for the misconduct arose out of a counseling situation. The danger is twofold: first, many pastors participate in counseling situations for which they are not adequately trained or qualified; and second, insufficient measures are taken to avoid the opportunity for misconduct to arise.

The denominational official wrote that the best advice he could give to pastors who have members who could benefit from counseling is "refer, refer, refer."[21] In the name of therapeutic counseling, the lives of many counselees, as well as their pastors and congregations, have been severely damaged.

How did the church come to a point in which internal matters assumed such primacy? More detail about the third reform is enlightening at this point. In the early twentieth century, a handful of reformers began a strategy to introduce psychology into the theological curriculum.[22] Eventually they called themselves the "clinical training movement." Their thought was that the pastor had to have available in his or her pastoral ministry insights from Freud and Jung, whose works were becoming well known. Their strategy was to develop a powerful training movement with high standards of accreditation so they could control the quality of what happened in the training process. They succeeded very well: the clinical training movement has had enormous impact, not only upon practical theology, but also upon the whole curriculum of theological education. The movement started with, perhaps, ten, fifteen, or twenty persons who stayed with it over an extended period of time. It took some twenty-five to thirty years to implant the concept on the North American scene. Now, virtually every pastor who has finished seminary in the past couple of generations has been affected by this movement.

Most pastors have accepted the internal, therapeutic model of pastoral ministry built on the foundation of the "clinical training movement." Powerful indications are emerging, however, that the movement is another symptom of the church's entrapment in modernity and that

21. Richard E. Rusbuldt, while serving as executive minister of American Baptist Churches of Pennsylvania and Delaware.

22. The historical information in this paragraph is excerpted from a presentation made by Robert Wood Lynn at a Colloquy for Theological Educators in June 1992 in Waterloo, Ontario.

change may be appropriate. In 1993, *Time* featured a cover article titled "Is Freud Dead?"[23] Paul Gray reported on the fierce debate going on in intellectual circles about the validity of Freudian theories and how widespread Freudian theories have become: "Sigmund Freud's rich panoply of metaphors for the mental life has evolved into something closely resembling common knowledge."[24] This "common knowledge," however, is being called into serious question by many scholars. Gray reported that Frank Sulloway, a visiting scholar at M.I.T and a long-time critic of Freud's methods, took a somewhat more apocalyptic view: "Psychoanalysis is built on quicksand. It's like a 10-story hotel sinking into an unsound foundation. And the analysts are in this building. You tell them it's sinking, and they say, 'It's O.K.; we're on the 10th floor.'"[25] Though not willing to declare Freud finished, Gray observed:

> Psychoanalysis and all its offshoots may in the final analysis turn out to be no more reliable than phrenology or mesmerism or any of the other countless pseudosciences that once offered unsubstantiated answers or false solace. Still, the reassurances provided by Freud that our inner lives are rich with drama and hidden meanings would be missed if it disappeared, leaving nothing in its place.[26]

Despite these evidences that the world of Freudian psychoanalysis may be sinking into quicksand, the world of psychology continues to have a strong hold on the language and mind-sets of ordained ministers. Richard Busch wrote that in his renewal programs with pastors from around the world, a pattern often emerged: "Someone will introduce himself using the language of the Myers-Briggs Type Indicator — as an introvert or extrovert, a feeler or thinker, a sensor or intuitive.

23. Two articles were included in the 29 November 1993 issue of *Time:* Paul Gray, "The Assault on Freud," pp. 47-51, and Leon Jaroff, "Lies of the Mind," pp. 52-59. Two years later, an article by John Leland titled "The Trouble with Sigmund" appeared in *Newsweek,* 15 Dec. 1995, p. 62. The thrust of the *Newsweek* article was similar to the two articles in *Time.* Leland reported that "Recent research has challenged not only Freud's conclusions, but his ethics as well." He added that Melvin Sabshin, medical director of the American Psychiatric Association, says university psychology departments have moved away from Freud toward more empirical fields, especially biology and pharmacology.

24. Gray, "The Assault on Freud," p. 49.

25. Gray, "The Assault on Freud," p. 51.

26. Gray, "The Assault on Freud," p. 51.

Faces light up. Most people understand this shorthand interpretive language, and respond by declaring their own personality type. With this 'Christian horoscope' we begin to tell each other who we are."[27] When participants are directed to tell their stories — to share how they understand God to have been acting in their lives over the years, people respond with excitement. He continued:

> Yet the goal of the assignment — to share how God has been acting in their lives — is not always realized. Traditional Christian language is rarely woven into the narrative. At least 80 percent of the personal stories do not integrate the individual's life with the Christian faith. The vocabulary has a professional, ecclesiastical, or psychological flavor. Because the narratives are powerful, and the connections and associations resonate among the listeners, many fail to notice what is missing.
>
> Christians are "self-interpreting animals." . . . In these renewal programs, competent and articulate leaders of the church are strangely silent about defining themselves in the light of theological and scriptural foundations. It is painful for me to realize that I too share in this silence.[28]

Busch voiced his suspicion that

> behind this silence is finally this: the gospel is not the center of our lives, and our spiritual life is disconnected from the things that interest, worry and excite us. We have so many pressing interests, priorities and passions in our lives that we no longer seek first the kingdom. We lack the singleness of heart to be attentive to God. In our desire to be like the people around us, we emphasize the outward *doing* dimensions over the inward *being* dimensions of Christian living.[29]

Are pastors talking about many things, yet keeping silent about the life-giving logic of the gospel? Are we/they stewards of the gospel?

---

27. Richard A. Busch, "A Strange Silence," *The Christian Century*, 22-29 March 1995, p. 316.

28. Busch, "A Strange Silence," p. 316.

29. Busch, "A Strange Silence," p. 317.

Pastoral Ministry: Theologian in Residence

Is there another model for pastoral ministry? What could be a model for ministry for the pastor? Meeks argued strongly for the role of the pastor as a theologian in residence for the congregation. Because the ministry of ordination is highly specialized, people who are given this ministry by the church should focus on using their time in Word and sacrament — preaching the gospel and administering communion and baptism in such a way that they come alive in the congregation. Time in Word and sacrament includes more than the worship experiences of the congregation: it includes educational settings, board and committee meetings, conversations, and calls in the homes. Such a holistic, integrated understanding of pastoral ministry will enable the pastor to help people understand the life-giving logic of the gospel in the totality of their lives.

Lay Ministry Is Not Second-Class Ministry

Meeks said that the ministry of Word and sacrament, the ministry of ordination, while important, "is not *the* ministry. *Every* member of the church is called to ministry. The ministry of ordination is highly specialized; people who are given this ministry by the church should spend 90 percent of their time in word and sacrament."[30] Ordination is not for the purpose of establishing a privilege; rather, it gives a new responsibility.

In most congregations, the ministry of the laity is defined in relatively narrow ways that indicate that lay ministry is not full or "real" ministry, but exists primarily to carry out the secondary tasks in the congregation and to help the pastor do the things that "the pastor doesn't have the time to do." The danger is that lay ministry is not viewed by the pastor or the lay members as full participation in ministry. Lay ministry may be regarded by both the pastor and lay leaders as second-class ministry. It is not!

Lay ministry is usually identified with such tasks as serving as a lay leader in worship, preparing the elements for communion, singing in the choir, greeting and seating people, serving as a congregational offi-

---

30. M. Douglas Meeks observed that he formerly used the figure of 95 percent, but later lowered the number to 90 percent.

cer or member of a board or committee, teaching in the Sunday school or youth ministry program, helping maintain the building, preparing budgets, and giving money to support the budget. Sometimes, if the congregation has an outreach program, a few lay leaders participate in ministries to the poor, the hungry, and the homeless. Largely, these in-house and outreach ministries are carried out in a near theological vacuum without an in-depth biblical understanding of *why* they are carried out. An in-depth exploration might even reveal that some of the ministries are inappropriate for a household of God.

Paul, in Ephesians 4:12, wrote that pastors are to help equip members of the church for the work of ministry. The pastor's role is a specialist whose main role is to bring biblical insights and theological reflection to bear on the ministries of that congregation. This does not imply that others in the congregation should not be expected to or are not capable of providing biblical insights and theological reflection. Nonetheless, as one who has received specialized training and is afforded time, the responsibility for the biblical/theological tasks falls mainly to the pastor. The pastor who forfeits this responsibility has abandoned the primary reason for being present as pastor.

A word of caution needs to be noted, however. The pastor's special knowledge and abilities are not to be used in an authoritative style. It is not a matter of the pastor saying, "This is what I have learned and therefore this is the way it is." Rather, it is the pastor saying, "God has given me particular gifts and called me to be your pastor. God has also given each of you gifts to be used in God's mission to the world. Our task together is to determine what are the ways that God wants us to use these gifts from God." Such mutuality will do much to lessen "pastor/people tensions" and help the congregation to be faithful to what God has called it to be — a household of God.

Pastor and People in Partnership

The congregation that views the relationship between its members and the pastor as being primarily an employer/employee relationship will find it difficult to become a household of God. Nor does the other extreme work. A congregation that looks to the pastor as a "pastor-messiah" who has all the answers and who carries great authority is not likely to become a faithful household of God.

"Kudzu" is a cartoon feature that offers insights into the life of the church in North America. One of the cartoon strips depicted a pastor standing at his pulpit saying, "Brothers and sisters, years ago, the Lord Jesus called me to be your pastor . . . and now I feel like the Lord Jesus is calling me elsewhere." The final box shows the pastor still standing at the pulpit with a somewhat dumbfounded expression on his face. Coming from the direction of the congregation, he hears the words of an old gospel song, "What a Friend We Have in Jesus."[31] This is probably an extreme example of pastor-people relations gone wrong. Nevertheless, it reflects a reality that in many congregations the relationship between the pastor and people is strained and tension-filled.

The need is for a pastor and people who work together in partnership, knowing that the ministry of the church belongs to the *whole* people of God. The role of the pastor is important when it is properly understood. Meeks's suggestion that the pastor's role is primarily that of theologian in residence provides a way for pastor and people to work in partnership and makes it possible for the pastor's specialized knowledge and expertise in biblical studies and theological reflection to be a basic part of the partnership relationship.

The Concept of "Steward" as a Unifying Purpose and Focus for the Several Dimensions of Theological Education and the Traditions of *Paideia* and *Wissenschaft*

Use of the concept of "steward" can serve as a unifying purpose and focus for theological education and as a model for congregational ministry.

Key Elements of the Concept of "Steward"

We have identified the following key elements of the concept of "steward":

(1) Individual Christians and the church collectively are called to be stewards of the gospel.

31. Marlette, "Kudzu," *The Christian Century*, 15 Nov. 1995, p. 1093.

(2) As individuals and the church recognize and respond to God's call to be stewards of the gospel, the motivation to participate in God's mission will increase. In this view, our identity is "steward"; the task to which God calls us is "mission." To envision one's primary identity as a steward can represent a summing up of the Christian life.

(3) Three theological lenses sharpen the image of our identity as Christian stewards:

    (a) God as creator and owner;

    (b) Jesus Christ as chief steward; and

    (c) The church as steward of the gospel

An Invitation to Paideia

The journey of a steward of the gospel is a recapturing of *paideia*. The journey may be long and difficult. The journey of the Christian steward will involve a transformation — a conversion. Such a conversion, while it must begin at some particular point, will take place over time as the journey of many steps continues. The transformation, when it occurs, will be greater than when a caterpillar becomes a beautiful butterfly. It will leave a mark, as Jacob experienced when he wrestled with God and received a new identity — Israel, the one who strives with God (Gen. 32:24-31). In that journey, we will learn about a treasure far greater than gold or silver — a treasure that we hold in trust as Christian stewards, the gospel of Jesus Christ. "Think of us in this way, as servants of Christ, and stewards of God's mysteries" (1 Cor. 4:1).

At its best and truest, the church, as a household of God, is a resurrection people who are called to be countercultural. This is to say that God calls the church to live by the logic of the gospel and not by the logic of the prevailing culture.

To move beyond being market-driven and member-driven is to be ministry-driven. It happens when the church is driven by the imperatives of the gospel, rather than by market surveys or member needs. It will happen when the church and its pastors and members are stewards living in covenant, not consumers trying to satisfy a market that is never satisfied. It will happen when the church remembers that it is called to be an alternative community living in covenant with God.

The Concept of "Steward" as Integrative for Theological Education

The concept of "steward" can provide a means for theological education to break away from the classic "fourfold model of theological education as functioning in a linear way." As Kelsey indicated, the linear way has led to "a movement from theory to practice that lacks integration."

The concept of "steward" can be consistent with the best of both the "Athens" and the "Berlin" models. The Berlin model can help in the acquiring of information and concepts from biblical texts, theological reflection, and history that undergirds the goal of the "Athens" model to let one understand oneself by them, so that one's identity is shaped by the concepts, and one understands oneself critically.

Proposed Thesis and Model

We think the time and circumstances are right for a serious look at this thesis: **The object of theological education is to develop stewards of the gospel who, in turn, can provide leadership for the development of stewards of the gospel in Christian congregations, denominations, and in the church at large.** (In this chapter, we are focusing on leaders of Christian congregations.)

Traditionally, the primary function of schools of theological education has been to prepare men and women to serve as pastors of Christian congregations. The traditional path has been a four-year undergraduate degree, followed by three years in a seminary or divinity college to secure an M.Div. degree (or a B.D. degree, its equivalent in an earlier era). After graduation, the pastor-to-be is called or appointed to serve as pastor of a Christian congregation. A *direct* and *ongoing* relationship between theological education and that pastor's new congregation has been relatively rare.

Perhaps the proposals that follow in the next chapter can help to resolve this dilemma. The training of pastors needs to extend both in time and also in scope. If Christian congregations are truly to become stewards of the gospel, the linkage and connections among theological education, denominations, and congregations will have to be built and then strengthened by including elements specifically designed to enable congregations to become stewards of the gospel.

CHAPTER 8

The Treasure in Earthen Vessels

But we have this treasure in earthen vessels. . . .

2 Corinthians 4:7

"The number of Americans who call themselves Christians has dropped dramatically over the past two decades, and those who do so are increasingly identifying themselves without traditional denominational labels, according to a major study of U.S. religion released today." So began the 2009 article "More in U.S. Losing Religion" by Michelle Boorstein.[1] The survey of more than 54,000 people was conducted between February and November 2008. The results showed that the percentage of Americans identifying themselves as Christians dropped to 76 percent of the population, down from 86 percent in 1990. Researchers at Trinity College in Hartford, Connecticut, conducted the survey. People calling themselves mainline Protestants dropped from 19 percent to 13 percent during the same time period. The only group that grew in every U.S. state during that same period was people who said they had "no" religion. The survey said that this group is now 15 percent of the population.

Although such numbers in and of themselves are not the most im-

---

1. Michelle Boorstein of *The Washington Post,* "More in U.S. Losing Religion," *The Post-Standard,* Syracuse, New York, 9 Mar. 2009, p. A-1. For more comment on the study, see Jon Meacham, "The End of Christian America," *Newsweek,* 13 Apr. 2009, pp. 34-38.

portant factor in determining the vitality and faithfulness of the Christian faith in the United States, this survey does indicate a major shift in religion in the United States, especially in the Christian faith, and even more especially among mainline Protestants of whom I am one. The number (15 percent) who said they had "no" religion outnumbering the 13 percent who identified themselves as mainline Protestants is startling.

Earthen Vessels

Do the findings of this study reflect a full-blown crisis for the Christian faith in the United States? Or, do the numbers perhaps offer an opportunity? Is the gospel of Jesus Christ itself falling short, or is it the way in which the gospel is understood, packaged, and presented? The reflections of Daniel Aleshire are helpful in looking at this question. In the introduction to *Earthen Vessels,* Aleshire recalled his experience as a first-year assistant professor as he prepared to preach a seminary chapel service for the first time. Preaching to other members of the faculty seemed intimidating to him, more so than preaching to the students who would also be present. He scoured texts and settled on 2 Corinthians 4:7, where Paul defended his ministry from attack: "But we have this treasure in earthen vessels. . . ." Since then, Aleshire wrote, "the image of 'earthen vessels' has been part of my association with theological schools."[2]

What does it mean to have this treasure in earthen vessels? For me, the treasure is the gospel of Jesus Christ. The vessels are the instruments that God uses not only to "contain" the treasure but also to interact with the gospel and the surrounding environment or culture to carry out God's mission. The primary vessel that God has "called out" is the *ekklesia* (the church). The church, however, exists in many forms throughout the earth. Its primary form is in congregations, bands of individual Christians who have been captured by God's call in Jesus Christ. Likewise, many congregations work with one another to carry out God's mission. These groupings of congregations sometimes bear the name of "church" or "denomination," which are also vessels of the treasure of the gospel. Congregations and denominations need leaders

---

2. Daniel O. Aleshire, *Earthen Vessels: Hopeful Reflections on the Work and Future of Theological Schools* (Grand Rapids: Eerdmans, 2008), p. x.

(ordained and lay), who serve best if they have training in schools of theological education. These schools are also vessels of the gospel. In this book, I have attempted to show that schools of theological education are pivotal as vessels of the treasure, and that there is a disconnect among schools, denominations, and congregations.

Need for Integration Among All the Vessels

In Chapter 1, I noted the 2003 conference that was cancelled for a number of reasons. One of the papers that had been prepared for the conference was written by Bruce C. Birch.[3] In the paper he asked and addressed the central question that the conference was to address: "Can the concept of steward serve as an integrating center for theological education?" Birch wrote:

> If the concept of steward is to become an integrating center in theological education I believe that we must recognize that above all else we are called to be *stewards of the gospel* — the good news that God is at work reconciling the world through Jesus Christ. All other arenas of our stewarding work are derivative from this central task of the steward. We have been entrusted with this good news of the gospel and this makes sense out of all other arenas where the role of steward might be acted out. Theological education organized around the concept of steward would understand itself to be missional in character. What equips the ministries of the church to form disciples who will, as communities of stewards, witness to and live out of the gospel entrusted to their care? No discipline in the theological curriculum would serve as an end in itself but would be considered in relation to the overarching task of being faithful stewards of the gospel. (Emphasis added)

Birch also observed that if the concept of steward is to serve as an integrating role,

- It must be presented in community and not individual terms. We live in a culture increasingly marked by a utilitarian individual-

3. Bruce C. Birch, "The Bible, Stewards, and Ministry," paper written for a conference planned for 2003. See excerpts of Birch's paper in Chapter 9.

ism. . . . I have increasingly felt it important to talk about the "community of stewards" and to emphasize that our biblical faith always relates our individual experience of God to a community of believers. . . .

- An integrating concept of theological education necessarily implies an interdisciplinary approach to curriculum and learning. No integrating central concept can have effect if the disciplines stay unintegrated. There must be efforts to protect interdisciplinary integrity while encouraging the crossing of disciplinary boundaries so that students can see how a concept like steward can integrate a ministry or a congregation. It is important that the concept of steward not be relegated to the practice of ministry disciplines alone, or primarily.
- The role of steward can play a role in a shift that I think is already taking place in theological education to some degree. It is a rejection of *Wissenschaft* as a model adequate in itself, and it is a movement in the direction of *paideia*.

Birch added:

I think a new model may be struggling to be born. It is informed more by the church and its needs than by the university, but it remains informed by the knowledge gained in academic disciplines. It would be frankly and unapologetically theological, but would remain open to a wide range of theological approaches. It would be grounded in religious experience as well as rational discourse. It would remove the separation, still expressed in so many places and ways, between the so-called classical and practical disciplines. It would be particularistic but within an ecumenical framework. It will require a new pedagogy as well as a new curricular approach. It must insist on community experience beyond the classroom.

Disconnect

My own observations over the past fifteen years working with the more than three hundred congregations of American Baptist Churches of New York State — including rural, suburban, and urban — confirm much of what both Aleshire and Birch wrote. The trend is toward a greater number of churches being served by part-time pastors and by persons who complete a lay study program and then seek and obtain ordination recognized by the denomination. The overall result is that fewer congregations are being served by full-time pastors and an increasing number of churches are served by persons with no training in a school of theological education. This trend accentuates the *disconnect* between the world of theological education and the life of the congregation. My reflections earlier in this book about the role of laypersons in Fredonia Baptist Church illustrate a step toward breaching the disconnect.

These problems and possible solutions go much deeper than lack of financial support and differing views as to the role and importance of theological education. I believe the solutions include a clearer understanding of "What is the gospel (the treasure)?" as I have discussed in Chapter 3 and a willingness not to treat laypeople as second-class Christians.

Aleshire described what I call a disconnect between schools and congregations in these words:

As I listen to some church leaders and read some analyses of the needs of the church, the intellectual work of research or learning more than strategies for ministry seems to be in disrepute. It is perceived as a luxury that can no longer be afforded or a useless way to engage the practical difficulties that churches face. To some, intellectual work that does not have an immediate application feels like counting and color-sorting the deck chairs on the Titanic. Even a cursory glance at church history, however, refutes this assessment. The church was struggling to define what it was and what it believed when St. Paul wrote his letters. The church was struggling with new life in an ancient world when Augustine wrote the *City of God*. Paul's letters have practical advice, but it is often housed in complex theological affirmations that had never been made before. Augustine had a lot to do as the Bishop of Hippo, and in the middle of leading a young church, he wrote theological treatises that have informed the understanding of Christian believers to this day. I wonder if someone in his day complained that he didn't get done what needed to be done because he was writing that book. We live in a time in which useful and relevant information is crucial for congregational life and vitality, but Christian faith is not just about the problems of parishes and congregations at a given point in time. It is about an understanding of faithfulness and hope that emerges from thousands of years of study and research. Good intellectual work may be an important way in which the Spirit speaks afresh to guide this and future ages.

Another verse in that King James Bible my parents gave me that was especially difficult to understand was in John 3 [verse 8]: "the wind bloweth where it listeth, and thou hearest the sound thereof, but canst not tell whence it cometh, and whither it goeth. . . ." I remember thinking that I should be able to understand this verse — after all, it was from the chapter I had been taught was central to the New Testament message — but I couldn't. I remember writing it out in longhand, dropping the "eths," but it remained a mystery. Fifty years later, I have discovered that my not understanding was, in some ways, an accurate understanding. God's presence, like the wind, does not reveal its origin or destination; its movement can be felt, and its effect experienced, but the ways of God are, from beginning to end, mysterious. The God of ages past is the God of ages to come. The wind will blow. The purposes of God will sustain communities of faith and call new ones into being. Those communities will need pastors and teachers who know the story, who have learned a theological wisdom pertaining to responsible life in faith, and who are capable of leading communities in pursuit of God's vision for the human family. These pastors and teachers will need schools because schools provide the kind of learning they most need. Schools are earthen vessels that serve this particular function exceedingly well. The Spirit of God moves, and we do not know "whence it cometh or whither it goeth," but we can be confident that God will be up to something, working out God's purpose, calling into being what those purposes require for any age.[4]

Missio Dei

God's mission *(missio Dei)* is best understood when it is viewed as being derived from the nature of God. Mission has its origin and its life in the hands of God. Since the initiative comes from God, mission is a movement from God to the world and the church is an instrument for that mission. The church exists because there is mission, not vice versa.

4. Aleshire, *Earthen Vessels,* pp. 171-72.

It is customary in church circles to speak about the mission of the church, to say that the church has a mission. It would be more accurate and faithful to say that *God's mission has a church* (congregations, denominations, schools of theological education, etc.). This simple thought could revolutionize the way the church views itself and how it prepares and engages leaders for the church. It could lead to a clearer understanding that we (individual Christians, congregations, denominations, and schools of theological education) are stewards of the gospel — not containers only but actively interacting with God, with one another, and with God's creation.

A Medical Analogy

In January 2007, when I first met with my current oncologist, Dr. John J. Gullo, I was jolted, but not dismayed, when he told me that my prostate cancer, which had first been diagnosed in 2002, was "treatable but not curable." His words did lead me to reflect long and hard on the difference between the two words "treatable" and "curable." Healing is not simply a process of treating symptoms, but of finding a cure for an illness.

Part of that reflection led me to ask myself this question, "Is the reforming of theological education about which I have been writing the seeking of a treatment, or is it a cure?" This is not an easy question to answer. In medicine, treatment refers to management of an illness through the application of medicines, surgery, etc. By contrast, a cure is successful remedial treatment and restoration to health.

Is it possible that reforming theological education and bridging the disconnect between theological education and life of the congregation could effect a cure, or would it be only a treatment of symptoms that leaves the course of the underlying illness slowed but not stopped or reversed? Perhaps the answer cannot be known until the reforming of theological education is under way sufficiently to make observations and to draw conclusions. Of course, we will not know the answer unless we take steps towards reformation. My fervent hope is that a sufficient number of schools of theological education, several denominations, and a variety of congregations might join together to take such steps and that the position of ministry integrator be implemented in a number of different contexts: geographic, denominational, and socio-economic. The goal underlying these efforts would be to better know "What is the gospel?" and to have it lived out faithfully in the lives of congregations and in the church at large. Some of the steps may falter and stumble, but they must be taken. To stand still and take no action is to let the condition grow steadily worse.

What is needed, in my view, are partnerships among schools of theological education, denominations, pastors, and congregations that will model in various ways how they can become more faithful stewards of the gospel and how the position of ministry integrator can be part of the process.

Questions arise: How can this be funded?[5] Will members of the partnerships be willing to take on the challenges of being stewards of the gospel and the inevitable risks to the institutions involved? Will pastors be willing and able to let laypersons take on actual and real leadership in the congregations, even if this results in diminishing power and prestige for the pastor?

In 2008, Sharon Begley wrote a penetrating article on "why cancer is on track to kill 565,650 people in the United States this year — more than 1,500 a day, equivalent to three jumbo jets crashing and killing everyone aboard 365 days a year."[6] This is about 230,000 more Americans — 69 percent more — than it did in 1971, the year in which U.S. President Richard Nixon signed the National Cancer Act. Even when adjusted for population growth and age-related factors, the statistics are hardly more encouraging. "[C]ancer is poised to surpass cardiovascular disease and become America's leading killer."[7]

As one who has prostate cancer and, so far, has been treated by surgery, radiation, and hormone manipulation, I have more than a passing interest in these data. Yet that interest pales in comparison to the significance of what I think are important parallels between the world of oncology (both cancer research and the treatment of patients) and the world of the church (theological education, the congregation, and more).

My hypothesis in this book — that there is a disconnect among the worlds of theological education, denominations, congregations, pas-

5. See Walter Brueggemann, "From Anxiety and Greed to Milk and Honey," *Sojourners*, February 2009, pp. 20-24, for his comments on what the Bible has to say about "bailout" and economic crises.

6. Sharon Begley, "We Fought Cancer . . . ," *Newsweek*, 15 Sept. 2008, pp. 42-66.

7. Begley, "We Fought Cancer . . . ," p. 46.

tors, and individual Christians — seems to have a strong parallel in the world of medicine as it relates to research on cancers and the treatment of patients with cancer.

Dr. Harold Varmus, president of Memorial Sloan-Kettering Cancer Center in New York City, observed that basic-science studies of the mechanisms leading to cancer and efforts to control cancer "often seem to inhabit separate worlds."[8] If we think of cancer researchers (the bench of research) as parallel to theological educators and the doctors who treat cancer (the bedside) as parallel to pastors, the analogy takes on a frightening dimension. It raises the troubling possibility that the world of theological education inhabits a different world than that of denominations, congregations, and practicing pastors. Even though, to use the metaphor employed by me in this book, all are called to be stewards of the gospel, such a disconnect would be a major blocking force in responding to that call to be stewards of the gospel.

In response to the above paragraph, Dr. Victor Ling wrote:

> This is generally true. Universities, research institutes, and governments have invested heavily on the discovery aspects of cancer (how does it occur? what is the cause, etc.) and the research infrastructure (funding) is slanted towards these kinds of activities. The recognition that we need to invest in the application of these discoveries (called translational research) is a more recent phenomenon. The initiation of the Terry Fox Research Institute, which I head, is in response to the need of translational research (see www.tfri.ca). We need to apply the theory to practice and we need to invest in that process.[9]

An example of the disconnect between the world of cancer research and the treatment of cancer patients is the reality that the human tu-

---

8. Begley, "We Fought Cancer . . . ," p. 58.

9. Dr. Victor Ling in a note to the author, July 2009. Dr. Ling is an award-winning Canadian researcher in the field of medicine. Ling's research focuses on drug resistance in cancer. He is best known for his discovery of P-glycoprotein, one of the proteins responsible for multi-drug resistance. Ling was born in China and immigrated to Canada as a child. He received his bachelor's degree in 1966 from the University of Toronto and his Ph.D. in 1969 from the University of British Columbia. In 2006, he was awarded an honorary doctorate from Trinity Western University. He undertook post-doctoral training with Nobel-laureate Dr. Fred Sanger at Cambridge University. Ling is currently Assistant Dean of the Faculty of Medicine at the University of British Columbia and Vice-President of Discovery at the B.C. Cancer Agency in Vancouver, British Columbia.

mors that scientists transplant into mice almost never metastasize. Even though metastatic cells are responsible for 90 percent of all cancer deaths, scientists continue to rely on animal models where metastasis didn't even occur. Money was spent on elegant biology that cured millions of mice, rather than on the search for more practical advances.[10] Ling noted, however:

> This is a very specific example of how some of the models used in cancer research may not accurately predict how cancers behave in humans. However, one should not be misled that if the cancer did metastasize in mice that it would be more predictive of the human situation. So I have a scientific logic problem with that statement. If the point is that any theory needs to be tested by the real thing, i.e. a trial in human patients, then I totally agree.[11]

Fran Visco, a breast cancer survivor since 1987 and the first president of the National Breast Cancer Coalition and Fund, observed that throughout the 1980s and 1990s "researchers drilled down deeper and deeper into the disease," looking for ever-more-detailed molecular mechanisms behind the initiation of cancer, "instead of looking up and asking really big questions, like why cancer metastasizes, which might help patients sooner."[12] It appears that the focus was not on the human patient.

On the other hand, Begley's article points out a major difference between the world of pediatric oncologists and those who deal with adult cancers. Pediatric oncologists collaborated to such a degree that at times 80 percent of the children with a particular cancer were enrolled in a clinical trial testing a new therapy. In adults it had been less than 1 percent. In 2008, 80 percent of children with cancer survive well into adulthood. Adult scientists who work on adult cancers have observed that childhood cancers are simpler cancers. The reality seems to be that pediatric cancers are less wily than adult cancers, but also that the novel, practical approach of pediatric oncologists has made a difference.[13]

This suggests that the world of theological education may want to consider more novel, practical approaches to the preparation of men

---

10. See Begley, "We Fought Cancer . . . ," especially pp. 58, 60, 62.
11. Ling, note to the author, July 2009.
12. Begley, "We Fought Cancer . . . ," p. 60.
13. Begley, "We Fought Cancer . . . ," p. 60.

and women to serve as pastors and other leaders in the church. This is not to say that no efforts in this direction have been made in the past few years. A disconnect among the worlds remains, however.

John J. Gullo, M.D., a noted oncologist, following my request to him to critique part of this chapter, told me that, in general, he agreed with the Begley article in *Newsweek,* but he also thought the "disconnect" between the research and the treatment of cancer patients has lessened in the past few years.[14]

My own observation is that the "disconnect" between the world of theological education and the life of the congregation and the larger church has also lessened in the past few years. This observation was strengthened as a result of the six conferences held in 2007 and 2008. On the other hand, my direct experience with the life of numerous congregations of many different denominations does not convince me that the "disconnect" is lessening *significantly.* There is a continuing problem.

I recall again words from Walter Brueggemann written to me:

Thank you so much for sending along the information about the project on "Reforming Theological Education." It is a thoughtful piece, and I think you are taking on an enormously important project. *It may well be that you will find the seminaries endlessly intransigent, but at least one must try.*

I do wish you well and will look forward to being kept informed about the matter, as I have no doubt that it is of enormous importance. With good wishes and gratitude for what you are doing. (Emphasis added)

To continue the medical analogy, what are the "cancers" that afflict the world and the life of the church? I believe they are rooted in the prevailing culture that assumes many forms and takes devious twists and turns in its influences and effects on the church.

Clergy

In most churches, the primary leader of a Christian congregation is a full-time, ordained person. Is the maintenance of full-time, paid clergy

14. Dr. John J. Gullo is my oncologist in Syracuse, New York. Our conversation took place 24 Oct. 2008.

210

a fatal flaw for many churches? Is this a question that needs to be explored more fully? If full-time pastors are not paid adequately, will the "supply" of persons willing to spend years in theological education and then become a part-time pastor, paid little or no salary, be diminished?

This is a vexing question for the church in North America. Can the Christian church maintain a core of seminary-educated, full-time, full-salaried persons as the church's primary leaders? Or should the church even try?

In the early Christian church, the picture in regard to financial support of leaders is mixed. Some leaders gave themselves entirely to ministry and lived off the offerings of church members. This seems to be true of Peter and some other apostles. By contrast, Paul frequently did outside work, not wanting to be a financial burden to the churches he founded. Paul wrote that he and his companions "worked night and day, laboring and toiling so that we would not be a burden to any of you" (2 Thess. 3:8). In doing so, Paul probably increased his credibility.

Many Christian congregations struggle to find full-time, theologically-trained pastors. Consider these words: "The only group vanishing faster than the population in rural America is its pastors, stranding farm congregations and challenging church leaders to find new models." So began an article in *Time*.[15] The article went on to state: "America's rural congregations, thinned by age and a population drain that plagues much of farm country, have gotten too small and too poor to attract pastors. *No pastor means no church*" (emphasis added).

This last sentence, however, makes a sweeping assumption with which I strongly disagree. Can there be a Christian congregation without a full-time pastor? I believe there can be.

In his article, Van Biema mentions possible responses and solutions to the rural exodus of pastors: yoking two churches to share a circuit-riding minister; allowing laypeople to preach; allowing laymen and laywomen to be ordained but restricting them to their home pulpit.

In actuality these are neither new problems nor new solutions, but methods that have been used for many decades. For example, my first pastorate in New York State was that of Howard Union Church. Located in a Southern Tier dairy farming community, I served this federated church from 1957 to 1960. Two congregations had "federated" in

---

15. David Van Biema, "A Rural Exodus," *Time*, 9 Feb. 2009, pp. 44-45.

the 1920s when the local Baptist and Presbyterian churches had joined together while still maintaining ties to their respective denominations. The problem of decreasing numbers of full-time, theologically trained pastors is not new, but it is increasing. The trend is clear. Aleshire offered this observation:

> Mainline Protestant denominations are credentialing an increasing number of clergy without post-baccalaureate theological education because many of their congregations can no longer support full-time pastors. Evangelical megachurches have argued that theological education should be centered in successful congregations rather than theological schools, and there is some evidence that larger Evangelical congregations discount the education provided by theological schools. Roman Catholics are experiencing an unprecedented growth in the number of lay professional parish staff who are responsible for many aspects of parish life and ministry. Parishes and Episcopal leaders, however, are unsure of the amount of theological education these persons need to do their work well. These changes in the perceptions and practices of parishes and congregations result in questions about the value of theological schools. Is there a continuing role for their historic missions as the new century develops? Should the pattern of theological education that has served North American Christianity well in the past be jettisoned in the future?[16]

ATS Standards

The Association of Theological Schools in the United States and Canada (ATS) lists these "General Institutional Standards":

1. Purpose, Planning, and Evaluation,
2. Institutional Integrity,
3. Learning, Teaching, and Research: Theological Scholarship,
4. The Theological Curriculum,
5. Library and Information Resources,
6. Faculty,
7. Student Recruitment, Admission, Services, and Placement,

16. Aleshire, *Earthen Vessels,* pp. xii-xiii.

8. Authority and Governance,
9. Institutional Resources,
10. Multiple Locations and Distance Education.[17]

Standard number 4 is particularly worth noting:

> 4. THE THEOLOGICAL CURRICULUM
> The theological curriculum is the means by which teaching and learning are formally ordered to educational goals.
>   4.1 Goals of the theological curriculum.
>   4.1.1 In a theological school, the overarching goal is the development of theological understanding, that is, aptitude for theological reflection and wisdom pertaining to responsible life in faith.
>   4.1.2 The emphasis placed on particular goals and their configuration will vary, both from school to school . . . and within each school.[18]

The Work and Value of Theological Education

When the cost per M.Div. student is calculated, based on three years at a cost of $100,000 per year, the total cost is $300,000. Assuming that the person receiving a theological education spends twenty years (or more) in ministry, the amortized cost of his or her education is $15,000 per year. If the length of ministry is forty years, the amortized cost drops to $7,500 per year. The question is, will congregations and/or denominations be able and willing to contribute such an amount (in constant dollars) to schools of theological education? Presently, I fear, the answer is no. I do believe, however, that over time the valuation that congregations and denominations place on theological education can be increased significantly. The key is that congregations see more clearly the work of the schools and its value to the life and work of the congregation.

What is the value of theological education beyond the current fig-

17. Bulletin 47, Part 1, 2006, The Association of Theological Schools, The Commission on Accrediting, pp. 141-84.

18. Bulletin 47, Part 1, 2006, The Association of Theological Schools, The Commission on Accrediting, pp. 148-49.

ure of $100,000 per year mentioned by Aleshire? He listed these ele-
ments as the work of theological schools:

1. Theological schools are an "indispensable resource for learning for
   the religious vocation";
2. "The Christians tradition is a teaching tradition, and theological
   schools are ideal settings for teaching."
3. Theological schools are "centers of research."
4. "Theological schools generate more than the sum of learning,
   teaching, and research. When learning for religious vocation,
   teaching ministers and church members, and theological research
   are done in close connection with each other, over time, in communities of common interest, the result is fundamentally different
   than if these activities are done separately. Each is enhanced when
   performed in the context of the others, and a school provides a singular context that brings them together in both expectation and
   practice."
5. "Theological schools are worth the money. The education they
   provide is worth the effort."[19]

An earthen vessel, Aleshire wrote, "has instrumental value, not ter-
minal value. . . . Theological schools are not good because they have
great histories, or wonderful facilities, or distinguished faculties. They
are good to the extent that they cultivate the learning, knowledge, skills,
sensitivities, and perceptions that the church needs for its leaders."[20]

What, then, are the value of theological education and the work of
theological schools? When ATS conducted discussions with presidents
and deans across the Association a few years ago, ATS Executive Director Daniel Aleshire reported that one question leaped out at him: "Is
there value in the church having *educated* clergy?"[21] He continued:

Theological education takes many forms: institutes and congrega-
tion-based programs, training programs for part-time and bi-
vocational clergy, undergraduate programs in ministry, and the
post-graduate, professional education conducted by ATS schools.
What is the value of *seminary-educated* religious leaders? As the first

19. Aleshire, *Earthen Vessels*, pp. 162-64.
20. Aleshire, *Earthen Vessels*, p. 165.
21. Aleshire, *Earthen Vessels*, p. 161.

decade of this century is nearing its end, it costs about one hundred thousand dollars per student for theological schools to provide a three-year M.Div. education. Compared to other forms of graduate professional education, like medicine and law, the cost of a theological degree is relatively low. But to the world of forever-strained finances in North American Christianity, it's hardly pocket change. What good does this education do?[22]

Pedagogies

In their volume *Educating Clergy,* Charles R. Foster, Lisa E. Dahill, Lawrence A. Goleman, and Barbara Wang Tolentino named four signature pedagogies for theological education:

> At the heart of this volume is the authors' claim that there are four signature pedagogies of theological education: pedagogies of interpretation, pedagogies of formation, pedagogies of contextualization, and pedagogies of performance. Thus, the teachers of clergy must instruct their students in the disciplined analysis of sacred texts; in the formation of their pastoral identities, dispositions, and values; in the understanding of the complex social, political, personal, and congregational conditions that surround them; and in the skills of preacher, counselor, liturgist, and leader through which they exercise their pastoral, priestly, and rabbinical responsibilities.
>
> These four pedagogies are not limited to the education of clergy, however. They are powerful instances of the kinds of teaching needed in every profession. Every profession rests on a body of text, whether philosophical, scientific, mathematical, or literary. Every profession expects that those who master those texts also are formed into women and men of integrity who can be trusted to use their knowledge and skill in the responsible service of others. Every profession expects its members to serve society by understanding critically the nature of the society it is called upon to serve, and to be more than slavish responders to the demands of their clients. And every profession rests on a body of skilled practice without which neither theory nor character is sufficient. Thus pedagogies of interpretation, formation, contextualization, and performance will re-

22. Aleshire, *Earthen Vessels,* p. 161.

appear in our future studies of other professions, often under different names, but predictably with similar functions. To be a professional requires understanding, character, and practical skill that can be employed with sensitivity to the conditions and contexts within which one works. This is no small challenge.[23]

These four signature pedagogies of theological education listed above — pedagogies of interpretation, pedagogies of formation, pedagogies of contextualization, and pedagogies of performance — seem to leave a faint trace of *Wissenschaft*. These statements about signature pedagogies would be much stronger, I think, if the interdisciplinary, decompartmentalizing possibilities were emphasized.

The authors also wrote about three pedagogical challenges:

In discussing their roles in cultivating — in an academic setting — the distinctively religious dimensions of clergy leadership, seminary educators often spoke of the need to address **three pedagogical challenges**. First, however formed or unformed students may appear to be in their religious traditions, they have been, at the same time, quite well formed by other personal, cultural, and spiritual forces. Students enter seminary deeply rooted in family traditions and local or regional subcultures.

The second pedagogical challenge, clergy educators noted, is the task of helping many students grow out of the naïve, precritical, sentimental, or quasi-fundamentalist piety with which they enter seminary and into what nineteenth-century German Protestant theologian Friedrich Schleiermacher called a "pietism of a higher order," or what philosopher of religion Paul Ricoeur called a "second naïvete."[24]

The third pedagogical challenge for many seminary educators originates in the tension they experience between helping ground students deeply enough in a religious tradition for it to be truly "formative" in the face of conflicting cultural and societal values, and at

23. Charles R. Foster, Lisa E. Dahill, Lawrence A. Goleman, and Barbara Wang Tolentino, *Educating Clergy: Teaching Practices and the Pastoral Imagination* (San Francisco: Jossey-Bass, 2006), pp. xi-xii.

24. Paul Ricoeur: "In every way, something has been lost, irremediably lost: immediacy of belief. But if we can no longer live the great symbolisms of the sacred in accordance with the original belief in them, we can, we modern men, aim at a second naïvete in and through criticism. In short, it is by interpreting that we can hear again." In *The Symbolism of Evil* (New York: Harper & Row, 1967).

the same time wanting them to remain open enough to engage truths in other religious traditions. Despite this widely shared goal, the *degree* of openness seen as desirable in approaching the beliefs and practices of "others" varies widely from tradition to tradition and from school to school.[25]

In regard to these challenges, I am in agreement. One of the most difficult tasks for those would-be stewards of the gospel is to be able to discern their differences with the prevailing culture and to be willing to take the risks necessary to be countercultural.

Ministry Integrator

During 2007 and early 2008, Rose Marie Vallet and I participated in six conferences that were very helpful. One of the important learnings was that an earlier model diagram in the first draft needed to be expanded, especially so as to include denominations as one of the important elements. It was also clear that we needed to list possible ways to make the model a reality by helping potential participants envision the program both as important and financially and logistically feasible.

The position of ministry integrator could be a vital *connection* among schools of theological education, denominations, pastors, and congregations. The graphic model on page 219 is suggestive; that is, the model would probably vary in different contexts, especially depending on the polity of the church bodies involved.

My vision now includes a number of theological schools of different denominations, in different geographic settings, that would each partner with their denomination to establish a "ministry integrator" program involving a selected number of their pastors and congregations. For example, a Presbyterian Church (USA) seminary might work with a Presbytery or Synod to recruit a number of pastors and congregations for the program. In the same vein, an American Baptist seminary might work with an American Baptist region or association. Likewise, a United Methodist seminary might work with a bishop and heads of conferences or district superintendents. The possibilities extend far beyond these three examples. The paths and structures would

---

25. Foster et al., *Educating Clergy*, pp. 102-03.

vary from one denomination to another. In effect, a customized approach would be used for each grouping of a school, a denomination, and selected congregations. Denominations vary in their systems of governance (church polity), and this would be a major factor in how the position of ministry integrator would function in a particular denominational setting.

It is also a reality that not all denominations and congregations would agree with the way I defined "gospel" in Chapter 3 of this book. It is important, however, that theological educators, denominational officials, pastors, and members of congregations struggle with the biblical texts and seek to find a faithful answer to the question "What is the gospel?" and then strive to be stewards of the gospel.

Even with the reality of the diversity of church polity and varying definitions of the gospel mentioned in the previous two paragraphs, I believe that mainline churches, evangelical churches, the Roman Catholic Church and its dioceses and parishes, and Orthodox churches and parishes could gain strength and faithfulness from seeking to be stewards of the gospel and seeking a greater connectedness among the various dimensions of the church.

Consider the graphic model on page 219.

Very often a man or woman who finishes seminary becomes pastor of a small, often struggling, congregation. In this situation, the support of the seminary for the pastor and the congregation is usually not there, or at least does not seem to be there. Even if the pastor takes a continuing education seminary course once in a while, the congregation does not feel a vital connection to the seminary. (Perhaps this helps to explain why congregational support for theological education is usually minimal.) The primary impact of theological education comes through the pastor, and often only through the pastor. As a result, in the mind of the congregation and, perhaps to a lesser extent, in the mind of theological educators, the connection between the two is nil or minimal. If the potential connection was not made when the seminary student graduated, how can the connection be made or strengthened? How can the "chasm" be bridged?

Notice in the model below that the positions of pastors and lay leaders of the congregation lie in their own boxes, between the congregation and theological educators. These are not new positions, but I think they can be viewed in new and exciting ways. Their placement in separate boxes is used as a visual reminder of their important role in

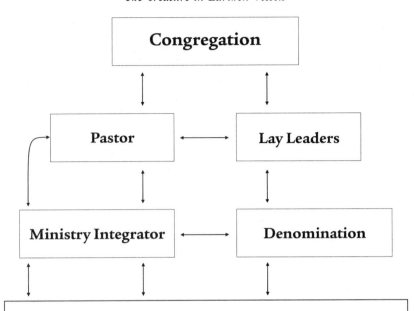

Theological Educators

A variety of faculty specialists who know well their area of "expertise" and who also value and practice an interdisciplinary approach and who willingly and gladly coordinate their work with ministry integrators, denominational leaders, and congregational leaders. The faculty and students are backed by the administration, board, and the full resources of the school in this endeavor.

the linkages between the congregation, the larger church, and the world of theological education.

A second element is new: the position of *ministry integrator*. Notice the linkage between the ministry integrator and all the other parts of the *schema*. All the arrows run in both directions. This is to indicate that communication and learning must always flow in two directions. The ministry integrator learns from and interacts with the theological educators about their special areas of expertise.

The ministry integrator meets periodically with denominational leaders, pastors and lay leaders (and ideally with theological educators at the same meetings) to mutually share insights and ideas. The ministry integrator coordinates the sharing of learnings and insights (including his/her own) from the denominational leaders, pastors and lay leaders about what is going on in the life of the congregations and the larger church, as all strive to be stewards of the gospel.

These learnings and ideas are then shared with other theological educators, with the hope and expectation that the sharing will help theological educators as they prepare syllabi and plan future courses, leading to a growth in interdisciplinary approaches among the theological educators.

Meanwhile, the insights gained by pastors and lay leaders from these meetings are shared with the whole congregation and put into practice in the life of the congregation. The insights and learnings gained directly by the pastor from theological educators and others become part of the total mix of communication and learnings. At this point, the pastor can fulfill the important role of "theologian in residence."

In a similar way, the position of ministry integrator is placed in a box separate from the box of theological educators. One of the major decisions that will have to be made in the implementation of this model is the "placement" of this position. To whom will he or she be accountable? How will funding for the position be secured and maintained on an ongoing basis? My personal hope is that the position would be funded by a mix of support from congregations, the larger church, and schools of theological education. The mix will vary from one context to another, probably based significantly on the polity of the church involved.

The net result in the model is that there is an ongoing flow from the world of theological education to the world of the larger church, the world of congregations, and back again. The position of ministry integrator will impact what happens in the life of the congregation as well as what happens in the other worlds. Part of that flow in both directions will involve having a periodic evaluation of how the process is working and making changes and adjustments as needed. Part of the ongoing evaluation will be to determine if and how congregations are becoming the salt in the cultural caldron.

The question arises: What about students in theological schools who plan to become pastors upon completion of their theological studies, but who are not serving as a pastor while in school? These students would become familiar with and experience the model, with the expectation that, after graduation, they would work with the theological school and ministry integrator(s) in the congregation they are serving. Ideally, while still in theological school, they would begin their work with the ministry integrator(s) with whom they will work in their first pastorate.

When possible, the same ministry integrator(s) with whom they work while in school will also have begun a relationship with the congregation that the student will be serving as pastor. The implementation of this part of the model would involve establishing a long-term relationship between schools of theological education and congregations. As already noted, a variable factor in accomplishing this would be the polities of different congregations and their relationship with the denomination of which they are a part. Thus, a strong relationship between schools of theological education and the denomination that relates to a particular congregation would be essential. Depending on the particular polity in place in a particular case, the implementation might well be facilitated or take longer.

An overall, long-term strategy would necessitate building strong relationships among schools of theological education, denominations, and congregations. In some denominations, such relationships may already exist, and the task would be to strengthen such relationships. In other denominations, because such relationships do not exist at a significant level, much groundwork and interpretation would be required over a period of time.

In a conversation with Bruce Birch, dean of Wesley Theological Seminary, he pointed out the layout of the campus in Washington, D.C. The chapel and library of the seminary are aligned in such a way that when one is in the chapel, looking outward through the main entrance, the library is in view. And when one stands at the main entrance to the library, looking outward, the chapel is in view. Both head and heart are involved.

The Scope of Stewardship: More Implicit Than Explicit

The role of the steward in the Christian faith is not often expressed in explicit terms that use the word "steward." Yet, as Birch wrote:

> the concept of the steward is amazingly comprehensive. It appears in
> a broad range of materials, but what I think impresses me more is
> that without appearing explicitly as a term (in any of its iterations)
> the role of steward usefully illumines so many other biblical con-

cepts. It is an exceptionally resilient concept for relating divine and human agency in the effort to bring wholeness to a broken world. As an example, consider the concept of covenant community. I have found it very helpful to ask students and church people to think of covenant as a community of stewards. The various elements of covenant responsibility (economic, political, social, religious) are all related to a trust from and accountability to God as the sovereign covenant partner. And this covenant responsibility can only be discharged as a corporate community, responsible to God and neighbor. I find the notion of a community of stewards to be a very helpful way of looking at the covenant concept. It gives missional thrust to what is often seen in more legalistic categories.

I suppose that, as a biblical scholar, I have come to regard the concept of the steward as one of my main integrating lenses in seeing the larger whole of biblical theology. It is so readily usable in this way that I am dismayed at how few biblical scholars/teachers have actually discovered this. I think most of them are suffering from the narrow restriction of stewardship to budget and fundraising that still afflicts many in the church. Since my own broadened concept was a result of being challenged by stewardship leaders to relate my work to their own, an issue of strategy may suggest itself. Before redoing theological curriculum there may need to be a strategy of challenge to the various arenas of theological scholarship to consider the role of steward. Perhaps what I am suggesting is a strategy to convert more faculty to the usefulness of the steward image in their own work.[26]

I believe that, even though more implicit than explicit, the word "steward" is a powerful integrative force for all parts of the church.

God's Grace

For the Christian who strives to be a faithful steward of the gospel, the text of Luke 4:16-30 is particularly significant. Luke 4 begins with a recounting of the temptations of Jesus in the wilderness. Then, we read, Jesus began teaching in the synagogues and received praise. When he came to Nazareth, his "hometown," he went to the synagogue and read

26. Birch, "The Bible, Stewards, and Ministry."

from the book of Isaiah, including 61:1-2a — the very verses that talk about the principles of the Jubilee year. At the beginning of his ministry, and in his hometown, Jesus placed emphasis on the year of Jubilee, or the year of the Lord's favor. The themes in the text from Isaiah were to be the major emphases of Jesus' ministry. Jesus taught, preached, healed, and cast out demons. He ministered to those who were poor, outcast, sick, and blind. There Jesus read the words of Isaiah: "The spirit of the Lord is upon me, because he has anointed me to bring good news to the poor"; the congregation was pleased.

Yet, as Vincent Alfano wrote:

> Jesus goes on, "Remember in the Old Testament, when Elijah and Elisha tried to preach to their own people, to people like you, nobody would believe them. So I'm going to go back, back [to Capernaum] to where the rejects and foreigners, and the poor and the sick, and the homeless, and the imprisoned are, back where you never go, because maybe there they will believe what I have to say."
>
> That did it. The crowd went wild. They couldn't and wouldn't believe that the walls they had erected had cut them off from the word of God and, in their anger, they tried to throw Jesus off a cliff. This time, Jesus escaped.[27]

At first, those who heard Jesus that day in the synagogue were pleased with his words. But when Jesus reminded his listeners about Elijah's ministry to a widow who was not of Israel and Elisha's healing of Naaman the Syrian, they became enraged and tried to kill him. The people in the synagogue had read Scripture as promises of God's exclusive covenant with them. The deliverance that Jesus announced was for all peoples.

R. Alan Culpepper reminded us that this scene is paradigmatic of Jesus' life and ministry:

> God's grace is never subject to the limitations and boundaries of any nation, church, group, or race. Those who would exclude others thereby exclude themselves. Human beings may be instruments of God's grace for others, but we are never free to set limits on who may receive that grace. Throughout history, the gospel has always been

27. Vincent Alfano in a sermon, "The Mob Will Always Be There," preached 25 Jan. 1998 to Cosburn United Church, Cosburn, Ontario.

more radically inclusive than any group, denomination, or church, so we continually struggle for a breadth of love and acceptance that more nearly approximates the breadth of God's love.[28]

When Jesus spoke against trying to limit, or to create boundaries around, God's grace, he met resistance. Likewise, Jesus' disciples, who live and speak the gospel of grace, will encounter hostility, ridicule, and resistance. The church, as a steward of the gospel, must guard against viewing itself as the sole guardian of the gospel that bears God's grace.

For the Christian church, Jesus is seen as the Servant of God who suffered and was executed on a cross. His righteousness was vindicated by God through the Resurrection. Jesus, the Suffering Servant, serves as a model for the Christian steward who desires to live in covenant with God.

The Christian church, as a covenant community, may legitimately use the Old Testament as a basis for understanding Yahweh and what it means to live as a steward in covenant with God. This use of the text should not be construed as exclusive, however. The text of the Old Testament must not be reduced to the simple rendering of any one faith community. In particular, the Christian church must remember that the Jewish community is "co-reader, co-hearer, and co-practitioner of this text, whereby the community that Christians have long demonized becomes a heeded truth-teller," wrote Walter Brueggemann.[29] The implications of this statement argue against, correctly in my opinion, a supersessionist reading of the Old Testament in which the New Testament and teachings of the Christian church supersede the teachings of the Old Testament, which is, of course, the Hebrew Bible. Brueggemann also wrote that, in his judgment, "theologically, *what Jews and Christians share is much more extensive, much more important, much more definitional than what divides us.*"[30]

The next chapter contains responses and conversations related to the first eight chapters of this book.

---

28. R. Alan Culpepper, *Luke-John*, The New Interpreter's Bible, vol. 9 (Nashville: Abingdon Press, 1995), p. 108.

29. Walter Brueggemann, *Theology of the Old Testament: Testimony, Dispute, Advocacy* (Minneapolis: Fortress Press, 1997), p. 745.

30. Brueggemann, *Theology of the Old Testament*, p. 108.

CHAPTER 9

Contributions by Theological Educators

With one exception, the six contributions in this chapter were written in 2009 in response to reading the first eight chapters of this book. (The exception is the contribution by Bruce C. Birch, which is excerpted from an article that he wrote in 2003 in response to my proposal for reforming theological education, written in 2001.) The contributors are Daniel Aleshire, David L. Bartlett, Bruce C. Birch, Terry Parsons, Eugene F. Roop, and L. E. "Ted" Siverns.

*   *

Daniel Aleshire
Executive Director
The Association of Theological Schools in the United States and Canada
Pittsburgh, Pennsylvania

"Response to *Stewards of the Gospel*"

Stewards of the Gospel conveys the voice of a pastor and ecumenical agency executive who cares deeply about the mission of God in the world. It reflects the culmination of thought that has grown through decades of work in service to that mission.

Stewards reaches broadly to include individual Christians; the congregations in which those individuals gather for worship, fellowship, education, and service; the theological schools that educate leaders for those congregations; and the agencies that advance the church's mission in the world. Not only is the reach breathtakingly broad; the focus is also penetratingly deep. Ronald Vallet wants to re-vision the fundamental metaphor of Christian identity as "Stewards of the Gospel." "Stewardship" is not as much about the care of material resources as it is an all-consuming thirst of the believer for God, and "gospel" is not so much about an undefined "good news" as it is about the cross by which humankind is reconciled to God and kingdom in which the reign of God is expressed as Christians embody God's love and justice.

I work with theological schools and want to reflect on *Stewards of the Gospel* from the perspective of that world in terms of (1) the ecology in which theological schools are embedded, (2) the curriculum of theological education, (3) the character of change in these schools, and (4) the relationship of Vallet's call to reform theological education to other calls for reform. I also want to comment on the ways in which each of these four areas may advance or impede the proposal for reform that Ronald Vallet makes in *Stewards*.

The Ecology of Theological Schools

Theological schools are embedded in an educational ecology that includes ecclesial bodies and higher education. If "the object of theological education is to develop stewards of the gospel who, in turn, can provide leadership for the development of stewards of the gospel," then both the schools and the ecclesial communities to which they are related will need a common understanding about this kind of stewardship. The change for which the book is arguing is a systemic change, not just a change in theological schools. If the church does not think that it is a community of stewards of the gospel, then there is little chance that a change in the schools would affect the church. The ecological system includes the broader church, not just schools and the particular ecclesial communities to which they relate. This book gives closer attention to one part of American Christianity, mainline Protestantism, than other parts, such as the Roman Catholic Church or evangelical Protestantism. Mainline Protestantism has experienced four decades of decline in members, cultural influence, and institutional capacity while evangelical Protestants have witnessed four decades of increasing membership and cultural influence. Roman Catholics have experienced growth in numbers and decline in priestly vocations. How this book's argument is perceived will vary, in part, on the reader's location in American Christianity. Denominations in decline behave differently from denominations that have experienced growth and increased capacity. Both deal with change, but they deal with it quite differently. Because theological schools are also embedded in higher education, the intellectual and professional quality of this proposal will be assessed in multiple ways, because that assessment is at the core of the intellectual work of the schools. Thus, if change is to come, it will occur because a system of influences has interacted in such a way that the change occurs both in the broader ecology and in individual schools. Ecological systems are more difficult to re-orient than individual institutions. *Stewards* is correct in understanding that multiple parts of an ecological system must be changed to effect significant change in any one of those parts.

The ecological embeddedness of theological schools and church bodies complicates the potential adoption of these proposals.

The Curriculum of Theological Schools

Stewards reviews the history of the curriculum of the modern seminary, but it is a more complex history than this volume has space to rehearse. What is perhaps most important to note about the core curriculum of theological study is its stability over time. It is stable because much of what the curriculum covers does not go out of date. As a result, changes typically occur by addition, not by substitution. For example, seminarians need to learn both the theological formulations of the early church fathers and the contemporary feminist critique of patriarchal religion. One does not replace the other. Students need to learn the history of the Reformation, but they also need to learn the most recent history of the church. Other professions have a body of literature that tends to replace itself with time (medical students are not learning much about scientific ideas of the third century), but the theological curriculum accrues over time — new ideas are added but older ones are seldom discarded. A call to rethink theological curriculum needs to understand that that space is crowded and that new ideas need to find homes in existing areas, to the extent possible.

Fortunately, *Stewards* does just that. The ATS Commission on Accrediting Standards states that the overarching goal of the theological curriculum "is the development of theological understanding, that is, aptitude for theological reflection and wisdom pertaining to responsible life in faith." The argument forwarded in this book does not require a new course or a new professor; rather, it provides a proposal for the core metaphor of this theological understanding and wisdom — "Stewards of the Gospel."

Theological schools are frequently encouraged to add more courses to cover what is perceived to be missing in the skill set of new graduates, and one course often requested is on stewardship. Seminary deans and presidents, to whom the question most often comes, graciously explain that the curriculum likely does not have room for a course devoted to stewardship alone, and that the subject is covered in some course that does not bear that name. The course is requested, I think, because some pastors have trouble asking for money or don't know how to do it well. After significant ecumenical service dealing with stewardship that was typically understood as focused on monetary issues, Vallet wants to relocate stewardship in a much deeper theological context than organized religion's need for money, and in relocating it, perhaps undergird the small part of stewarding the gospel that has to do with money.

The theological curriculum can accommodate the proposal forwarded by this book without adding courses and without a focus on congregational fund-raising and finance. This enhances the potential of the proposal being implemented.

The Character of Change in Theological Schools

Anyone who works around congregations has heard the adage "we never did it that way before." Whether it is the order of service or the arrangement of the chancel furniture, congregations are places where change can be threatening and resisted. While theological schools tend to be open to new ideas, they are often resistant to changes in fundamental structures. Like other organizations that must change but are slow to do so, theological schools tend to make institutional changes by layering the new on top of the old. They add something new without abandoning what the "new" was supposed to replace. While this is necessary with the curriculum, as discussed above, it is problematic for institutional changes. Many congregations are faced with the question of what will meet the needs of the gospel and gathered community next week. Theological schools have the luxury of a longer time frame: they are addressing the question of what students will need next year, or the year after that. Surprising as it may seem to people who spend their lives in congregational work, congregations change faster than theological schools change.

Stewards of the Gospel wants change in a fundamental metaphor for understanding Christian life and ministry. Seminaries will be open to the theological idea of this new metaphor, but it will be in a context with other metaphors. They will be more likely to add it as another metaphor of study than to replace existing metaphors. The reform that is proposed will require fundamental change in the church's self-understanding and work, and that may prove more difficult than adding a new theological metaphor to the crowded theological curriculum.

Calls to Reform Theological Education

American Christianity spent the nineteenth and the first seven decades of the twentieth century building a system of theological schools that served a wide range of denominations and religious constituencies. These schools served their constituencies with a growing academic quality and institutional capacity. In the past forty years, however, there have been increasing calls to reform theological education, especially Protestant theological education. Some of these calls to reform have been academic in nature, conveying a perception that newer interpretations of texts or newer theological construals (e.g., liberation theology, feminist biblical interpretation) are not advancing theological understanding. Other academic calls to reform have reflected a perception that theological education has become too focused on clerical, professional education and insufficiently attentive to the theological center of theological education. Still other calls for reform have come from the church. Some of these calls have emerged from evangelical Protestants, especially pastors of larger membership churches, who think that many theological schools are too removed from the rapidly changing work of the congregational Christianity. They want reform in theological education that focuses on the new paradigms of congregational work in fast-growing, large congregations. Other calls to reform that have come from the church reflect the perception that theological schools have strayed doctrinally or substituted religious knowledge for religious fervor. The enduring struggle in mainline Protestantism has called for reform in the theological education that serves this part of American Protestantism. It is not always clear what the pattern of reform should be, but these calls convey a perception that the decline in membership and loss of cultural influence that mainline Protestants have experienced is, at least in part, a function of what seminaries have failed to teach, have taught inadequately, or taught wrongly.

Stewards of the Gospel calls for reform in theological education in the context of calling for a commensurate reform in the church. That is unique among the many calls for the reform of theological education. Other arguments for reform have been more focused on the seminary, arguing in one way or the other, that the church has been right and poorly served by the seminary or that if the church is wrong, the seminary was at least partly to blame. *Stewards* argues that the church needs a renewed root theological metaphor for Christian identity and ministry and that the seminaries must help the church by educating leaders to live into and minister out of this metaphor. It is not so much a call to rethink what stewardship has come to mean as it is a call to find the theological resource that the church needs in order to be a home for the reign of God that claims the cross and the world.

Reform is difficult in both the church and the theological school. It is not impossible, and the present historical moment in mainline Protestantism may be calling enough assumptions into question that destabilized institutions will be ready to consider changes that they may not have considered decades ago. The challenge, I think, will be the pull toward institutional and organizational survival on the one hand and the pull toward theological integrity and faithfulness on the other. *Stewards* offers a valuable image for the church and the theological school.

* * *

David L. Bartlett
Professor of New Testament
Columbia Theological Seminary, Decatur, Georgia

"Stewards of the Gospel: A Response"

For me this book accomplished what it set out to accomplish. It caused me to rethink my understanding of stewardship biblically, theologically, and practically. It persuaded me that the metaphor of the steward provides an invaluable picture for thinking of the church's ministries and of the ways in which seminaries and divinity schools can help prepare faithful stewards.

Ronald Vallet moves us far beyond the old picture of stewardship as a once-a-year chore the churches take on to make sure they can meet their budget. Stewardship becomes a lens through which we are enabled to view a whole range of Christian beliefs and practices more clearly. Most powerfully, he reminds us that the church does not practice stewardship for its own sake but for the sake of the "cauldron" of the world, which is, after all, God's world.

In response to this book I want only to expand briefly on the insights concerning "gospel" in Chapter 3 and the insights concerning biblical interpretation in Chapter 4 and then to add a closing query about the place of models and metaphors in our ecclesiology.

Reflections on Chapter 3

Historically, it is quite right to acknowledge that there is more than one way of understanding gospel in the New Testament. For the synoptics, the gospel is in large measure the proclamation of God's Kingdom. For Paul the stress is much more on Christ crucified and risen. John's Gospel does not use the term "gospel" at all. For the Fourth Gospel, the faithful are invited, not to the Kingdom, but to "eternal life" and Christ, though of course he is crucified and risen, is above all the living bread of life to be received by faith.

The divisions among our churches (and our seminaries) are in part divisions about which aspect of the gospel we take to be central. The hope for unity among our churches and our seminary lies in the claim

Ronald Vallet rightly makes in the introduction to this book. The gospel is first of all about God and only secondly about us. And the gospel is first of all about the God whose kingdom, power, glory, and humility are all known in Jesus Christ.

It is helpful to remember, as this book suggests, that the usual translation of the term "gospel" as "good news" may miss some of the distinctive features that the term took on in early Christian worship and literature.

Nonetheless the familiar translations remind us of two features of "gospel" that are still pertinent to the discussion of faithful stewardship. First, gospel does have to be *good* news. The powerful appeal of prosperity preachers comes in part from their ability to comfort people. The deep mistake in prosperity preaching is the tendency to confuse the human appetite for goods with the human hunger for the good God. Second, the gospel does have to be good *news* — that is, it has to make a difference. However we declare the gospel, it is really always a huge headline: the world is changed.

In the context of Ronald Vallet's helpful use of Walter Brueggemann's claim that we tell a story that competes with the world's stories, it might help to think of gospel as the "Good Story" as opposed to all the inadequate stories that we keep telling ourselves.

This book rightly reminds us that the competing, not-so-good story that we tell ourselves in North America is often a story that treats us as consumers who can be satisfied by stuff, when in fact we are seekers who will be restless till we find our rest in God.

As we seek to understand stewardship of the gospel I would only add that sometimes the competing stories represent other false gods. In the academic world, scholarly acclaim is far more apt to be an idol than wealth is. In other "worlds," some hunger for power, others for a kind of familial security that can stand in the way of loyalty to God's family.

Reflections on Chapter 4

All of us are informed and helped by the wise way in which the author presents the issues of scriptural authority.

One helpful way to pick up on the discussion is to draw on the suggestion — mediated in our time first by Hans-Georg Gadamer and then by David Tracy — that interpretation is always conversation, and therefore biblical interpretation is always a conversation with the biblical text.

If this is the case, it is neither surprising nor frightening that our understanding of the text changes as we change, as we bring to the conversation new insights about science, for instance, or about the human cost of slavery. What Christians also want to insist, however, is that the Bible itself is the senior partner in that conversation. It is not simply that our ideas change so we reinvent the text; it is rather that in the light of our own changing selves we understand the text's own message in new and different ways.

This also implies that while the Protestant rallying cry of *sola Scriptura* was polemically powerful, all of us who read scripture are in conversation not only with scripture, but with the interpreters of scripture around the world and across the ages. *Sola Scriptura* is enriched by the communion of saints.

Further, the excellent suggestions for biblical interpretation in the chapter might be augmented by remembering that biblical interpretation is always a matter of conversation among the interpreters themselves. The way we keep our interpretations from being entirely self-serving is to talk about the texts with other selves who can call us to account.

In many ways the present book is a conversation starter. It will be most effective if Christians talk about the Bible with each other in the light of these new insights. Given the fact that the book is a conversation starter, it will not be surprising if different congregations, denominations, and seminaries learn from the book different lessons and apply the book in a variety of ways.

A Modest Caveat

Finally, I have to confess my skepticism that any single paradigm — even one as powerful as the paradigm of stewardship — will be able to provide an organizing metaphor that will be equally acceptable for the range of theological seminaries, mainline and evangelical Protestant, Roman Catholic and Orthodox, denominational, inter- and non-denominational, self-standing and university-based.

Avery Dulles's book *Models of the Church* provides a very helpful typology of the different ecclesial models that predominate in our different churches and denominations.[1] I suspect that one could do a similar typology of seminaries and divinity schools in North America. For example, to borrow from Dulles's categories, Catholic and Anglican schools will almost certainly center on the church as sacrament and Baptist schools on the church as herald. Powerful as the model of church (and minister) as steward may be, I doubt that it will replace those deeply-entrenched (and rich) ecclesial perspectives.

In the discussion of the role of the churches in the public realm, we have been helped by the distinction between public and confessional theology. Appropriately, faith communities have confessional language that shapes them and informs their worship, study, and action. However, some theologians have urged the churches also to find a public theology that can inform conversation between believers and unbelievers.

Within the world of the seminaries, denominations, and congregations, we are eager for a rich language that transcends the confessional and provides opportunity for conversation, revision, and mutual correction. I suspect the gift of this study will not be that most seminaries will revise their curricula and their mission statements to put stewardship at the center of their vision, though of course some will do so faithfully and imaginatively.

Rather, the metaphor of stewardship gives us an image both deep and broad that can enable us to engage with one another around a common theme and indeed a common vision. It will not be the only theme or the only vision for our seminaries, but it will be a theme or vision that keeps us talking with each other and joining with each other as stewards of the mysteries of God.

*　　　*

Bruce C. Birch
Academic Dean, Wesley Theological Seminary
Washington, D.C.

"The Bible, Stewards, and Ministry" (2003)

Can the image of steward function to integrate theological education? I find that I cannot address this question in the abstract. To some ex-

1. New York: Doubleday, 1987.

tent I must address the question autobiographically, since the concept of steward was not on my horizon when I began my teaching career. How it came to be so central in my own work is a piece of experiential learning that I think is instructive to our focal question.

As a matter of self-identity I can claim three designations, but my formal education and training prepared me for only one of them. I am a biblical scholar, prepared in graduate school to be a scholar-educator, primarily in Old Testament theology and its related subjects. Because I obtained a faculty position in a theological school, I also became a theological educator. This was not merely incidental. I am ordained in the United Methodist Church and deeply committed to the ministries of the church, so I welcomed the opportunity to relate my scholarship and teaching to the task of equipping persons for leadership in the church. I think of my combined roles as biblical scholar and theological educator as a calling in my own ministry. In many ways these roles were those for which I had aimed, aspired, and prepared.

What is more surprising to me is that I now also consider myself to be a stewardship educator. Since 1979 a major part of my professional life has been devoted to events, projects, publications, and courses that relate to the role of steward in the life of the church. This was an arena of work and commitment that I had never anticipated and only gradually came to accept as a part of my calling. I want to speak about a few elements in my own journey to become a stewardship educator. My thoughts on the possibilities for the role of steward as an integrating focus for theological education grow out of my own discovery of its centrality to my work as a biblical scholar and a theological educator.

A Biblical Scholar Among the Stewards

In 1978 I co-authored with Larry Rasmussen a book entitled *The Predicament of the Prosperous*. This book grew out of our previous work together relating the Bible to Christian Ethics and our mutual involvement at that time in issues of hunger, poverty, and environmental responsibility. Any mention in this book of the words "steward" or "stewardship" was only incidental. I have now come to understand this book as primarily concerned with stewardship.

Following the publication of this book, I was invited to the Winter Meeting of the NCCC [National Council of the Churches of Christ]

Commission on Stewardship in San Antonio in 1979. The other speaker at that meeting was Douglas John Hall. I began to acquire a vocabulary and a set of colleagues that drew me, and my own biblical work, increasingly into the arena of stewardship issues. I began to receive regular invitations to speak and teach in a wide variety of stewardship venues. That involvement has continued to the present.

In 1979 I undoubtedly associated the word stewardship primarily with the annual budget pledge campaign in a local church. To hear Douglas John Hall (and to read his book as I quickly did) and to find a multitude of convergences with my own interests as a biblical theologian was for me an intellectual and spiritual opening to an unexpected arena. I could never think of stewardship in such a narrow way again.

I was struck by the comprehensiveness of the role of steward. All that we are, all that we have, all that we do is by virtue of the gifts of God entrusted to our care and use. Almost all of the themes important to me as a biblical theologian relate in some genuine way to the role of the steward.

As a biblical theologian I am naturally suspicious of centering themes in biblical theology. In today's scholarly context I could not imagine writing a theology of the Old Testament organized around a single centering concept or image (e.g., Eichrodt and covenant, or von Rad and *Heilsgeschichte*). I have no desire to write an Old Testament or biblical theology centered on the concept of the steward, and I do not think it would do justice to the complexity and diversity of scripture. This probably also predisposes me to be reluctant to center theological education on a singular theme. I will return to this later.

Nevertheless, the concept of the steward is amazingly comprehensive. It appears in a broad range of materials, but I think what impresses me more is that without appearing explicitly as a term (in any of its iterations) the role of steward usefully illumines so many other biblical concepts. It is an exceptionally resilient concept for relating divine and human agency in the effort to bring wholeness to a broken world. As an example, consider the concept of covenant community. I have found it very helpful to ask students and church people to think of covenant as a community of stewards. The various elements of covenant responsibility (economic, political, social, religious) are all related to a trust from and accountability to God as the sovereign covenant partner. And this covenant responsibility can only be discharged as a corporate community, responsible to God and neighbor. I find the notion of a community of stewards to be a very helpful way of looking at the covenant concept. It gives a missional thrust to what is often seen in more legalistic categories.

I suppose that, as a biblical scholar, I have come to regard the concept of the steward as one of my main integrating lenses in seeing the larger whole of biblical theology. It is so readily useable in this way that I am dismayed at how few biblical scholar/teachers have actually discovered this. I think most of them are suffering from the narrow restriction of stewardship to budget and fundraising that still afflicts many in the church. Since my own broadened concept was a result of being challenged by stewardship leaders to relate my work to their own, an issue of strategy may suggest itself. Before redoing theological curriculum there may need to be a strategy of challenge to the various arenas of theological scholarship to consider the role of steward. Perhaps what I am suggesting is a strategy to convert more faculty to the usefulness of the steward image in their own work.

The Theological Educator as Steward

I was never content to pursue the scholarly interests of my own discipline and let others worry about how the disciplines fit together as a theological education. I thought of myself almost from the beginning as a theological educator. I have been deeply involved in curricular issues. I have been concerned for the work of bridging between academy and church. Now, I serve as the Academic Dean in my institution, and I have formal responsibility for integrating what David Kelsey called "a clutch of courses" into a theological education that serves God's church in the world.

Wesley Theological Seminary has been a particularly congenial place to nurture a concern for stewardship themes. I have found it a school with a particular commitment to relate theological scholarship to the life and ministry of the church. I had two predecessors in my role as Dean who were deeply committed to this connection, Marjorie Suchocki and Douglas Meeks, and I now stand on their shoulders in continuing this commitment to vital partnership with the ministries and congregations of the wider church. We say in our strategic plan that we have moved from being a "church-related school" to being a "church-based school."

I have been surrounded by colleagues in other disciplines who have spoken, taught, and written about stewardship issues: Larry Rasmussen, Douglas Meeks, Marjorie Suchocki, Sondra Wheeler, David Watson, Lovett Weems, Sue Zabel, Alan Geyer, and Lewis Parks. We have a new D.Min. track on "The Role of Steward in Christian Ministry." I have had many lively conversations on stewardship matters with the colleagues named above.

Yet, for all this, there is little discernible impact of stewardship on the approach to theological education at Wesley. The curriculum is still organized around the traditional *theological encyclopedia* noted by Farley in his study. There is actually no regularly offered course on stewardship in the curriculum. If there is a discernible shift at Wesley where stewardship concerns on the part of so many faculty have had an effect, it is in ethos not curriculum. I believe that teaching and scholarship at Wesley have become less driven by the concerns of *Wissenschaft* and are moving in a direction more in keeping with *paideia*, although the present reality is somewhere in between. The engagement of many of our faculty, myself included, in the wide discussions that are broadening the scope of stewardship in the life of the church, have had an impact less on the formal shape of curriculum than on the way things are taught. There is less concern for a body of knowledge as an end in itself and a greater concern for teaching that informs ministry. It is here that I think the influence of the concept of "steward" can be found, for ministry itself is a stewarding role. Ministry is an enterprise in which men and women are entrusted by God — for God's Word, for God's people, for the mission of the church in the world. Ministry itself becomes an issue of stewardship. My article on "Leadership as Stewardship" (*Quarterly Review*, Dec. 2002) is informed by this shift in ethos at Wesley.

All of this suggests that even with a school and faculty culture congenial to the concept of "steward," the entrenched patterns by which we organize theological education will be very difficult to change.

The same is true for the life of the church. In spite of many years during which I have observed the dedicated work of stewardship leaders to broaden the scope and meaning of the concept of steward, much of the stewardship culture in the church has stayed focused on meeting budgets and raising money.

Steward at the Center?

Can the concept of steward serve as an integrating center for theological education? This is an attractive notion for many reasons, but a challenging one. I offer only some concluding thoughts that might serve more as a direction than as a conclusion.

1. *If the concept of steward is to become an integrating center in theological education, I believe we must recognize that above all else we are called to be stewards of the gospel — the good news that God is at work reconciling the world through Jesus Christ.* All other arenas of our stewarding work are derivative from this central task of the steward. We have been entrusted with the good news of the gospel and this makes sense out of all other arenas where the role of steward might be acted out. Theological education organized around the concept of steward would understand itself to be missional in character. What equips the ministries of the church to form disciples who will, as communities of stewards, witness to and live out of the gospel entrusted to their care? No discipline in the theological curriculum would serve as an end in itself, but would be considered in relation to the overarching task of being faithful stewards of the gospel. This provides the framework for understanding what it means to be a steward in the varied arenas and communities that define our life in the world. Out of our role as stewards of the gospel, we consider our stewardship of the earth, economics, politics, family, relationships, and the church itself. Considered eschatologically our stewardship of the gospel is also our stewardship of hope. Theological education should produce ministerial leadership that sees beyond present challenge to envision God's future as that has already been glimpsed in Jesus Christ. To be stewards of the gospel is also to be stewards of that hopeful vision. Theological education ought to challenge students to such stewardship.

2. *If the concept of steward is to serve an integrating role, it must be presented in community and not individual terms.* We live in a culture increasingly marked by a utilitarian individualism (cf. Bellah, et al.). Even with reports of a current rising generation interested in spirituality it tends to be a highly selective spirituality, tailored to individual tastes. The images of steward and stewardship can easily be heard in highly individualistic, even privatistic, ways. The popular tie of these terms to money and economic matters contributes to this since people are highly private about these matters in our culture.

I have increasingly felt it important to talk about the "community of stewards" and to emphasize that our biblical faith always relates our individual experience of God to a community of believers. I have appreciated Ron Vallet's two most recent volumes because of their strong community emphases.

This has implications for theological education and the role of the steward concept there. Theological schools are struggling with issues of community formation as a dimension of theological education. Increasing numbers of students are part-time, tied to jobs or families, perhaps using online learning options, and commuting rather than residential. The use of the concept of steward as an integrating element in theological education will require working at an ethos appropriate to the concept. Issues of community and formation in community must loom large to provide an appropriate context for the use of the concept of steward. There is no hope for the full impact of the steward concept if there is no experience of the community of stewards in the theological school. Alongside curriculum, issues of worship, community life, spiritual disciplines, mutual support and openness of communication must receive attention.

3. *An integrating concept in theological education necessarily implies an interdisciplinary approach to curriculum and learning.* No integrating central concept can have effect if the disciplines stay unintegrated. There must be efforts to protect disciplinary integrity while encouraging the crossing of disciplinary boundaries so that students can see how a concept like steward can integrate a ministry or a congregation. It is important that the concept of steward not be relegated to the practice of ministry disciplines alone, or primarily.

4. The role of steward can play a role in a shift that I think is already taking place in theological education to some degree. At an ATS/ Luce-sponsored consultation to assess the state of theological scholarship, Nicholas Wolterstorff challenged the gathering to let theology be theology. He argued that theology too often adapts its agenda to an effort to find acceptability to the wider culture in terms defined by that culture. He believes that the theology that will make a difference will be a theology that sets its own agenda, uses its own language and traditions, and engages the world and its issues in its own terms. He believes that theological scholarship, and the theological schools where it is nurtured, has too often let its agenda be set by the culture rather than by the needs of the church. In the end, he called for what he labeled

"formation theology" focused not on academic disciplines but on formation of community.

I find myself in general agreement with this analysis and summons. Increasingly at Wesley, we use the term "formation" to describe our general goals, not as the term for the non-academic elements of the program. As I go to meetings of others in theological education I find a growing yearning for something that transcends the university-shaped academic models that still dominate us. Many voices in theological education have been urging and chronicling such changes. It is a rejection of *Wissenschaft* as a model adequate in itself, and it is a movement in the direction of *paideia*. Yet, I think a new model may be struggling to be born. It is informed more by the church and its needs than by the university, but it remains informed by the knowledge gained in academic disciplines. It would be frankly and unapologetically theological, but would remain open to a wide range of theological approaches. It would be grounded in religious experience as well as rational discourse. It would remove the separation, still expressed in so many places and ways, between the so-called classical and practical disciplines. It would be particularistic but within an ecumenical framework. It will require a new pedagogy as well as a new curricular approach. It must insist on community experience beyond the classroom.

In the emergence of a new model that moves in this direction I believe that the concept of steward could play an important centering role. It is both expansive and particular, and it contains within itself an inherent message of the important partnership between divine and human agency in the reconciling work of the church.

If the concept of steward has a place in theological education it will be as a part of an unapologetic effort to claim our own language for the task of preparing theologically educated persons for the ministries of the church. What may focus today on a reclaiming of the steward concept may be a part of a larger effort to reclaim a particularistic theological language embedded in our texts and traditions, unapologetic in its confessional commitments, diverse in its voices and methods, and open to a wide range of dialogues in the wider world.

*   *

Terry Parsons

Terry Parsons is the former Stewardship Officer for the Episcopal Church. She has served as vice president of the Ecumenical Stewardship Center; as a keynote speaker for stewardship conferences throughout the United States, Canada, and an international conference in England; and as an adjunct professor of stewardship at The General Theological Seminary in New York.

"What about Tithing?"

Tithing is a funny thing. I raise this question because it seems to be the one most often deliberately avoided. Sometimes it feels like a silent conspiracy in the meeting. Sometimes whoever has invited me handles the entire matter when we arrange the visit by asking me not to talk about "the 'T' Word."

I bring up the question here because I believe a simple exploration of the origins of this concept brings us into a useful discussion of that intersection of money story and gospel story that is the practical application of a theology of stewardship. In order to make the point, let us briefly explore the biblical story that introduces tithing and see where it takes us.

When explaining tithing to children, I like to ask: "Now who do you suppose thought that up?" If you can wait just a moment or two, there will usually be a hesitant voice that responds, "Was it God?" The correct response here is "No," at least not according to the Bible stories that we have.

There are some who will tell you it was Abraham, but if you look up the most cited support for that theory you will find it was not God directly to whom Abraham gave one-tenth but Melchizedek, the king of Salem and a priest.

> After his return from the defeat of Chedorlaomer and the kings who were with him, the king of Sodom went out to meet him at the Valley of Shaveh (that is, the King's Valley). And King Melchizedek of Salem brought out bread and wine; he was priest of God Most High. He blessed him and said, "Blessed be Abram by God Most High, maker of heaven and earth; and blessed be God Most High, who has delivered your enemies into your hand!" And Abram gave him one-tenth of everything. (Gen. 14:17-20)

A much more likely suspect is Jacob.

Jacob left Beer-sheba and went toward Haran. He came to a certain place and stayed there for the night, because the sun had set. Taking one of the stones of the place, he put it under his head and lay down in that place. And he dreamed that there was a ladder set up on the earth, the top of it reaching to heaven; and the angels of God were ascending and descending on it. And the LORD stood beside him and said, "I am the LORD, the God of Abraham your father and the God of Isaac; the land on which you lie I will give to you and to your offspring; and your offspring shall be like the dust of the earth, and you shall spread abroad to the west and to the east and to the north and to the south; and all the families of the earth shall be blessed in you and in your offspring. Know that I am with you and will keep you wherever you go, and will bring you back to this land; for I will not leave you until I have done what I have promised you." Then Jacob woke from his sleep and said, "Surely the LORD is in this place — and I did not know it!" And he was afraid, and said, "How awesome is this place! This is none other than the house of God, and this is the gate of heaven." So Jacob rose early in the morning, and he took the stone that he had put under his head and set it up for a pillar and poured oil on the top of it. He called that place Bethel; but the name of the city was Luz at the first. Then Jacob made a vow, saying, "If God will be with me, and will keep me in this way that I go, and will give me bread to eat and clothing to wear, so that I come again to my father's house in peace, then the LORD shall be my God, and this stone, which I have set up for a pillar, shall be God's house; and of all that you give me I will surely give one tenth to you." (Gen. 28:10-22)

Now here comes the important question. Why did Jacob make this promise? God's promise was unconditional. Was there something in his memory of his grandfather's gift to the priest-king that prompted it, or something in the culture of the time? We do not know, but four reasons have occurred to me.

1. It was an act of remembrance. Knowing what we do of Jacob up to this time in his life makes it easy to imagine that it was his way of helping God remember the generous promise God had just made to him. After all, at the moment Jacob is fleeing the fury of his brother Esau after not only securing Esau's inheritance as first-

born but also receiving the firstborn's blessing by tricking his father Isaac. As we know his whole history, however, it is equally easy to imagine that, over time, the return of one-tenth became the means by which Jacob remembered that God was the source of all that he had.

2. It was a tangible expression of gratitude. The story of our human relationship with God is rich with stories of God acting and humans thanking, usually with a sacrifice. Perhaps the memory of his grandfather Abraham's gift to Melchizedek had taught Jacob that this was the way to say "thank you." Whatever prompted it, there is something in this God-human exchange of gifts that grounds the relationship in gratitude rather than gifts of supplication. It distinguished the Children of Israel from every culture that surrounded them. Those gods sought gifts of petition. God gave without being asked or demanding a return, thus granting freedom and dignity to his human creation.

3. It allowed Jacob to experience generosity. We believe we are created in the image of God, and generosity is one of God's distinctive attributes. When we are generous, we touch some small part of ourselves that calls up the possibility of the God in us. One of the greatest gifts God has given us is the ability to give, even to God. Generosity feels good! Friends who give freely and often have told me that giving is much more fun than spending. I would like to think that over the years Jacob found great delight in keeping his tithing promise and giving back to God.

4. Tithing is an act of faith. The promise to return one-tenth to God assumes that 90 percent is enough and that the God who gave it will continue to give enough to provide for us. Jacob had no way of knowing how richly God would bless him in the years to come, which makes the promise an expression of his hope and belief that God would keep God's own promise to him.

Curiously, although the story of Jacob's ladder is told so often and so well that it has its own song, most readings of the story end before the last two verses that contain Jacob's promise. This story appears only once in the three-year cycle of lectionary readings and is often omitted then. Have you ever heard a sermon on Jacob's promise? Why do we omit that? "Why did he do it?" is a question that invites us not just to a new understanding of tithing but to a practical discussion of stewardship — what it is, how it places us in relationship with God, and how behaviors shape that relationship. The great benefit of a stewardship perspective on theological education is that it takes it from intellectual exercise into practical behavior. It calls us to the moment Jacob seems to have had in which he looked at what God had promised and asked himself how he should respond. Through the Gospels we can know of God's greatest gift. We know of its capacity to transform individual lives and the world. We become stewards when we ask ourselves, what do we do with what we know?

*   *

Eugene F. Roop
President Emeritus and
Wieand Professor Emeritus of Biblical Studies
Bethany Theological Seminary, Richmond, Indiana

"Conversation with Ron Vallet: *Stewards of the Gospel: Reforming Theological Education*"

One cannot respond to the wide-ranging discussion in *Stewards of the Gospel* by Ron Vallet without first expressing appreciation for the incredible wealth of information available in this book. Most specifically, the reader will find a brief history of "stewardship" in the North American Protestant church as well as valuable background material related to theological education in the United States. While this material may be available in other books and articles, with the publication of *Stewards of the Gospel* we have the material collected in a single resource. In addition, the reader will learn much from Ron's discussion defining "the gospel" as well as his reflections on the disputes surrounding biblical interpretation and his perspective on the issues facing the Christian church in North America. Of course, for Ron, all these elements lead to and serve a single purpose — his proposal to redesign education for ministry. Thank you, Ron. I appreciate the opportunity to add my thoughts to your discussion.

The book's value is visible in the myriad of ideas that came to my mind, all of which I would enjoy discussing. Instead, I will confine my remarks to a couple of items: (1) observations related to use of the metaphor of the "steward" and (2) the impact of educational technology on ministry education.

Steward as a Metaphor

For more than a quarter of a century, we have explored the word "steward" as a broad metaphor for Christian ministry and discipleship. During these decades "steward" and "stewardship" have gained widespread use both in the church and the culture.

Use of the metaphor "steward" in the church encouraged congregations to think and talk in new ways about Christian discipleship. The biblical roots of this metaphor enabled Christians to recognize ourselves as commissioned and trusted by God. The metaphor reminded believers not only of the trust God placed in us but also of the responsibility and accountability that come with divine trust. The metaphor of the "steward" nourished a generation eager to move beyond clergy-centered congregational life to fully embrace the ministry of all believers.

That being the case, I notice that the "steward" does not seem to have the same compelling metaphoric power for the newer generations of Christians in North America. Undoubtedly, there are many reasons for this development.

The word "steward" has found widespread use in American culture, especially in connection with the current emphasis on the environment, the animate and inanimate world in which we live. In this cultural context, "stewardship" has been disconnected from its biblical roots and become a code word naming our accountability and responsibility for our natural environment.

Certainly this use of "steward" in the broader culture has greatly increased everyone's familiarity with the word. However this broad use of "stewardship," unrelated to its biblical roots, seems to have diminished its value as a compelling metaphor in the church.

I recognize that, even as we appropriated "steward" from the biblical tradition and transformed it into a metaphor, the Christian community disconnected "steward" from its biblical roots and culture. A degree of disconnect from the originating context is inherent in the "creation" of any metaphor.

In both Testaments the word "steward" refers to an office, a specific leadership responsibility in the civic and/or economic life of the community. Even in the church, the metaphor "steward" has lost that sense of an official position. Its connection with the "ministry of all believers" has commissioned us all as "stewards." It has become the work of all members of the household of God rather than an office in the household. Ron Vallet's definition of the work of the steward in Chapter 2 illustrates the distance between the metaphor and the work of the ancient office: "Stewardship then may be defined as drinking deeply from the waters of the living God by moving from the stagnant waterholes of 'more' to the living water of the gospel of Jesus Christ, and inviting others to do the same."

We see a similar transformation in the church's use of "servant/slave" as a metaphor for leadership. Perhaps the same can be said of "shepherd," although with "shepherd" the biblical agrarian context and reference has been sustained to a greater extent than for "servant/slave" and "steward."

I repeat, a disconnect is inherent as we transform a biblical word from the concrete to the metaphorical. Nevertheless, the church expects that we will maintain an active conversation between the metaphors we use in the church and their concrete biblical roots. When that conversation becomes less visible and/or no longer provides the word/metaphor with discernible content, the metaphor loses some of its compelling character *in the church*. Frequently we see its use fade — not disappear, but diminish.

One suspects that the metaphor of the "shepherd" has lost much of its compelling character largely because of the urban character of contemporary culture. We have clearly maintained a conversation between the concrete biblical word "shepherd" and its use as a metaphor for leadership. Nevertheless, the distance between the job of the ancient shepherd and employment in our culture has reduced the power of the metaphor. We have seen its use fade.

As for the metaphor "servant/slave," we have almost entirely lost its biblical roots in the practice of slavery in the ancient Near East and the Roman Empire. Having largely dropped the conversation with the biblical referent, we have filled the metaphor of the word "servant" with content from other contexts, as for example the use of "servant leadership" among corporate and denominational executives. That too seems to have drained the metaphor of much of its power, especially among younger generations in the church.

While not as dramatic as with the metaphor "servant," the metaphor of the "steward" has taken a similar path — resulting in a diminished capacity to stir energy. Does this mean that "steward" cannot be reclaimed for the task Ron Vallet has proposed? Of course not! However, it does mean that employing "steward" as the guiding metaphor for ministry and ministry education faces a very different set of challenges now, compared to three decades ago when Douglas John Hall dramatically directed our attention to the value of "steward" as a metaphor.

Reforming Ministry Education

Writing a book with the intention of having a significant impact on, indeed "reforming" theological education is a bold undertaking — a challenge few have accepted. Those of us deeply committed to education for ministry welcome all ideas into the ongoing conversation about the emerging shape and character of that education. Thank you, Ron, for your contribution to this discussion.

Education for Christian ministry is changing, changing in response to many of the challenges named by Ron Vallet — leadership for small membership congregations, the emergence of large non-denominational congregations, as well as other fundamental changes in our culture. These changes have profoundly altered the character and role of the Christian community in North American society.

I have neither the time nor the wisdom to explore all of the elements that are impacting and will impact education for ministry. Hence, I'll focus on one element whose impact will only grow in the coming years and decades: *educational technology (ET)*.

Educational technology has changed and will change the educational practice and process in the traditional campus setting as well as provide an alternative educational path to ministry. The value of the changes brought by educational technology has and will be debated both inside the academic community and in the broader church. Be that as it may, the dramatic impact of technology is no longer debatable. A friend teaching a summer math course in a "camp" setting, a "classroom" not equipped with the latest educational technology, told me that he could not buy "blackboard chalk" at any of the national or local office supplies stores!

Educational technology has not only changed the classroom activities; ET has also made it probable that many, perhaps most, students will receive their education for ministry without leaving their home area. To be sure, the localization of ministry education was already under way before the invasion of educational technology. Many denominational seminaries had become regional inter-denominational institutions, enrolling large numbers of local/commuter students. Many women and men had already made the decision that their study preparation for Christian ministry would/could not involve residency on a traditional campus.

The use of educational technology has increased the localization of a student's education for Christian ministry. Ron Vallet rightly talks about the emergence of certificate education for ministerial leadership (programs not designed to lead to an M.Div. or equivalent degree). It seems certain that most, if not all, certificate education will take place on a local/regional basis in the form of short-term intensive courses and distance courses delivered through the various venues provided by educational technology.

While increasing the localization of both degree and certificate programs, ET does enable students to take distance courses at their own denominational seminary without relocating to a campus setting. Hence educational technology may have made preparation for ministry through one's denominational seminary more available at the very time when students were opting to remain at home for their graduate or certificate educational program.

The localization of education for Christian ministry raises a very different set of educational challenges from those we know at the "set apart" (residential) seminary campus. Appropriately, Ron discussed the disconnect between "the world of theological education and the life of the congregation." Such a disconnect, attributed to the "ivory tower" isolation of the seminary, has long plagued the ministry education on the "set apart" seminary campus. Field education may have helped to narrow the gap, but it did not silence the refrain: "Seminary did not train me for ministry in a real congregation."

In the future, many (most?) students will complete their ministry education without leaving their home area, their local congregation. Their educational program may be carried out under the supervision of the regional offices of their denomination and/or the "ministry committee" of their local congregation. Throughout their program, their primary community will be the congregation, not the seminary.

For obvious reasons, this local committee and the student himself/herself may be inclined to focus the educational program, formation, and *Wissenschaft* in a direction appropriate for that particular congregation at that moment in its life cycle.

While localization may close the gap between an academic program and the reality of congregational ministry, it raises other issues. Will the localization of ministry education pose a challenge just the opposite of the residential campus? I expect that to be the case. We will ask: How can we provide the students with significant educational space in and analytical distance from the local setting to allow for thoughtful, creative reflection on Christian faith, practice, and ministry?

Without some educational space, energy that might be used to explore the roots of faith and practice will be needed for the constant but unanticipated interruption of local ministry. Without some analytical distance, the distinctive and pressing character of each community will tempt students to filter all their study through a very local prism. Without time for wonder the energy may not be available

- to explore Christian practices in distant times and places,
- to discuss faith using the unfamiliar vocabulary of theology, and
- to listen to both Testaments in the languages in which they were first written.

Be that as it may, the continuing development of educational technology will provide us new educational opportunities and a new set of pedagogical challenges as we seek to prepare students for ministry now and tomorrow, at home and far away.

I do not intend this discussion of educational technology to diminish the value of Ron Vallet's proposal, e.g., the development of a "ministry integrator." Ron's proposal comes at a time of great change in the preparation of women and men for leadership in the ministry and mission of the church. Perhaps we all have moments when we wish it would all go away and we could return to education as usual. Ron has reminded us, first, that education "as usual" had its own problems — it served some students well and others not so well — and second, that the ancient words from the prophet still ring true:

This is what the Lord said . . .
Behold, I am doing a new thing,

It is growing,
Do you not perceive it? (Isa. 43:19)

I am grateful that Ron Vallet's book *Stewards of the Gospel* keeps us focused on God's new world coming.

*   *

L. E "Ted" Siverns

Acting Dean, St. Andrew's Hall, Vancouver School of Theology,
Vancouver, British Columbia
and
Scholar in Residence, Tainan Theological College and Seminary in Taiwan

"The Known Unknowns and the Unknown Unknowns"

Donald Rumsfeld had a point, or at least would have had a point if he had stopped after the third unknown rather than continue for a total of eleven "knowns" and six "unknowns," enough to leave even careful listeners shaking their heads.[1]

What for us are the knowns? Dr. Ron Vallet, the indefatigable dean of stewardship, has brought together much of the history, theology, and practice of stewardship and seeks to use "stewardship" as the way of expressing the totality of the Christian life. This in itself is not new as there have been many variations on this theme, as Vallet knows better than anyone. As an example I quote two definitions from the past. Stewardship is

... the practice of the Christian religion. It is neither a department of life nor a sphere of activity. It is the Christian conception of life as a whole, manifested in action. (W. H. Greever, 1937).

... what I do after I've said I believe. (Clarence Stoughton, 1949)

We know the word has been around a long time and there are many definitions of "steward" and "stewardship." We also know that as there is a disconnect between definition and practice. A word that is descrip-

1. Former U.S. Secretary of Defense Donald Rumsfeld at a press conference at NATO Headquarters in Brussels in June 2002.

tive of the Christian life is often defined in practice as "money" or "support of the church." We tend to speak of stewardship only when the church coffers are bare or there is a project to be completed. Vallet knows all this, and though a new word might allow us to shirk off the sometimes-dark past of stewardship, he cannot find a better word that will carry the meaning; neither can I.

Is it possible to close the disconnect and redeem the dynamic of "stewardship"? This is an unknown. Is it worth the effort? Is there an alternative? We know that words are constantly shifting meaning, even forgotten and revived again. There is some evidence that the business world, having discovered "steward" and "stewardship," may prove to be an ally in a return to the biblical meaning.

We also know that the church is in the midst of a major storm (a cauldron?) and our ark is being tossed to and fro. The voice of Jesus has not yet told the winds to "Be still!" (Mark 4:39). How can we be the people of counter-culture in our little boat on the wild secular sea?

As long as the issue is definition Vallet is not facing serious criticism, but by focusing on the seminaries as a way of redeeming authentic stewardship he has moved into more difficult territory. Could authentic stewardship taught and lived in our seminaries be the lever that moves the church into a future not yet envisioned? Theological education is venturing into a future of unknown unknowns.

A known about the seminary is the continued tension between providing a practical versus a scholarly education. In the words of one of my former teachers: "A rather persistent conflict obtains between the scholars and the practising clergy. . . . [I]t is likely to be productive of two types of graduate — young scholars who are not at heart inclined to the ministry and young ministers who are not at heart inclined to scholarship."[2] To keep the doors open, seminaries may conclude that they have to cater to the marketplace, which seeks a clear emphasis on the practical. Recently, after several years in pastoral ministry, a former student informed his seminary that though he enjoyed studying the Hebrew language and exegesis, it had proven no benefit and what he really needed was a course on being CEO of a volunteer organization. Isn't this the easy road that leads to knowledge without wisdom? As T. S Eliot asked even before all questions were seemingly answerable on

---

2. Stanley Glen, *The Recovery of the Teaching Ministry* (Philadelphia: Westminster Press, 1960), p. 23.

the Internet: "Where is the wisdom we have lost in knowledge? / Where is the knowledge we have lost in information?"[3]

Teaching often offers questions and potential answers that are not immediately understood, or practical. Robertson Davies remembered that at the age of eight he had to memorize F. W. Bourdillon's poem "The Night Has a Thousand Eyes." The poem meant little to him for fifteen years, and then as a "mind stretcher" the poem reached its target and "exploded." The teaching and example of stewardship may carry with it explosive elements that will result in something new.

Becoming CEO or "professionalizing" the role of minister is a temptation. Though here I rush to say that there is nothing inherently wrong with the term "professional." A professional is one who is prepared to live life for others that justice may be done (law), that health may be experienced (medicine), and that God may be acknowledged and served (religion). In each of these professions practitioners are called to be stewards for the sake of others and, we would add, on behalf of God (see John 3:16; 1 John 3:17, 18; 4:7-12).

It is when the role of steward is forgotten that the French phrase *déformation professionale* may be quoted. In the words of Eugene Peterson, *déformation professionale* refers

> to maladies that we are particularly liable to in the course of pursuing our line of work. Physicians are in constant danger of becoming calloused to suffering, lawyers in danger of cynicism about justice, and those of us who think and talk and read and write god are in danger of having the very words we use about God, separate us from God, the most damning *deformation* of all.[4]

As H. L. Mencken observed: "Every profession is a conspiracy against the laity." It is not my task here to illustrate the disconnect between seminary and congregations, though I readily agree with Vallet that it is real. Indeed, with many seminaries gaining enrolment in spirituality and general religion courses, those seeking preparation for pastoral ministry have become a minority, making a connect more difficult. Add to this the reduced grants from denominations and other sources, the growing deficits, and the competition for survival.

3. T. S. Eliot, *Choruses from "The Rock."*
4. Eugene H. Peterson, "The Seminary as a Place of Spiritual Formation," Fuller Theological Seminary, *Theology, News and Notes,* October 1993.

I underline a point made by Vallet that in New Testament steward-ship we are called not only to be stewards of God (if that were possible), but stewards one to another (1 Peter 4:10). Preaching and practice that emphasizes being stewards of God, but fails to connect with being God's stewards for the sake of the world, has missed the mark.

Ron Vallet has chosen the parables to emphasize the role of the biblical steward. The parables are always fresh and challenging with in-terpretation now shifting to what is not said but implied in the realities of first-century poverty and the role of Rome and Temple. That is, the concern is not only with me as steward, but with an invitation to con-sider what that means in a world where Rome demanded more taxes and the Temple insisted on greater financial support for its own pur-poses. In the meantime, the common people were fodder for the wealthy.

The meaning and significance of "steward" in the epistles is also challenging with such phrases as "stewards of God's mysteries" (1 Cor. 4:1-2), "good stewards of the manifold grace of God" (1 Peter 4:10), "the stewardship of God's grace which I was given for you" (words attrib-uted to Paul in Eph. 3:2), and a bishop is to be "God's steward" (Titus 1:7).

As I write this, I am preparing to leave for Tainan Theological Col-lege and Seminary in Taiwan for a five-month appointment as Scholar in Residence. I remind myself that I know too little of stewardship and seminary outside of North America. Would you call this one of the known unknowns? I wonder how it is that a mere 3 percent of the pop-ulation of Taiwan is Christian, but that same 3 percent has an impact far greater than its number suggests. Why does this bit of "salt" so in-fluence Taiwan's education, health care, politics, social services, and re-ligions? Though not the whole answer, I might hear echoes of Dr. Vallet's insistence that stewardship is a focus of heart, mind, and hands. It is not a program, but it is relational and it is that which per-vades the curriculum.

Vallet has concluded that the teaching of stewardship for an hour or two or as a one-term subject is counter-productive. I wonder if in-stead of calling such classes "stewardship," we might better remove the ambiguity and confusion and simply call them "Funding for the Church 101." Let "stewardship" be integral to the entire curriculum and let it name our reasonable service.

In the seminary as in the church, we teach what we do even more than what we say. I've heard the lament of several students that when they submitted the required budget in applying for bursaries, "church contribution" was struck off. The bursar's office has concluded that financial support of the church is not a legitimate expense and therefore not part of a student's budget.

There is much more that could be said under both the title "knowns" and "unknowns," but these few words simply illustrate the challenging nature of this book.

CHAPTER 10

Final Reflections

In this final chapter, I offer reflections on the contributions in Chapter 9. I am deeply appreciative to Daniel Aleshire, David L. Bartlett, Bruce C. Birch, Terry Parsons, Eugene F. Roop, and L. E. "Ted" Siverns.

Upon reading their responses, I am glad to note that there is much common ground among their insights and the thoughts I have put forth in this book. Using a question-and-response format (using excerpts from their contributions), I will point out some of this common ground.

Question: What is the scope of the concepts of steward and stewardship?

BRUCE C. BIRCH: I was struck by the comprehensiveness of the role of steward. All that we are, all that we have, all that we do is by virtue of the gifts of God entrusted to our care and use. I could never think of stewardship in such a narrow way again.

L. E. "TED" SIVERNS: We know the words have been around a long time and there are many definitions of "steward" and "stewardship." We also know that as there is a disconnect between definition and practice. A word that is descriptive of the Christian life is often defined in practice as "money" or "support of the church." We tend to speak of stewardship only when the church coffers are bare or there is a project to be completed. Vallet knows all this, and though a new word might allow us to shirk off the sometimes-dark past of stewardship, he cannot find a better word that will carry the meaning; neither can I.

SIVERNS: As long as the issue is definition, Vallet is not facing serious criticism, but by focusing on the seminaries as a way of redeeming authentic stewardship he has moved into more difficult territory. Could authentic stewardship taught and lived in our seminaries be the lever that moves the church into a future not yet envisioned?

SIVERNS: The teaching and example of stewardship may carry with it explosive elements that will result in something new.

DAVID L. BARTLETT: I have to confess my skepticism that any single paradigm — even one as powerful as the paradigm of stewardship — will be able to provide an organizing metaphor that will be equally acceptable for the range of theological seminaries. . . . Rather, the metaphor of stewardship gives us an image both deep and broad that can enable us to engage with one another around a common theme and indeed a common vision. It will not be the only theme or the only vision for our seminaries, but it will be a theme and vision that keeps us talking with each other and joining with each other as stewards of the mysteries of God.

BARTLETT: Ronald Vallet moves us far beyond the old picture of stewardship as a once-a-year chore the churches take on to make sure they can meet their budget. Stewardship becomes a lens through which we are enabled to view a whole range of Christian beliefs and practices more clearly. Most powerfully, he reminds us that the church does not practice stewardship for its own sake but for the sake of the "cauldron" of the world, which is, after all, God's world.

EUGENE F. ROOP: Use of the metaphor "steward" in the church encouraged congregations to think and talk in new ways about Christian discipleship. The biblical roots of this metaphor enabled Christians to recognize ourselves as commissioned and trusted by God. The metaphor reminded believers not only of the trust God placed in us but also of the responsibility and accountability that come with divine trust. The metaphor of the "steward" nourished a generation eager to move beyond clergy-centered congregational life to fully embrace the ministry of all believers.

ROOP: The word "steward" has found widespread use in American culture, especially in connection with the current emphasis on the environment, the animate and inanimate world in which we live. In this cultural context, "stewardship" has been disconnected from its biblical roots and become a code word naming our accountability and responsibility for our natural environment.

ROOP: I recognize that, even as we appropriated "steward" from the biblical tradition and transformed it into a metaphor, the Christian community disconnected "steward" from its biblical roots and culture. A degree of disconnect from the originating context is inherent in the creation of any metaphor. . . . [E]mploying "steward" as the guiding metaphor for ministry and ministry education faces a very different set of challenges now, compared to three decades ago when Douglas John Hall dramatically directed our attention to the value of "steward" as a metaphor.

RONALD VALLET: I appreciate the common ground that the words "steward" and "stewardship" reach far beyond the traditional understanding in the church that the words refer almost exclusively to fundraising and meeting budgets.

Question: What is the gospel?

BARTLETT: The divisions among our churches (and our seminaries) are in part divisions about which aspect of the gospel we take to be central. The hope for unity among our churches and our seminaries lies in the claim Ronald Vallet rightly makes in this book [Chapter 3]. The gospel is first of all about God and only secondly about us. And the gospel is first of all about the God whose kingdom, power, glory, and humility are all known in Jesus Christ.

VALLET: It is my hope and prayer that a common understanding by the church of "what the gospel is" will draw the church closer to God and the fulfillment of God's mission in the world.

Question: What are some of the principles of biblical interpretation?

BARTLETT: All of us are informed and helped by the wise way in which the author presents the issues of scriptural authority. . . . [O]ur understanding of the text changes as we change, as we bring to the conversation new insights about science, for instance, or about the human cost of slavery. What Christians also want to insist, however, is that the Bible itself is the senior partner in that conversation. It is not simply that our ideas change so we reinvent the text; it is rather that in the light of our own changing selves we understand the text's own message in new and different ways.

BARTLETT: [T]he excellent suggestions for biblical interpretation in [Chapter 4] might be augmented by remembering that biblical interpretation is always a matter of conversation among the interpreters themselves. The way we keep our interpretations from being entirely self-serving is to talk about the texts with other selves who can call us to account.

BARTLETT: In many ways the present book is a conversation starter. It will be most effective if Christians talk about the Bible with each other in the light of these new insights. Given the fact that the book is a conversation starter, it will not be surprising if different congregations, denominations, and seminaries learn from the book different lessons and apply the book in a variety of ways.

VALLET: Thank you, David, for the important reminder that biblical interpretation is "always a matter of conversation among the interpreters themselves."

Question: What are the disconnects among schools of theological education, denominations, and congregations?

SIVERNS: A known about the seminary is the continued tension between providing a practical versus a scholarly education.

SIVERNS: It is not my task here to illustrate the disconnect between seminary and congregations, though I readily agree with Vallet that it is real. Is it possible to close the disconnect and redeem the dynamic of "stewardship"? This is an unknown. Is it worth the effort? Is there an alternative? We know that words are constantly shifting meaning, even forgotten and revived again. There is some evidence that the business world, having discovered "steward" and "stewardship," may prove to be an ally in a return to the biblical meaning.

BARTLETT: This book caused me to rethink my understanding of stewardship biblically, theologically, and practically. It persuaded me that the metaphor of the steward provides an invaluable picture for thinking of the church's ministries and of the ways in which seminaries and divinity schools can help prepare faithful stewards.

VALLET: There is general consensus that the disconnects are real.

Question: What change in theological education is being sought in this book?

DANIEL ALESHIRE: The change for which the book is arguing is a systemic change, not just a change in theological schools. If the church does not think that it is a community of stewards of the gospel, then there is little chance that a change in the schools would affect the church. The ecological system includes the broader church, not just schools and the particular ecclesial communities to which they relate. . . . *Stewards of the Gospel* is correct in understanding that multiple parts of an ecological system must be changed to effect significant change in any one of those parts.

ALESHIRE: *Stewards of the Gospel* calls for reform in theological education in the context of calling for a commensurate reform in the church. That is unique among the many calls for the reform of theological education.

ALESHIRE: It is not so much a call to rethink what stewardship has come to mean as it is a call to find the theological resource that the church needs in order to be a home for the reign of God that claims the cross and the world.

VALLET: The change needed is, indeed, systemic and will require change in the broader church — individuals, congregations, denominations, and schools of theological education.

Question: How difficult is it to rethink the theological curriculum?

ALESHIRE: What is perhaps most important to note about the core curriculum of theological study is its stability over time. . . . A call to rethink theological curriculum needs to understand that that space is crowded and that new ideas need to find homes in existing areas, to the extent possible. Fortunately, *Stewards of the Gospel* does just that.

BIRCH: All of this suggests that even with a school and faculty culture congenial to the concept of "steward," the entrenched patterns by which we organize theological education will be very difficult to change.

ALESHIRE: The argument forwarded in this book does not require a new course or a new professor; rather, it provides a proposal for the core metaphor of this theological understanding and wisdom — "Stewards of the Gospel."

ALESHIRE: The theological curriculum can accommodate the proposal forwarded by this book without adding courses and without a focus on congregational fund-raising and finance. This enhances the potential of the proposal being implemented.

VALLET: I agree that the stability and entrenched patterns of the core curriculum will make it difficult to rethink theological curriculum. Yet I still feel hope.

Question: Can theological education be centered on a singular theme?

ALESHIRE: *Stewards of the Gospel* wants change in a fundamental metaphor for understanding Christian life and ministry. Seminaries will be open to the theological idea of this new metaphor, but it will be in a context with other metaphors. They will be more likely to add it as another metaphor of study than to replace existing metaphors. The reform that is proposed will require fundamental change in the church's self-understanding and work, and that may prove more difficult than adding a new theological metaphor to the crowded theological curriculum.

BIRCH: [I am] reluctant to center theological education on a singular theme. Nevertheless, the concept of the steward is amazingly comprehensive. It appears in a broad range of materials, but I think what impresses me more is that without appearing explicitly as a term (in any of its iterations) the role of steward usefully illumines so many other biblical concepts. It is an exceptionally resilient concept for relating divine and human agency in the effort to bring wholeness to a broken world. As an example, consider the concept of covenant community. I have found it very helpful to ask students and church people to think of covenant as a community of stewards.

BIRCH: [A]s a biblical scholar, I have come to regard the concept of the steward as one of my main integrating lenses in seeing the larger whole of biblical theology.

BIRCH: If the concept of steward is to become an integrating center in theological education, I believe we must recognize that above all else we are called to be stewards of the gospel — the good news that God is at work reconciling the world through Jesus Christ. All other arenas of our stewarding work are derivative from this central task of the steward.

BIRCH: What may focus today on a reclaiming of the steward concept may be a part of a larger effort to reclaim a particularistic theological language embedded in our texts and traditions, unapologetic in its confessional commitments, diverse in its voices and methods, and open to a wide range of dialogues in the wider world.

SIVERNS: Vallet has concluded that the teaching of stewardship for an hour or two or as a one-term subject is counter-productive. I wonder if instead of calling such classes "stewardship," we might better remove the ambiguity and confusion and simply call them "Funding for the Church 101." Let "stewardship" be integral to the entire curriculum and let it name our reasonable service.

VALLET: While not all agree that a single metaphor can be used to integrate the disconnect, there is general agreement that viewing the life of the church through a lens such as stewardship can be an integrating factor.

Question: How is the culture of the church affected (infected) by the culture of the surrounding society?

BIRCH: Let theology be theology. . . . [T]heology too often adapts its agenda to an effort to find acceptability to the wider culture in terms defined by that culture. . . . [This] is true for the life of the church. In spite of many years during which I have observed the dedicated work of stewardship leaders to broaden the scope and meaning of the concept of steward, much of the stewardship culture in the church has stayed focused on meeting budgets and raising money.

VALLET: There is a consensus that the church is called by God to be countercultural.

Question: How does ministry relate to stewardship?

BIRCH: Ministry is an enterprise in which men and women are entrusted by God — for God's Word, for God's people, for the mission of the church in the world. Ministry itself becomes an issue of stewardship.

TERRY PARSONS: Have you ever heard a sermon on Jacob's promise? Why do we omit that? "Why did he do it?" is a question that invites us not just to a new understanding of tithing but to a practical discussion of stewardship, what it is, how it places us in relationship with God, and how behaviors shape that relationship. The great benefit of a stewardship perspective on theological education is that it takes it from intellectual exercise into practical behavior. It calls us to the moment Jacob seems to have had in which he looked at what God had promised and asked himself how he should respond. Through the Gospels we can know of God's greatest gift. We know of its capacity to transform individual lives and the world. We become stewards when we ask ourselves, what do we do with what we know?

VALLET: Ministry is indeed an issue of stewardship. Terry concluded that we become stewards when we ask ourselves, what do we do with what we know? This is indeed an important step — necessary, but not sufficient. Eventually we are called to drink of the waters of the living God. If being a steward is understood as I wrote in Chapter 2 — "drinking deeply from the waters of the living God by moving from the stagnating waterholes of 'more' to the living water of the gospel of Jesus Christ, and inviting others to do the same" — then it is intertwined with Christian ministry, and the form that Christian ministry takes is itself an issue of stewardship. It becomes more of a verb than a noun.

Question: What are the interrelationships between having an integrating concept in theological education and an interdisciplinary approach?

BIRCH: An integrating concept in theological education necessarily implies an interdisciplinary approach to curriculum and learning.

VALLET: The disciplines of theological education will need to be less compartmental and more permeable.

Question: What strategies might be employed?

ROOP: Writing a book with the intention of having a significant impact on, indeed "reforming" theological education is a bold undertaking

— a challenge few have accepted. Those of us deeply committed to education for ministry welcome all ideas into the ongoing conversation about the emerging shape and character of that education. Thank you, Ron, for your contribution to this discussion.

ROOP: Education for Christian ministry is changing, changing in response to many of the challenges named by Ron Vallet — leadership for small membership congregations, the emergence of large non-denominational congregations, as well as other fundamental changes in our culture. These changes have profoundly altered the character and role of the Christian community in North American society.

ROOP: The use of educational technology (ET) has increased the localization of a student's education for Christian ministry. Ron Vallet rightly talks about the emergence of certificate education for ministerial leadership (programs not designed to lead to an M.Div. or equivalent degree). It seems certain that most, if not all, certificate education will take place on a local/regional basis in the form of short-term intensive courses and distance courses delivered through the various venues provided by educational technology.

ROOP: While increasing the localization of both degree and certificate programs, ET does enable students to take distance courses at their own denominational seminary without relocating to a campus setting. Hence educational technology may have made preparation for ministry through one's denominational seminary more available at the very time when students were opting to remain at home for their graduate or certificate educational program.

ROOP: The localization of education for Christian ministry raises a very different set of educational challenges from those we know at the "set apart" (residential) seminary campus. Appropriately, Ron discussed the disconnect between "the world of theological education and the life of the congregation." Such a disconnect, attributed to the "ivory tower" isolation of the seminary, has long plagued the ministry education on the "set apart" seminary campus. Field education may have helped narrow the gap, but it did not silence the refrain: "Seminary did not train me for ministry in a real congregation."

ROOP: While localization may close the gap between an academic program and the reality of congregational ministry, it raises other issues. Will the "localization" of ministry education pose a challenge just the opposite of the residential campus? I expect that to be the case. We will ask: How can we provide the students significant educational space in and analytical distance from the local setting to allow for thoughtful, creative reflection on Christian faith, practice, and ministry?

Roop: I do not intend this discussion of educational technology to diminish the value of Ron Vallet's proposal, e.g., the development of a "ministry integrator." Ron's proposal comes at a time of great change in the preparation of women and men for leadership in the ministry and mission of the church. Perhaps we all have moments when we wish it would all go away and we could return to education as usual. Ron has reminded us, first, that education "as usual" had its own problems — it served some students well and others not so well — and second, that the ancient words from the prophet still ring true:

This is what the Lord said . . .
Behold, I am doing a new thing,
It is growing,
Do you not perceive it? (Isa. 43:19)

Birch: Since my own broadened concept was a result of being challenged by stewardship leaders to relate my work to their own, an issue of strategy may suggest itself. Before redoing theological curriculum there may need to be a strategy of challenge to the various arenas of theological scholarship to consider the role of steward. Perhaps what I am suggesting is a strategy to convert more faculty to the usefulness of the steward image in their own work.

Vallet: I agree with Bruce on the strategy that might be employed. The question that I struggle with is: How and by whom? My hope is that the concept of "ministry integrator" will receive serious attention and exploration.

Question: Are the hopes for reform and change realistic?

Aleshire: Reform is difficult in both the church and the theological school. It is not impossible, and the present historical moment in mainline Protestantism may be calling enough assumptions into question that destabilized institutions will be ready to consider changes that they may not have considered decades ago. The challenge, I think, will be the pull toward institutional and organizational survival on the one hand and the pull toward theological integrity and faithfulness on the other. *Stewards of the Gospel* offers a valuable image for the church and the theological school.

BIRCH: Many voices in theological education have been urging and chronicling such changes. It is a rejection of *Wissenschaft* as a model adequate in itself, and it is a movement in the direction of *paideia*. Yet, I think a new model may be struggling to be born. It is informed more by the church and its needs than by the university, but it remains informed by the knowledge gained in academic disciplines.

BIRCH: In the emergence of a new model that moves in this direction I believe that the concept of steward could play an important centering role.

VALLET: I pray that a new model *is* struggling to be born. Again, my thanks to all who have helped in the development of this book with its hopes, dreams, and prayers.

Final Words from the Author

Years ago, when I started working on this project, I envisioned the beginning of a revolution in theological education that might reach to the mid-point of the twenty-first century. Now I better understand that the transformation should involve all parts of the church and could extend even further into the twenty-first century.

Old Testament stories — especially those that describe God's covenant making — make it clear that God's covenants and workings are neither quickly made nor quickly ended. We in North America, by contrast, are conditioned to expect rapid conclusions and instant gratification. Films and television programs seldom teach the lessons of patience and perseverance. Business planning often reaches only as far as the bottom line of the next quarter.

A "modern" example of long-range thinking was described by Larry Rasmussen, recounting a story told by Gregory Bateson. When the oak beams (forty feet long and two feet thick) in the main hall at New College of Oxford University suffered from dry rot, the college administrator was concerned about how he would be able to locate oak beams of that size to replace the oak beams that had been used when the building was built in the 1600s. After a number of inquiries, he finally consulted the college forester. The forester said to the administrator, "We've been wondering when you would ask the question. When the present building was constructed three hundred fifty years ago, the architects specified that a grove of trees be planted and maintained to replace the beams in the ceiling when they suffered from dry rot."[1]

Only in 2009 did I become aware of Kosuke Koyama, an ecumenical theologian — one who also took a long view. Koyama had died earlier that year at age 79. Once, in discussing death, Koyama recalled the story of Jesus washing the feet of his disciples. He said Jesus would be with others the same way: "Looking into our eyes and heart, Jesus will say: 'You've had a difficult journey. You must be tired, and dirty. Let me wash your feet. The banquet's ready.'"

As I close this book, the words of Paul in 1 Corinthians come to mind:

> What, after all, is Apollos? And what is Paul? I planted the seed; Apollos watered it. What's important is that God made it grow. It's not important who plants nor who waters, but only God, who makes things grow. The one who plants and the one who waters have one purpose, for we are both God's workers. (3:5a, 6-8a, 9a, paraphrased)

Am I helping to plant a seed, or am I one who is watering a seed already planted? I do not know, nor does it matter. In the deepest sense, the planter and the waterer are one. It is the working of God's Holy Spirit that will determine the outcome. My days are pledged to be a steward of the gospel of Jesus Christ and to be part of a community of stewards. The gospel *is* the treasure held in earthen vessels.

1. Larry Rasmussen, *Earth Community Earth Ethics* (Maryknoll, NY: Orbis Books, 1996), p. 332.

267

Appendix

2007-08 Conference Participants

The six conferences held from October 2007 to February 2008 included fifty-one participants (thirty-five men and sixteen women), whose names are listed here. I am humbled and deeply impressed both by the number of participants in the conferences and by the quality of their contributions. It is amazing to me that so many agreed to read the manuscript prior to the conference in which they participated and to engage actively in a full-day conference.

A breakdown of the participants by categories is as follows. The total is greater than fifty-one because some persons carried more than one role.

Theological Educators	28
Pastors	18
Denominational Executives	7
TE21 Board Members	5
Theological Consortium	5

The last category refers to the executive director and two other staff members of the Association of Theological Schools, the executive director of the Washington Theological Consortium, and the executive director of The Churches' Council on Theological Education in Canada.

Participants in the Six *Stewards of the Gospel* Conferences

Palmer Theological Seminary
Wynnewood, Pennsylvania
October 16, 2007

Donald Brash, Associate Professor of Historical Theology, Palmer Theological Seminary, Wynnewood, Pennsylvania

Elizabeth Congdon-Martin, Director of Supervised Ministries, Palmer Theological Seminary, Wynnewood, Pennsylvania

Elouise Renich Fraser, Vice President and Dean, Palmer Theological Seminary, Wynnewood, Pennsylvania

George Hancock-Stefan, Associate Professor of Church History, Palmer Theological Seminary, Wynnewood, Pennsylvania

Wallace Smith, President, Palmer Theological Seminary, Wynnewood, Pennsylvania

Leo Thorne, Associate General Secretary for Mission Resource Development, American Baptist Churches in the USA, Valley Forge, Pennsylvania

Al Tizon, Assistant Professor of Evangelism and Holistic Ministry, Palmer Theological Seminary, Wynnewood, Pennsylvania

Ronald E. Vallet, President, Theological Education 21, Manlius, New York

Rose Marie Vallet, Secretary/Treasurer, Theological Education 21, Manlius, New York

Wesley Theological Seminary
Washington, D.C.
November 2, 2007

William O. Avery, Professor of Field Education, the Arthur L. Larson Professor of Stewardship and Parish Ministry, and Director of Internship, Lutheran Theological Seminary at Gettysburg, Gettysburg, Pennsylvania

Bruce C. Birch, Dean and Woodrow W. and Mildred B. Miller Professor of Biblical Theology, Wesley Theological Seminary, Washington, D.C.; Board Member of Theological Education 21

William A. Carlsen, Executive Minister, American Baptist Churches of New York State; Board Member of Theological Education 21

John W. Crossin, Executive Director, Washington Theological Consortium, Washington, D.C.

Stephen D. Foulk, Attorney; Member of First Baptist Church, Endicott, New York; Board Member of Theological Education 21

Scott Thomas Kisker, James Cecil Logan Associate Professor of Evangelism and Wesley Studies, Wesley Theological Seminary, Washington, D.C.

David McAllister-Wilson, President, Wesley Theological Seminary, Washington, D.C.

Ronald E. Vallet, President, Theological Education 21, Manlius, New York

Rose Marie Vallet, Secretary/Treasurer, Theological Education 21, Manlius, New York

First Baptist Church, Manlius, New York
(for Pastors)
November 8, 2007

Paul Bailey, Pastor, Camillus Baptist Church, Camillus, New York

Larry Bell, Pastor, United Church, Auburn, New York

Mark Caruana, Pastor, Tabernacle Baptist Church, Utica, New York

John Ferrie, Pastor, Good Shepherd Lutheran Church, Fayetteville, New York

Mark Frazier, Pastor, St. David's Episcopal Church, DeWitt, New York

David Movsovich, Pastor, Fay Road Baptist Church, Syracuse, New York

Leon Oaks-Lee, Pastor, First Baptist Church, Manlius, New York

Janice Robinson, Pastor, First Baptist Church, Geneva, New York

Mary Ann Short, Interim Pastor, First Baptist Church, Wolcott, New York

Doug Taylor-Weiss, Pastor, Sts. Peter and John Episcopal Church, Auburn, New York

Ronald E. Vallet, President, Theological Education 21, Manlius, New York

Rose Marie Vallet, Secretary/Treasurer, Theological Education 21, Manlius, New York

Keith Wimmersberger, Pastor, Tully United Community Church, Tully, New York

Appendix

Emmanuel College, Toronto, Ontario, Canada
November 19, 2007

Betsy Anderson, Coordinator for Continuing Education Programmes, Emmanuel College. Toronto

David A. Bruce, Minister, Leaside United Church, Toronto, and Chairperson, Don Valley Presbytery, Toronto

Linda Butler, Minister, Richmond Hill United Church and Adjunct Faculty, Pastoral Theology, Emmanuel College, Toronto

Sheila Campbell, Recent graduate, M.Div. Programme, Emmanuel College, Toronto

Ron Ewart, Associate Executive Director, Toronto United Church Council, Toronto

Robert Faris, Executive Director, The Churches' Council on Theological Education in Canada, Toronto

Barb Fullerton, Program Coordinator, Stewardship Development (Congregational, Educational, & Community Ministries Unit), The United Church of Canada, Toronto

Andrew Irvine, Coordinator of Theological Field Education and Director of D.Min. Program, Knox College, Toronto

Cathy MacDonald, Minister, Claremont United Church, Claremont, Ontario, and Member, Stewardship Studies Group, The United Church of Canada

Ted Reeve, Program Coordinator, Leadership and Theological Education (Congregational, Educational, & Community Ministries Unit), The United Church of Canada, Toronto

Brenda Simpson, Director, Francis Sandy Theological Centre, Paris, Ontario (Native Ministries)

Ronald E. Vallet, President, Theological Education 21, Manlius, New York

Rose Marie Vallet, Secretary/Treasurer, Theological Education 21, Manlius, New York

Susanne Vanderlugt, Minister, Humbercrest United Church, Toronto

Peter Wyatt, Principal, Emmanuel College, Toronto

Stewards of the Gospel

Columbia Theological Seminary
Decatur, Georgia
January 23, 2008

Margaret Aymer, Assistant Professor of New Testament, The Interdenominational Theological Center, Atlanta, Georgia

David L. Bartlett, Professor of New Testament, Columbia Theological Seminary

Laura S. Mendenhall, President, Columbia Theological Seminary

Cam Murchison, Dean of Faculty, Executive Vice President, and Professor of Ministry, Columbia Theological Seminary

Terry Parsons, Stewardship Officer, Congregational Development, The Episcopal Church; Adjunct Professor of Pastoral Theology, The General Theological Seminary, New York City

Charles E. Raynal, Director of Advanced Studies and Associate Professor of Theology, Columbia Theological Seminary

David Rensberger, Professor of New Testament, The Interdenominational Theological Center, Atlanta

Stanley P. Saunders, Associate Professor of New Testament, Columbia Theological Seminary

Ronald E. Vallet, President, Theological Education 21, Manlius, New York

Rose Marie Vallet, Secretary/Treasurer, Theological Education 21, Manlius, New York

Association of Theological Schools in the United States and Canada (Staff)
Pittsburgh, Pennsylvania
February 26, 2008

Daniel O. Aleshire, Executive Director, Association of Theological Schools, Pittsburgh, Pennsylvania

Stephen R. Graham, Director of Faculty Development and Initiatives in Theological Education, Association of Theological Schools, Pittsburgh, Pennsylvania

Carol E. Lytch, Assistant Executive Director, Association of Theological Schools, Pittsburgh, Pennsylvania

Ronald E. Vallet, President, Theological Education 21, Manlius, N.Y.

Rose Marie Vallet, Secretary/Treasurer, Theological Education 21, Manlius, N.Y.

Selected Bibliography

Books

Aleshire, Daniel O. *Earthen Vessels: Hopeful Reflections of the Work and Future of Theological Schools.* Grand Rapids: Eerdmans, 2008.

Brackney, William H. *Christian Voluntarism: Theology and Praxis.* Grand Rapids: Eerdmans, 1998.

Branch, Taylor. *Parting the Waters: America in the King Years, 1954-63.* New York: Simon & Schuster Paperbacks, 1988.

Brownson, James V., Inagrace T. Dietterich, Barry A. Harvey, and Charles C. West. *StormFront: The Good News of God.* Grand Rapids: Eerdmans, 2003.

Brueggemann, Walter. *Theology of the Old Testament: Testimony, Dispute, Advocacy.* Minneapolis: Fortress Press, 1997.

————. *Using God's Resources Wisely: Isaiah and Urban Possibilities.* Louisville: Westminster/John Knox Press, 1993.

Culpepper, R. Alan. *Luke-John.* The New Interpreter's Bible, volume 9. Nashville: Abingdon Press, 1995.

Daniels, Harold M. *To God Alone Be Glory.* Louisville: Geneva Press, 2003.

Douglas, Mark. *Confessing Christ in the 21st Century.* Boulder: Rowman & Littlefield, 2005.

Guder, Darrell L. *The Continuing Conversion of the Church.* Grand Rapids: Eerdmans, 2000.

Hall, Douglas John. *The Steward: A Biblical Symbol Come of Age.* New York: Friendship Press for Commission on Stewardship, NCCC, 1982.

Herzog, William R., II. *Parables as Subversive Speech: Jesus as Pedagogue of the Oppressed.* Louisville: Westminster/John Knox Press, 1994.

Hilton, James. *Good-bye, Mr. Chips.* Little Brown, 1934, 1962.

Hudnut-Beumler, James. *In Pursuit of the Almighty's Dollar: A History of Money and American Protestantism.* Chapel Hill: University of North Carolina Press, 2007.

J.D., a Minister of the Gospel. *The Glorious Progress of the Gospel Amongst the Indians in New England.* London: Edward Winslow, 1649.

Kelsey, David H. *Between Athens and Berlin: The Theological Education Debate.* Grand Rapids: Eerdmans, 1993.

————. *To Understand God Truly: What's Theological about a Theological School.* Louisville: Westminster/John Knox Press, 1992.

Martin, Robert M. *There are Two Errors In The The Title Of This Book: a source book of philosophical puzzles, problems, and paradoxes.* Peterborough, Ont.: Broadview Press, 1992.

Myers, Ched. *The Biblical Vision of Sabbath Economics.* Washington, DC: The Church of the Saviour, 2001.

Niebuhr, H. Richard. *Christ and Culture.* San Francisco: HarperSanFrancisco, 2001.

Noll, Mark A. *The Civil War as a Theological Crisis.* Chapel Hill: University of North Carolina Press, 2006.

Oden, Thomas C., ed. *Parables of Kierkegaard.* Princeton: Princeton University Press, 1978.

Steinbeck, John. *The Grapes of Wrath.* New York: Viking Press, 1939.

Swartley, William M. *Slavery, Sabbath, War, and Women.* Scottsdale, PA: Herald Press, 1983.

Tarnas, Richard. *The Passion of the Western Mind: Understanding the Ideas That Have Shaped Our World View.* New York: Ballantine Books, 1991.

Vallet, Ronald E. *Congregations at the Crossroads: Remembering to Be Households of God.* Grand Rapids: Eerdmans, 1998.

————. *The Steward Living in Covenant: A New Perspective on Old Testament Stories.* Grand Rapids: Eerdmans, 2001.

Vallet, Ronald E., and Charles E. Zech. *The Mainline Church's Funding Crisis.* Grand Rapids: Eerdmans, and Manlius, NY: REV/Rose Publishing, 1995.

Westerhoff, John. *Building God's People in a Materialistic Society.* New York: Seabury Press, 1983.

Wood, Charles M. *Vision and Discernment.* Atlanta: Scholars Press, 1985.

World Council of Churches. *Mission and Evangelism: An Ecumenical Affirmation,* ¶25. Geneva: WCC, 1982.

Wuthnow, Robert. *Acts of Compassion: Caring for Others and Helping Ourselves.* Princeton: Princeton University Press, 1991.

————. *Christianity in the Twenty-first Century.* New York: Oxford University Press, 1993.

————. *The Crisis in the Churches: Spiritual Malaise, Fiscal Woe.* New York: Oxford University Press, 1997.

Journal Articles and Chapters in Books

"Abolish Torture Now." *Christian Century,* 27 June 2006, pp. 14-15.

Alder, Jerry. "Evolution of a Scientist." *Newsweek,* 28 November 2005, pp. 49-58.

Alfano, Vincent. Sermon, "The Mob Will Always Be There." Preached 25 January 1998, Cosburn United Church, Cosburn, Ontario.

Alter, Jonathan. "Monkey See, Monkey Do." *Newsweek,* 15 August 2005, p. 27.

Begley, Sharon. "We Fought Cancer . . ." *Newsweek,* 15 September 2008, pp. 42-66.

Beinart, Peter. "Let Your Enemies Crumble." *Time,* 5 June 2006, p. 80.

Bell, Daniel M., Jr. "In War and in Peace." *Christian Century,* 6 September 2005, p. 26.

Bell, John. "Sing a New Song." *Christian Century,* 25 July 2006, p. 20.

Bendis, Debra. "Moving Mountains in Haiti: Dokte Paul." *Christian Century,* 2 November 2004, p. 30.

Birch, Bruce C., and M. Douglas Meeks. "Stewardship and Theological Education: A Dialogue." *Journal of Stewardship* 44 (1992): 44-49.

Boorstein, Michelle (of *The Washington Post*). "More in U.S. Losing Religion." *The Post-Standard,* Syracuse, N.Y., 9 March 2009, p. A-1.

Branson, Mark Lau. "Escaping a False Gospel: On Changing Stories." *Theology, News and Notes,* Spring 2004, pp. 16-19.

"Briars in the Cottonpatch: The Story of Koinonia Farm." DVDL, A Cottonpatch Production. (See also the interview with Millard Fuller in the December 1995 issue of *Christian Ethics Today,* found on the website www.christianethics today.com/Issue/004/An%20Interview%20With%20Millard%20Fuller_004 _6_.htm.)

Brueggemann, Walter. "Follow Your Thirst." *Journal of Stewardship* 49 (1997): 41-48.

———. "From Anxiety and Greed to Milk and Honey." *Sojourners,* February 2009.

———. "Life-or-Death, De-privileged Communication." *Journal for Preachers,* Lent 1998, p. 22.

———. "Living with the Elusive God: Counterscript." *Christian Century,* 29 November 2005, pp. 22-28.

———. "A Personal Reflection: Biblical Authority." *Christian Century,* 3-10 January 2001, pp. 14-20.

Buchanan, John M. "Gift Wrapped." *Christian Century,* 12 December 2006, p. 3.

———. "A Good Cry." *Christian Century,* 27 December 2005, p. 3.

———. "Hymn to Creation." *Christian Century,* 30 November 2004, p. 3.

Busch, Richard A. "A Strange Silence." *The Christian Century,* 22-29 March 1995, p. 316.

Butts, Calvin O., III. "A New Heaven and a New Earth." The Ministers and Missionaries Benefit Board of American Baptist Churches, 1999.

Byassee, Jason. "Documenting the Church's Failure: Theologians and Nazis." *Christian Century*, 30 May 2006.

Carter, Jimmy. Nobel Lecture, Oslo, 10 December 2002. The Nobel Foundation, 2002.

"Century Marks." *Christian Century*, 24 April–1 May 2002, p. 6.

"Century Marks." *Christian Century*, 28 November 2006, p. 6.

Chaves, Mark. "Analyzing the Trend Toward Larger Churches: Supersized." *Christian Century*, 28 November 2006, pp. 20-25.

Copenhaver, Martin B. "Formed and Reformed." *Christian Century*, 14 October 1998, p. 937.

Cose, Ellis. "Transition: Rosa Parks, 1913-2005: A Legend's Soul Is Rested." *Newsweek*, 7 November 2005, p. 53.

"Cosmic Design." *Christian Century*, 6 September 2005, p. 5.

Craddock, Fred B. "What We Do Not Know." *Journal for Preachers*, Advent 1998, p. 35.

Dart, John. "Up Against Caesar." *Christian Century*, 8 February 2005, pp. 20-24.

Davis, Ronald L. F. "Creating Jim Crow: In-Depth Essay." Internet Site: www.jimcrowhistory.org/history/creating2.htm.

Dickey, Christopher, and Melinda Henneberger. "The Vision of Benedict XVI." *Newsweek*, 2 May 2005, p. 43.

"Disparity Growing Between People Who Have and Those Who Don't." *The [Syracuse, N.Y.] Post-Standard*, 17 August 2004, p. A-3.

Easterbrook, Gregg. "The Real Truth about Money." *Time*, 17 January 2005, pp. A32-A34.

Gerlach, David. "How AIDS Changed America." *Newsweek*, 15 May 2006, pp. 36-41.

Gibbs, Nancy. "Stem Cells: The Hope and the Hype." *Time*, 7 August 2006, pp. 40-46.

Guelich, Robert A. "What Is the Gospel?" *Theology, News and Notes*, Spring 2004, pp. 4-7.

Hadaway, C. Kirk, and Penny Long Marler. "Did You Really Go to Church This Week? Behind the Poll Data." *Christian Century*, 6 May 1998, pp. 472-75.

Hall, Douglas John. "Stewardship as a Missional Discipline." *Journal for Preachers*, Advent 1998, pp. 19-20.

Harrell, Daniel. "Power Source." *Christian Century*, 27 June 2006, p. 17.

Hempfling, Robert J. "An Enlistment Plan That Fits." *Journal of Stewardship* 39 (1987): 22-29.

"ID Ruling Expected to Impact Other States." *Christian Century*, 24 January 2006, p. 12.

Jones, L. Gregory. "Answerizing." *Christian Century*, 18-25 November 1998, p. 1121.

―――. "Faith Matters: HallowThanksMas." *Christian Century*, 22-29 December 1999, p. 1258.

————— "Faith Matters: Why Are They Singing?" *Christian Century*, 8-15 September 1999, p. 864.

Kalb, Claudia, and Andrew Murr. "Battling a Black Epidemic." *Newsweek*, 15 May 2006, pp. 42-48.

Kern, Kathleen. "Victims as Pariahs." *Christian Century*, 24 January 2006, p. 9.

King, Martin Luther, Jr. "Letter from a Birmingham Jail." Internet site: http://www.africa.upenn.edu/Articles_Gen/Letter_Birmingham.html.

Kluger, Jeffrey. "By Any Measure, Earth Is at . . . the Tipping Point." *Time*, 3 April 2006, p. 35.

Jackson, Jesse L., Sr. "Appreciation." *Time*, 7 November 2005, p. 23.

Lovin, Robin. "What Would Bonhoeffer Do? Ethics for This World." *Christian Century*, 19 April 2005, p. 26.

"Lutherans, Catholics, Methodists in Accord." *Christian Century*, 22 August 2006, p. 11.

Marino, Gordon. "Beyond the Comfort Level." *Christian Century*, 13 May 1998, p. 492.

Marlette. "Kudzu." *The Christian Century*, 15 November 1995, p. 1093.

Martinez, Felipe N. "Are We There Yet?" *Christian Century*, 31 May 2005, p. 21.

Marty, Peter W. "Beyond the Polarization: Grace and Surprise in Worship." *Christian Century*, 18-25 March 1998, p. 284.

Meacham, Jon. "The End of Christian America." *Newsweek*, 13 April 2009, pp. 34-38.

Mead, Loren B. "Wealth and Stewardship: An Interactive Exploration of Law and Grace." *Journal of Stewardship* 49 (1997): 40.

Miller, Lisa. "Beliefwatch: On Purpose." *Newsweek*, 23 October 2006, p. 9.

Nessan, Craig L. "A Life Interrupted." *Christian Century*, 17 October 2006, p. 55.

Noll, Mark. "The Impasse over Slavery: Battle for the Bible." *Christian Century*, 2 May 2006, p. 20.

"Numbers." *Time*, 22 May 2006, p. 27.

Packer, James. "In Quest of Canonical Interpretation." In *The Use of the Bible in Theology: Evangelical Options*, edited by Robert K. Johnston. Atlanta: John Knox Press, 1985.

Powell, Luther P. "Stewardship in the History of the Christian Church." In *Stewardship in Contemporary Theology*, edited by T. K. Thompson. New York: Association Press, 1960.

"The Power of a Word." *Newsweek*, 12 July 2004, p. 30.

Quindlen, Anna. "The Last Word: Open to All: The Big Job." *Newsweek*, 9 January 2006, p. 64.

—————. "The Last Word: Separate, Not Equal at All." *Newsweek*, 2 May 2005, p. 74.

—————. "The Last Word: Undocumented, Indispensable." *Newsweek*, 15 May 2006, p. 78.

Quinn, Jane Bryant. "Health Care's New Lottery." *Newsweek,* 27 February 2006, p. 47.

"Revolt of British Farmers Against the Tithe." *The Literary Digest,* 23 September 1933, pp. 116-17.

Ruun, Haruum. "Meanwhile in Darfur." *Christian Century,* 19 October 2004, p. 5.

Sach, Jeffrey D. "The $10 Solution." *Time,* 15 January 2007, p. 65.

"Sojourners." *Christian Century,* 11 July 2006, p. 5.

Stendahl, John. "The Offense." *Christian Century,* 21 January 1998, p. 53.

"Stiffing the Poor." *Christian Century,* 14 June 2003, p. 5.

"10 Questions for Elie Wiesel." *Time,* 30 January 2006, p. 8.

"Ten Reasons for NOT Ordaining Men." *Christian Century,* 18 April 2006, p. 7.

"Theologians: No Need to Fight Evolution." *Vital Theology,* 30 October 2005 (Special Issue), p. 1.

Thompson, Marianne Meye. "Reflecting on the Gospel." *Theology, News and Notes,* Fuller Theological Seminary, Spring 2004, p. 2.

Tucker, Gene E. "The Book of Isaiah 1–39: Introduction." In *Isaiah-Ezekiel.* The New Interpreter's Bible, volume 6. Nashville: Abingdon Press, 2001.

Twain, Mark. "The Revised Catechism." *New York Tribune,* 27 September 1871. Quoted in Justin Kaplan, *Mr. Clemens and Mark Twain: A Biography.* New York: Simon and Schuster, 1966, pp. 124-25.

Van Biema, David. "God vs. Science." *Time,* 13 November 2006, p. 55.

Van Biema, David/Crookston. "A Rural Exodus." *Time,* 9 February 2009, pp. 44-45.

Volf, Miroslav. "Floating Along?" *Christian Century,* 5 April 2000, p. 398.

Wallis, Jim. "If All You Have Is a Hammer . . ." *Sojourners,* August 2006, p. 5.

Walsh, Bryan. "How Business Saw the Light." *Time,* 15 January 2007, p. 56.

Waskow, Arthur, and Phyllis O. Berman. "Courtesy or Clarity? A Jewish Response to Theologians Under Hitler." *The Progressive Christian,* January/February 2007, pp. 11-12, 48.

Willimon, William H. "Dispatch from Birmingham: First Year Bishop." *Christian Century,* 20 September 2005, p. 31.

Wilson, Stan. "On the Vine." *Christian Century,* 2 May 2006, p. 19.

Wright-Riggins, Aidsand, III. "Opposing Words of Horror." *Mission in America,* September/October 2006, p. 4.

————. "The Segregated Hour." *Home Mission Today,* American Baptist National Ministries, Summer 1998, p. 2.

Zakaria, Fareed. "How to Exploit the Opening." *Newsweek,* 19 June 2006, p. 39.

Index

yard and the laborers, 145; parable of the wicked tenants, 146

McCarrick, Theodore, 97

McLaren, Bruce, 97

McMaster Divinity College (Hamilton, Ontario), 3, 5

Mead, Loren B., 27-29

Meeks, M. Douglas, 190, 195, 197, 237-38

Megachurches, 24-25, 131-32, 133-34, 212

Memorial Sloan-Kettering Cancer Center (New York City), 208

Mencken, H. L., 253

Metaphors of Jesus, 135-41; light of the world, 140-41; "salty disciples," 136-40, 173; vine and branches, 135-36

Miller, Lisa, 131

Miller, Stephen, 107

Ministry integrator, 217-21; how position would work in different denominational settings, 217-18, 221; the "placement" of the position, 220

Missio Dei, 205-6

Models of the Church (Dulles), 233-34

Money and prosperity: biblical interpretations of prosperity, 23-24; common misunderstandings about financial stewardship and attitudes toward wealth and possessions, 23-25, 151-59, 174; megachurches and prosperity theology, 24-25; motivations for giving and notions of scarcity/abundance, 20-21; relationship between happiness and, 25-27; and stewardship, 23-25, 151-59, 174

Montgomery bus boycott, 84-87

Mott, John R., 21

Mouw, Richard, 97, 150

Moyers, Bill, 148

Murphy, Nordan, 2

Murr, Andrew, 103

Myers, Ched, 153-54, 155-56, 157-58

National Association of Evangelicals, 97

National Breast Cancer Coalition and Fund, 209

National Council of the Churches in Christ (NCCC), 126, 235-36; Winter Meeting of the Commission on Stewardship (San Antonio, 1979), 235-36

National Prayer Breakfast (2006), 93

Nazi Germany, 64-69, 75, 78

Nessan, Craig L., 67

New England, colonial, 12-14, 22

New Sudan Council of Churches, 94

Newsweek, 193n, 207, 210

Newton, Isaac, 57

New York Times, 97

Niebuhr, H. Richard, 120-21n

Niebuhr, Reinhold, 95-96

Nineteenth-century American churches: "benevolence" and "beneficence," 17; "charity," 16-17; church giving, 13-15, 22; Scripture and proslavery/antislavery views, 58-63, 72, 73, 75, 77-78, 81-82; the term "stewardship," 18-20

Noko, Ishmael, 54

Noll, Mark A., 61-63, 81-82

Nouwen, Henri, 166

Obama, Barack H., 89

O'Connor, Alice, 91

Oil companies, 112-14

Ordination Council of the Los Angeles Baptist Association, 50

Origen, 184

The Origin of Species (Darwin), 106

Osteen, Joel, 24-25, 132

Our Country: Its Possible Future and Its Present Crisis (Strong), 18

Packer, James, 188

Padgett, Alan, 107

Paideia tradition and theological education, 4-5, 183-86, 198, 203, 238

Palestinian peasants and Roman rule, 122-24, 154-55

Parables of Jesus: financial steward-

ship and Jesus' parable of the talents, 152-58; and gift of God's grace, 145, 146; parable of the vineyard and the laborers, 145; parable of the wicked tenants, 146; Siverns on using parables to emphasize role of biblical steward, 254
Parks, Lewis, 238
Parks, Rosa, 84-85
Parry, Martin, 111
Parsons, Terry: and the call to reform theological education, 242-45, 263; and story of Abraham's gift to Melchizedek, 242; and story of Jacob's ladder and Jacob's promise, 243-45, 263; on tithing, 242-45
Pastoral ministry and theological education, 189-97; external model, 190, 191; the frustrations of pastors, 189-90; how ministry relates to stewardship, 262-63; internal model, 190, 191-94; larger congregations, 191; lay ministry, 160, 176-77, 195-96, 204, 211-12; pastor and people in partnership, 196-97; role of pastor as theologian in residence, 195; sermon preparation, 190; therapeutical counseling and issue of clergy sexual misconduct, 191-92; therapeutical counseling model and the "clinical training movement," 192-94; trend toward part-time pastors and lay persons, 203-4, 210-12
Paul: on Christian identity and church membership, 45; exhortation to Christians at Philippi, 141; the "gospel" for, 122; and gospel of Christ crucified, 36-37; on ministry leaders and financial support, 211; on pastors' role in helping equip members of the church for ministry, 196; understanding of church membership, 142
Pedagogies of theological education, 215-17; interpretation, formation, contextualization, performance, 215-

16; and three pedagogical challenges, 216-17. *See also* Curriculum and theological education
Perera, Kingsley, 136
"A Personal Reflection: Biblical Authority" (Brueggemann), 49, 51
Peterson, Eugene, 253
Piccolomini, Ascanio (Archbishop of Siena), 57
Pitts, William S., 116-17, 125
Poverty and hunger, 91-93; growing gap/disparities between rich and poor, 91-93; health and, 104; Johnson's war on poverty, 91
Powell, Luther P., 10, 13, 15
"The Power of Faith: How Religion Impacts Our World" (Marty), 131-32
Preaching, 160-64, 176; and the contemporary cultural climate, 163-64; by ordained or non-ordained leaders, 161; purpose as not "answerizing," 163; purpose as not to offer comfort, 162-63; role of the preaching office in an alternative community, 169. *See also* Clergy
The Predicament of the Prosperous (Birch and Rasmussen), 235
Presbyterian Church in Canada, 19n, 144
Prete, Anthony, 79
Princeton Theological Seminary, 61
Prosperity theology, 24-25
Puritans of New England, tithing and, 12-13, 22
The Purpose Driven Life (Warren), 131

Quindlen, Anna, 89-90, 167-68
Quinn, Jane Bryant, 103-4
Racism, 63, 77, 80-91; Civil Rights movement, 84-88; contemporary, 77, 81n, 88-89; immigration issue, 89-91; Jim Crow system of legalized segregation and disenfranchisement, 82-88; late-nineteenth-century U.S. Supreme Court rul-